European Television Industries

Petros Iosifidis, Jeanette Steemers and Mark Wheeler

bfi Publishing

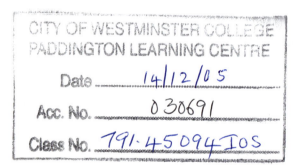
First published in 2005 by the
BRITISH FILM INSTITUTE
21 Stephen Street, London W1T 1LN

The British Film Institute promotes greater understanding of,
and access to, film and moving images culture in the UK.

Set by Fakenham Photosetting Limited, Fakenham, Norfolk
Printed in the UK by Cromwell Press, Trowbridge, Wiltshire

Cover design: ketchup
Cover illustrations: (front) *Tatort* (ARD); (back) *Cracker* (Granada Television).

British Library Cataloguing-in-Publication
A catalogue record for this book is available from the British Library

ISBN–1–84457–059–2 (pbk)
ISBN–1–84457–060–2 (hbk)

European Television Industries

This bc ⅃

Contents

Acknowledgments

We would like to express our thanks to the series editors Paul McDonald and Michael Curtin, who have been very patient with us, to Andrew Lockett, the former head of BFI Publishing, who commissioned this volume and to our editor at the BFI, Sophia Contento.

Introduction

Since the 1980s, the European television industries have been characterised by phenomenal change at many different levels. The most obvious reform has been the transformation from a system of heavily regulated, and predominantly publicly owned, monopolies to an abundance of televisual offerings operating in a less heavily regulated dual system of competing private and public television stations. Another major change involves the physical delivery of television into the home. Cable and satellite and, more recently, digital transmission have resulted in a massive expansion in the number of channels offered, creating relationships with audiences based on 'à la carte', on-demand and 'interactive' services. Through these changes, television has shifted from a service meeting distinct political, social and cultural objectives connected with citizenship, to become more of a consumer product as economic and industrial priorities take precedence.

Television industries in Europe, as in other parts of the world, face the challenges of technological innovation, the rise of global markets, deregulation and more intense commercial competition. Policy and regulation must contend not only with industry convergence but also with the growing transnational activities of multimedia companies and an environment in which audiences can choose from a wide range of television offerings. In this context, many uncertainties and issues remain. These include the difficulty of funding production in a fragmenting marketplace, uncertain public demand for new services, the future of public provision, the possible emergence of a two-tier society with the growth of subscription services and the consolidated power of a small number of large, vertically integrated and often multinational corporations controlling content, distribution and consumer access across different media.

This study sets out to explore the impact of technological development, changing ownership patterns, legislative revision and the much-heralded likelihood of convergence between telecommunications, broadcasting and computing on the European television industries. The findings are necessarily tentative because, as developments in digital television have shown, market predictions are always uncertain. When this book was first conceived, the industry was excited about the prospects of digital television and the opportunities for creating integrated media businesses that cut across television, publishing and the Internet. Yet, within a short space of time, several digital businesses in Europe collapsed and the dotcom boom dissolved into corporate failures, falling stock prices and company debt.

Concentrating on the historical, economic, cultural, technological, regulatory and political factors behind change, this book provides an opportunity to construct a conceptual and analytical base for judging recent developments in the European television industries and from which to assess future scenarios. It analyses, assesses and explains how the European television industries operate and seeks to identify the key factors defining the market. The objectives of the book are therefore:

- to place developments within a historical context
- to give an overview of organisational structures, trends and key players, taking into account both the public and commercial sectors
- to explain and analyse the impact of policy and legislative frameworks at both national and pan-European levels with regard to issues of pluralism, ownership, control and content
- to explain and assess the impact of new technologies on the European television landscape
- to identify and assess Europe's position within a global television marketplace

Throughout, we concentrate on the television institutions, policies and industries of those Western European countries who are members of the European Union (EU), and indeed one chapter deals specifically with the involvement of the EU. Over the next decade, the Union will incorporate the post-communist societies of Eastern and Central Europe and, while these are not covered here, future studies will need to consider developments in these territories and how they align within an EU framework. Although focusing on the television industries, some of the discussion around policy refers to broadcasting in general. Historically, the study describes the situation in European television as it stood at the end of December 2003. However, we recognise that the industry is continually undergoing changes in ownership, legislation and programming trends.

In compiling this volume, we found that our investigations raised as many new issues as the ones we sought to answer. This is understandable given the fast pace, uncertainty and scale of change. Consequently, the study gives prominence to certain themes over others, representing a range of particular viewpoints and thematic concerns about what has been happening and what may happen in the future with regard to regulation, policy and strategy.

Throughout the study, the transition from a heavily regulated television environment guided by social and cultural objectives to one driven by economic and global imperatives, over which governments have far less influence, remains a concern. At the same time, there is a strong sense of continuity because it is the established players from the analogue era, particularly in the commercial sector (e.g. BSkyB/News Corporation, Bertelsmann/RTL Group, Fininvest, Telefónica), who are emerging as key players in the digital era.

Any survey of television in Western Europe needs to place developments within a historical context through consideration of the public sector. Television in most EU countries began as public service or state-owned monopolies and, with the exception of Britain, Finland and Luxembourg, this was still the case well into the 1980s. Chapter 1, therefore, charts the origins and dominance of public television in EU countries until the 1980s and its decline thereafter, following the relaxation of regulation and consequent commercialisation in most European countries. It then considers how public service television differs across the EU in terms of its remit, funding and relationship with the political realm. Finally, it reviews the different responses from public service broadcasters to competitive challenges, both in respect of changes to existing channels and the launch of new services. The chapter suggests that, although public service television is likely to continue as an important counterweight to commercial television, the challenges it faces are likely to intensify. These challenges stem from uncertainties over funding, the dominance of a commercial logic and of multimedia conglomerates. Further difficulties arise from the perception (rightly or wrongly) that public television is no longer sufficiently distinctive in its objectives and programming output – whether through dependence on commercial revenues, the pursuit of 'commercial' programming policies or expansion into new activities. Individual case studies focus on aspects of public service television in Italy, the Netherlands, Germany and Britain.

Television began in Europe with largely vertically integrated public service or state-owned monopolies which were almost entirely responsible for the production (research, development and creation), broadcasting (commissioning, acquisition, scheduling) and physical distribution of programmes to the public. Since the 1980s, the story has been one of a shift towards a predominantly commercial model of television which, like its public service forebears, still exhibits a high degree of vertical integration, combined with greater horizontal integration and cross-media ownership transcending national boundaries. Chapter 2 explores the origins of commercial television within separate EU countries and provides an overview of the trends, channels and key players in the commercial television sector. Surveying different phases of commercialisation, it suggests that the most recent phase has been driven by the opportunities afforded by digital transmission and the convergence of television with other communications services. This has reinforced concentration within the industry and diversification into new areas of activity through merger, acquisition or corporate alliances. This chapter charts the processes of consolidation and conglomeration which have had mixed results for the different participants. Particular attention is paid to the collapse of the Kirch Group in Germany and the restructuring of the French-based company, Vivendi-Universal, in 2002, arguing that these companies took too many risks in an unproven marketplace, which was vulnerable to downturns in advertising revenue and consumer take-up.

Turning to the legal and regulatory issues associated with television in the EU, Chapter 3 considers what type of regulation is appropriate for a television landscape characterised by channel abundance, convergence and global media corporations. In the first instance, it examines the traditional basis for television regulation and the social and political considerations that underpinned and informed strict regulation of content and strong structural controls relating to market access, media concentration and cross-media ownership. It then describes and assesses how and why these rules have been adjusted and relaxed in a process of re-regulation to meet the demands of a 'lighter touch' approach towards commercial television in particular. It argues that, as technological developments have expanded channel provision and blurred the boundaries between different sectors of the communications market, traditional regulatory approaches based on sector-specific definitions have been undermined. It also suggests that the trend towards regulatory convergence at an institutional level (one regulatory body for all sectors of the communications industry) is being accompanied by a trend towards greater reliance on competition law to deliver policy objectives relating to access and competition in particular. At the same time, the role of the state is declining as national governments accept the inevitability of global market forces, relax regulatory controls and acquiesce to the limited role that external regulation has to play in controlling markets and content. This approach has been noticeable as a relaxation of ownership rules has allowed the rise of dominant players in key national markets. The chapter suggests, however, that the social and political considerations which justified regulation in earlier times still have a role to play and that regulation retains its relevance, particularly in relation to pluralism, diversity and access.

While Chapter 3 focuses on regulatory developments in different EU countries, Chapter 4 concentrates on pan-European developments, including cross-media investment, the emergence of pan-European channels and production companies (e.g. Endemol, FremantleMedia) operating on a pan-European basis. Pan-European cross-investment has emerged as one strategy which enables some European players to compete with US-based transnational corporations in the production and distribution of programming across Europe. Notable examples include the range of nationally targeted television channels operated by the RTL Group, Canal Plus and the Scandinavian Broadcasting System (SBS). However, cultural and linguistic barriers constitute significant obstacles to transnational activities, particularly pan-European channels, notwithstanding the hurdles of national regulation and the practice of selling programme and sports rights on a territorial basis. These barriers have led to the localisation of mainly US-owned thematic channels offering news, sport, music, children's programming and pornography in order to appeal to distinctive national audiences. In the light of pan-European developments, Chapter 4 also considers the interventions of the European Commission, designed to enhance the European television sector and allow it to compete more effectively on the global stage, exploring the unresolved conflict and tension between, on the one hand, the European Commission's desire to improve international competitiveness through market liberalisation, harmonisation and the creation of a single market with the Television Without Frontiers Directive, and the Commission's desire to intervene with measures designed to maintain European cultural diversity and pluralism. The EU's role in both protecting and stimulating the European television industry is examined through the implementation of quotas, support measures and its stance in international negotiations on the GATS (General Agreement on Trade in Services). It is argued here that these are a side issue in terms of what is happening in national markets. Here, relaxation of foreign ownership and content rules are proving a potent means of opening up markets to global market forces and multinational corporations at the expense of local considerations and cultural priorities.

Digital technologies promise to transform television both in terms of its technological capabilities and as a cultural form. In the words of Nicholas Negroponte, 'The key to the future of television is to stop thinking about television as television' (1995: 48). Chapter 5 starts by considering the extent to which digital television offers something entirely new and innovative, but goes on to suggest that the potential to enhance access and offer greater choice is limited by the small number of large multinational companies capable of funding these new ventures. The sector sought to attract consumers with expensively purchased sports and feature film rights, but for some companies the costs proved too high. This is illustrated in an overview of the European digital television landscape, which has seen low take-up rates in some countries, digital platform failures in Britain, Spain and Greece, and consolidation in the hands of a few companies. Evidence suggests that most national markets can only support one player with the 'deep pockets' to fund premium rights purchases and wait for subscriber levels to rise. This chapter argues that, to date, digital television has been about more channels and the recycling of existing programming rather than the creation of an interactive, information-based society. Notwithstanding the limitations imposed by consolidated ownership in the sector, it further suggests that the realisation of digital television's potential depends on a number of interrelated factors: regulation, affordability, availability and programming. Individual case studies focus on digital television in Britain, Spain, Greece and Italy.

In spite of the existence of one large EU market, Europe is still characterised by enormous cultural diversity. At the same time, there has long been considerable apprehension about the Americanisation of mass culture generally and television in particular. Chapter 6 concentrates on the trade in television programmes and starts by assessing the level and importance of US imports in European schedules and the reasons for the continuing popularity of certain types of American programmes with European television buyers. The popularity of American imports is contrasted with the performance of Britain as Europe's largest exporter of television programmes. With the exception of some formats (e.g. *Big Brother*, *Survivor* and *Who Wants to Be a Millionaire?*) and British programming with easier but restricted access to the large US market, the circulation of European programming within the EU and beyond is limited. However, it is suggested that while levels of US fiction imports continue to be high, the growing maturity of mainstream commercial networks in Western Europe has dented the appeal of US fiction as audiences demonstrate their liking for home-grown programming and schedulers seek to accommodate these preferences in peak time.

Analysis of the types of programming circulating across borders demonstrates the narrow range of content with international appeal, including crime drama, documentaries (natural history, wildlife, science), animation and pre-school programming, where cultural barriers are lowest. Trade between European countries remains minimal in spite of attempts to raise European collaboration through the co-production of high-cost fiction productions. The increasing importance of entertainment formats on European television underlines the growing demand for programming of local origination but also the trend towards the global dispersal of locally originated formats and programme concepts. In some cases, European players have even managed to achieve success in the highly competitive US marketplace while lacking the control of distribution (channels) to make this success more permanent.

The following is a jointly authored study in which individuals have taken responsibility for separate chapters. Chapters 1 and 6 were written by Jeanette Steemers while Mark Wheeler wrote Chapter 2. Mark Wheeler and Jeanette Steemers wrote Chapter 4 and Petros Iosifidis wrote Chapters 3 and 5. Through surveying the latest trends which have shaped the development of the European television economy and policy environment, it is our intention to contribute to the debates that have surrounded the reforms of this vital sector of the European economy and to enhance the reader's knowledge and understanding of the key issues involved.

1

The Public Sector – From Monopoly to Competition

Television in Western Europe is largely a post-war phenomenon, but within a short history, television services have undergone a radical transformation. One of the chief elements of that change has been the shift from a predominantly public service to a commercial model of broadcasting. Where public service monopolies largely prevailed at the beginning of the 1980s, most European countries now operate a dual system of commercial and public service television.

Public service broadcasters have not only had to compete with less heavily regulated commercial rivals but also with living in a television environment providing an overwhelming abundance of television on cable and satellite. While the political, social and cultural justification for public service broadcasting (PSB) seemed so self-evident in the days of monopoly, today the plethora of commercial channels has ultimately raised questions about the need for PSB. Public service broadcasters in Western Europe must now demonstrate much more clearly what distinguishes them from their commercial rivals. Some have proved more successful than others at adapting and reinventing themselves to meet the challenges of technology, competition and regulatory change, and some public services have become increasingly marginalised, particularly in the smaller territories of Belgium and Greece.

This chapter concentrates on the origins of public service television in Western Europe, the key players and the strategies they have pursued in the face of competition. The first part charts the origins of public service television in Western Europe, the reasons for its dominance until the 1980s and for its decline thereafter. The second part concentrates on public service players in both the larger and smaller territories of Western Europe. Case studies on Radiotelevisione Italiana (RAI) and Nederlandse Omroep Stichting (NOS) serve to highlight the different methods of operation public service television has in these territories. The final part looks at the prospects for public service television in a more competitive digital age, examining how and to what extent it is being redefined in an era of channel abundance. A case study on German public service television looks at how competition affected schedules, while the example of the

British Broadcasting Corporation (BBC) demonstrates how commercial strategies are pursued alongside public service principles.

PSB IN WESTERN EUROPE – FROM MONOPOLY TO MULTICHANNEL ABUNDANCE

Until the 1980s, television in Western Europe was largely run by public service monopolies, with a few exceptions in Luxembourg, Britain, Finland[1] and Italy (see Chapter 2). Public service and public ownership has therefore largely characterised television in post-war Western Europe, distinguishing it from the commercial system of the US, where ratings, advertising revenues and profit have taken priority (see Gitlin, 2000).

So why did most countries choose a heavily regulated public service monopoly (or duopoly) rather than unfettered commercial television? The simple answer is that radio had already provided a model of how television could be organised, and in most nations after World War II, radio services were re-established as monopolies. Historically, monopolies in radio and television were justified on technical grounds, as frequency scarcity prevented the accommodation of many competing services, and there was a desire to avoid the overcrowded airwaves which had impeded reception during the early days of radio in the US. In Europe, state authorities, usually in the form of the PTTs (postal, telegraph and telephone authorities), formed such monopolies to license, regulate and fund broadcasting in the public interest to ensure universal provision and prevent market abuse (Humphreys, 1996: 112–13).

A raft of political and social justifications were added to the technical and economic arguments for monopoly, because it was assumed that broadcast media had the potential to exert a powerful influence and were therefore in need of strict regulation. In post-war Europe, this approach reflected the mood for collective solutions to serve society as a whole in the interests of democracy (see Dahlgren, 2000: 25). Concerns about the social and political impact of television were reflected in issues over content. Like radio before it, television was regarded not simply as an entertainment medium but as an important contributor to realising democracy in the public interest (see Blumler, 1992: 12; Scannell, 1989: 160). As a 'public good', the underlying philosophy of PSB rested on non-commercial purposes and values including:

- the provision of diverse content encompassing varied schedules of information, education and entertainment
- a plurality of viewpoints including those of minorities
- a universal service for all regardless of income or geographical location

- public accountability
- impartial news
- the maintenance of national cultural identity, through the production and presentation of programmes that reflected domestic culture[2]

Arguably, governments could also more easily control publicly owned monopolies (see McQuail, 1995: 149). Some governments, for example in France, Italy and Greece, intervened unnecessarily in the running of television, influencing the implementation of and effectiveness of public service television, which became tainted by party political interference (see Hibberd, 2001; Papathanassopoulos, 2004: 95; Smith, 1998: 41).

During this early period, public television in Western Europe could afford to transmit programming without broad appeal. Even into the 1980s, the relative lack of competition allowed public service broadcasters to transmit categories of programmes at peak time which today would be regarded as distinctly uncompetitive, namely plays, political discussions, highbrow arts and information programming. Even those television stations partially funded by advertising (in Germany and Italy) did not have to let commercial considerations affect their programme strategies because there was no competition for advertising revenue.

Why then were public service monopolies ultimately unsustainable? The shift towards a more commercial environment can be traced back to the introduction of satellite and cable channels in the 1980s. Satellites promised channel abundance because they overcame the technical limitations of free-to-air transmission. They also offered opportunities for transnational services as satellite footprints did not respect national boundaries. The arrival of satellites made it difficult to justify regulatory regimes, which had favoured a small number of nationally based broadcasters operating according to public service principles. Governments could not prevent satellite transmissions from neighbouring territories. Countries like Sweden and Germany legislated to allow domestic commercial television rather than have this imposed externally with the possible loss of jobs, advertising revenues and control.

However, the removal of technological barriers and growth in television channels also involved a broader ideological shift, seeing collective, welfare-based solutions displaced by market-led thinking, not only in the regulation of television but in society in general (Dahlgren, 2000: 25; Murdock and Golding, 2001: 113–14). Deregulation in most West European countries not only diminished the dominance of public service television but also led to the prioritisation of commercial principles and funding, together with a relaxation of rules relating to the content and ownership of commercial channels (see Chapter 3).

This ideological shift went hand in hand with broader social changes, empha-sising the needs of the individual and consumption rather than the communal or social principles which had underpinned PSB (see Brants and De Bens, 2000: 17). Governments accepted pro-market arguments about greater individual consumer choice and the need to relax regulation in the expectation of econ-omic benefits, thereby weakening arguments for PSB (see Chapter 3). In the larger European countries, this shift saw the emergence of larger and more inter-nationally competitive media companies, together with an expansion of the audiovisual industry as an important sector of the economy (Humphreys and Lang, 1998: 17–18).

The perception that the non-commercial purposes of PSB allow it to meet a broader range of societal goals than its profit-seeking commercial counterparts still forms the principal justification for its continued existence (see Graham, 2000: 93–5). However, the market failure argument, which holds that PSB is a support for democracy counterbalancing the failings of the market, sits uneasily next to the growing commercial activities of some public service broadcasters. These commercial tendencies, which might undermine the public service remit and continued justification for public funding, include (McQuail, 1986; Steemers, 2001: 75–6):

- increased popular entertainment and fiction on PSB's core channels, at the expense of information and cultural programming
- externalisation of services and adoption of commercial management prac-tices
- breaching of universal access by the introduction of subscription funding and/or satellite or cable channels
- increased reliance on commercial income from advertising, co-production finance, programme sales and sponsorship, allowing commercial priorities to impinge on public service objectives, leaving public service television only marginally distinguishable from commercial television

ORIGINS AND DEVELOPMENT OF PSB IN WESTERN EUROPE

While all public service broadcasters have broadly similar purposes, in practice national variations are very noticeable in the organisation and relationship of public service television to 'the political realm' (see Humphreys, 1996: 122). One salient difference relates to variations between public (predominantly licence fees) and commercial (e.g. advertising) funding mechanisms (see table 1.1). In Sweden, Denmark, Finland, Flemish-speaking Belgium and Britain, public broadcasters SVT, DR, YLE, VRT and the BBC, respectively, take no advertising, but commercial revenues are generated from programme sales and

Table 1.1: Public Service Television Funding in Western Europe (%)

Country	Channel	Public Funding	Commercial Revenues	Other
Austria (2002)	ORF	44.3 (licence fee)	41 (mainly advertising)	14.7
Belgium (Wallonia) (2003)	RTBF	63.2 (licence fee)	31.8 (mainly advertising)	5
Belgium (Flanders) (2002)	VRT	67.9 (government subsidy)	15.1 (no television advertising)	17
Denmark (2003)	Danmarks Radio	91.3 (licence fee)	8.7 (no advertising)	–
Denmark (2003)	TV2	10.1 (licence fee)	89.9 (mainly advertising)	–
Finland (2002)	YLE	95.8 (licence fee)	4.2 (no advertising)	–
France (2002)	France 2	56.3 (licence fee)	40 (mainly advertising)	3.7
France (2002)	France 3	66.9 (licence fee)	29.6 (mainly advertising)	3.5
Germany (2002)	ARD	83 (licence fee)	15.7 (mainly advertising)	1.3
Germany (2002)	ZDF	84.7 (licence fee)	13.2 (mainly advertising)	2.1
Greece (2002)	ERT[1]	94 (levy on electricity bill)	6 (mainly advertising)	–
Ireland (2003)	RTE	50.3 (licence fee)	49.7 (mainly advertising)	–
Italy (2002)	RAI	50.4 (licence fee)	42.9 (mainly advertising)	6.7
Netherlands (2002)	NOS	65.1 (levy on income tax)	26.7 (mainly advertising)	8.2
Portugal (2002)	RTP	60.7 (government grant)	32.8 (mainly advertising)	6.5
Spain (2003)	TVE	9.1 (government grant)	86.4 (mainly advertising)	4.5
Sweden (2002)	SVT	93 (licence fee)	5.3 (no advertising)	1.7
United Kingdom (2004)	BBC	73.7 (licence fee)	26.3 (no advertising)	–
United Kingdom (2004)	Channel 4	–	100 (mainly advertising)	–

Source: EAO (2004)

other forms of commercial exploitation. In most other European countries, advertising is an important source of income ranging from less than a third of total income in Germany, the Netherlands and French-speaking Belgium, to over 86 per cent in Spain. In Greece, public television is funded by a levy on electricity bills with some income from advertising. Since 2000, Dutch public television has been funded by a levy on income tax, while in Portugal, Spain and Flemish-speaking Belgium, public funding is provided by government grant.

Britain

Originally formed in 1922 as the British Broadcasting Company by a group of leading wireless manufacturers, the BBC was granted its Royal Charter in 1927, becoming a public corporation and giving Britain an uninterrupted PSB tradition ever since. The British model was influential in other countries, notably in post-war Germany, but what marked Britain out from its neighbours was that public service principles, in respect of range and diversity of content, were also applied to free-to-air commercial television, introduced much earlier than in other countries with the launch of Independent Television (ITV) in 1955.

The BBC's foundations were laid down by its first Director General, John Reith, who imposed his personal vision of public service based on the provision of information, education and entertainment to a national audience regardless of geographical location. Over time Reith's paternalistic emphasis on education and information has been superseded by entertainment as the BBC has sought to justify public funding by appealing to mass audiences.

Following an experimental service between 1936 and 1939, the BBC resumed television broadcasting in 1946. Pressure from commercial interests and dissatisfaction with the BBC's approach to television resulted in the establishment of ITV, creating a duopoly of public and private services. Largely due to the perceived failings of ITV, the BBC was granted a second channel, BBC2, in 1964. It was not until 1982 that another service, Channel 4, appeared. As a public corporation, funded by advertising, the new channel's public service remit required it to cater for minority and neglected audiences. Channel 5[3], the last terrestrial channel, was launched in 1997 with a reduced set of public service obligations.

With increased competition from multichannel television, all the free-to-air broadcasters, including the BBC, have become more aggressive in their pursuit of ratings. BBC1, the BBC's flagship service, had the largest viewing share (i.e. the percentage of all television viewers) of 25.6 per cent in 2003, followed by ITV (23.7 per cent, down from 41 per cent in 1992). This represented a declining share for BBC1 from 38 per cent in 1982 and 34 per cent in 1992 (Broadcasters Audience Research Board, 2003; *Broadcast*, 2004). BBC1's mainstream approach centres on serial drama (e.g. *EastEnders* four nights a week), high-profile drama, news and light entertainment during peak time. BBC2, with a stronger focus on innovative and therefore risky drama, comedy, factual entertainment, lifestyle formats and high-profile imports (e.g. *The Simpsons*[4], *24*) maintained a steady share of 11 per cent in 2003, down slightly from 12 per cent in 1982. Since the BBC's launch of its own digital channels, it is noticeable that more traditional public service content including children's programming (CBeebies, CBBC), news (BBC News 24), youth content (BBC3), arts programming and documentaries (BBC4) is finding a home on these lower rating services. This trend indicates the continued fragmentation of the television audience and constitutes a strategy of using digital to meet public service requirements targeting different groups and interests in society (see Tunstall, 2004: 270).

France

After World War II, in 1945 broadcasting was re-established in France as a state monopoly under Radiodiffusion de France (RTF), a civil service department. TF1 (Télévision Française), the first post-war television channel, was launched in 1947, joined in 1964 by Antenne 2 and in 1972 by France Régions 3 (FR3).

Between 1945 and 1970, the state exercised centralised managerial and financial control, using broadcasting as an instrument of presidential propaganda, and providing little exposure for those who were not close government supporters (Lamizet, 1996: 89; Smith, 1998: 41). In June 1964, RTF was replaced by ORTF (L'Office de Radiodiffusion-Télévision Française), which was broken down in 1974 into seven autonomous public companies covering television (TF1, Antenne 2, FR3), radio, programme production, transmission and archives. The state monopoly over television remained but autonomy from government was enhanced.

This monopoly came to an end in 1984 with the launch of the terrestrial, pay-television service, Canal Plus. In 1986, Prime Minister Jacques Chirac's government privatised TF1. Antenne 2 and FR3 were re-christened France 2 and France 3 in 1989 and amalgamated as two constituent parts of a holding company, France Télévision, with common resources, management structures and complementary production and scheduling strategies (Palmer and Sorbets, 1997: 61).

France 2 is the flagship public service channel while France 3 provides both a national service and regional opt-outs. La Cinquième was launched in 1994, and since 2002 has been incorporated into France Télévision as France 5, with a strong educational remit. It broadcasts during the day, sharing a frequency with Arte, the Franco-German arts channel established in 1992. All are typical public service channels with an obligation to provide wide-ranging programming and a plurality of viewpoints. Fierce competition following the privatisation of TF1 resulted in greater reliance on cheaper entertainment formats in order to attract audiences and advertisers (Humphreys, 1996: 233). According to Jean-Marie Charon, there has been little clarification of the public service mission, with a consequent drift towards commercial priorities, reinforced by partial funding from advertising (2004: 72). This was reduced from ten minutes to eight minutes per hour in 2002 in return for higher licence fees (TBI, 2002: 39). In terms of ratings, during 2001 France 2 came second (20.8 per cent) after TF1 (32.7 per cent), with France 3 securing a 16.4 per cent share in third place (EAO, 2003a, p.82). France 5 and Arte averaged a combined 5.1 per cent and 3 per cent share respectively (ibid.).

Germany

In Germany, there are two national public television networks. Established in 1950 as a federation, ARD (Arbeitsgemeinschaft der Rundfunkanstalten Deutschlands) comprises ten regionally based broadcasting stations of varying size that contribute proportionately to a nationally networked television service, Erstes Deutsches Fernsehen, launched in 1954. After a constitutional dispute in 1961 that saw central government unsuccessfully try to install commercial television, ZDF (Zweites Deutsches Fernsehen) was launched in 1963 as the second national television channel, run as a centrally organised broadcaster based on agreement by the federal states. Since 1969 the ARD stations, either individually or in collaboration, offer eight regionally based channels with higher levels of cultural and regional content, which are now available throughout Germany on cable and satellite. This decentralised structure indicates that federalism is a key feature of the German television landscape, reflected in Länder (federal state) rather than central government control of cultural and media policy.

Public service television has its origins in that part of occupied Germany which emerged in 1949 as the Federal Republic of West Germany. Counter to their own experience of state-controlled and commercial broadcasting, the French and American authorities followed the lead of the British in establishing corporations of public law in their zones of occupation, in order to promote democracy after years of National Socialism (see Bausch, 1980; Flottau, 1978; Tracey, 1983). Following (re)unification with the former German Democratic Republic during 1989 and 1990, the dual system of public and private television was adopted by the whole of Germany.

Private television was never unconstitutional but appeared late due to constitutional hurdles relating to diversity of content and socially representative internal boards (see Bundesverfassungsgericht, 1971: 255). The Constitutional Court modified its rulings when it became clear that cable and satellite would allow more channels, and the first private stations (Sat.1, RTL) were launched in 1984. Initially these services hd little impact on public television but ARD and ZDF's advertising revenues and audience shares have dropped sharply since. Efforts to relax rules restricting advertising on public television to twenty minutes a day on weekdays before 20.00hrs have not been successful.

In the highly fragmented German market, in terms of audience share, during 2002 ARD came second (14.3 per cent) to commercial rival, RTL (14.6 per cent), with ZDF securing 13.9 per cent followed by the regional channels with a combined 13.3 per cent share, giving the mainstream public television services a combined share of 41.5 per cent (Darschin and Gerhard, 2003: 159). At peak time (20.00–23.00 hrs), ARD (15.6 per cent) and ZDF (14.5 per cent) trailed behind RTL (16 per cent) (p. 161).

Spain

After the Franco regime (1936–75), Spain became a constitutional monarchy in 1978, and this political change heralded wide-ranging transformations in the nation's television, which previously had operated under tight government control (Vilches, 1996: 174). TVE 1 (Televisión Española) was launched in 1956 as a government-controlled state monopoly. A second channel was launched in 1965. From the start TVE was funded predominantly by advertising and a small state subsidy, except during the period between 1982 and 1992 when it did not

Operación Triunfo

receive any state funding at all (de Mateo, 2004: 229). In 1983, Spain's seventeen autonomous regions were allowed to create their own publicly owned channels. This occurred in the Basque region (ETB-2/Euskal Telebista, RTB-1), Catalonia (TV-3, Canal 33), Galicia (Televisiín de Galicia/TVG), Andalucía (Canal Sur, Canal 2), Valencia (Canal 9, Noticies 9), Aragón (TVA) and Madrid (Telemadrid). In 1988, legislation was passed allowing the introduction of private television, and in 1989, Antena 3, Telecinco and pay channel Canal Plus all launched services.

Commercial competition saw TVE's audience share decline from 90 per cent in 1990 to 28 per cent in 1995, contributing to a decline in TVE's financial situation (Vilches, 1996: 187). TVE is responsible for the mainstream La Primera, and information-based La 2 services. As a result of its dependency on advertising revenues and the competitive situation, there is a strong focus on La Primera on light entertainment, US films and series, Latin American telenovelas and sport, with little attention to cultural programmes. Consequently there is little to distinguish La Primera from its commercial rivals.

According to Lorenzo Vilches, there is no legal authority empowered to ensure either diversity of scheduling or minimum standards of programme quality, because the emphasis has always been on television's political and economic significance rather than its social and cultural dimension (1996: 186). TVE has been forced to take a commercial route and pursue ratings simply to ensure its share of commercial revenues and survival. In 2001, legislation was passed which aimed to redefine the role of public service broadcasting, requiring TVE to deliver a balanced mix of content and channels, to promote diversity at a regional level and to encourage the information society by offering digital and online services.[5]

In 2002, La Primera led the ratings with a 24.7 per cent share, ahead of Antena 3 (20.2 per cent) and Telecinco (20.2 per cent) (EAO, 2003a, p.79). La Primera's big hit of 2002 was *Operación Triunfo* (*Fame Academy*), a talent-based reality format, which secured a final audience of 13 million viewers and a 68 per cent share.

CASE STUDY: RADIOTELEVISIONE ITALIANA (RAI)

Among the larger Western European nations, Italy provides one of the clearest examples of public service television struggling amid new commercial and political pressures. Public service television in Italy is represented by RAI, which operates three terrestrial channels, Rai Uno, Rai Due and, since 1979, the more information and culturally focused, Rai Tre. RAI's position is defined by two factors. These are its highly competitive relationship with the three channels of Prime Minister Silvio Berlusconi's company, Mediaset – Canale 5, Italia 1 and Rete 4 – and the degree of influence exercised by political elites over its management and programming. RAI's relationship with the political elite has always been complex but its position became more difficult when Berlusconi became Prime Minister for a second time in May 2001, following a short period in office during 1994.

Established in 1946, RAI's regular television broadcasts began in 1954, and quickly proved popular reaching 20 million people by 1959, giving Italians for the first time 'a national collective frame of reference for their private actions and daily lives' (Sartori, 1996: 151). A second channel, Rai Due, was introduced in 1961, and the broadcaster held a monopoly until 1976 when a Constitutional Court ruling confirmed that private broadcasters should be allowed to participate in local television under a law passed in 1975. Hundreds of local television stations were established, which quickly consolidated under the leadership of the three Mediaset networks. With intense competition for advertising revenues, RAI faced a financial crisis and was forced to react. From the early 1990s, rationalisation resulted in improvements to RAI's financial position and there is now greater coordination in respect of scheduling, acquisitions and commissioning to prevent RAI channels competing with each other (Hibberd, 2001: 240).

Taking its inspiration from the BBC, RAI's original public service mission included information and education (Sartori, 1996: 148). In the 1980s, RAI gave up part of its public service remit (Achille and Miège, 1994: 34; Hibberd, 2001; McKinsey, 1999; Padovani and Tracey, 2003). Friday-night drama series disappeared, children's slots were reduced, and cultural offerings were marginalised to late-night slots in a period described by Carlo Sartori as 'tactical degeneration' (1996: 156). RAI could not afford to lose the ratings battle because almost half of its income came from advertising. At the same time, levels of imported feature films and series increased. A two-week survey in 1991 showed that almost half of the feature films and 90 per cent of the series shown by RAI were of US origin (see Humphreys, 1996: 234). According to Cinzia Padovani, hours of transmitted fiction on RAI grew from 2,259 hours in 1982 to 9,242 hours in 1992 (2003: 145). But fiction production plummeted to 220 hours in 1996, rising to only 357 hours in 1998 (p. 146). Similarly, light entertainment grew from 1,310 hours in 1982 to 3,147 hours in 1992 (p. 145). However, dependence on imports in prime time decreased in the late 1990s in favour of more locally produced programming such as *Un Medico in famiglia* on Rai Uno and the popular in-house detective series, *Commissario Montalbano*, which secured a 24 per cent share in 2000 (Muscara and Zamparutti, 2000).

However, RAI's most enduring troubles have resulted from party political interference. In the early days, Christian Democrat-led governments sought to influence senior appointments and news reporting while excluding other groupings, particularly the Italian Communist Party (Hibberd, 2001: 234). The 1975 Broadcasting Act led to the *Lottizzazione* system whereby Parliament was given the job of appointing RAI's Administrative Council. RAI's television channels were divided up as spoils between the Christian Democrats (Rai Uno) and Socialists (Rai Due) but as corruption scandals caused the collapse of the old Christian Democrat-Socialist regime in 1992, a power vacuum resulted which was soon filled by parties of the right, notably Berlusconi's Forza Italia. In 2002, the Berlusconi government proposed new communications legislation amid furore about the government's appointment of political allies to the posts of president of the RAI council and chief executive (Rodier, 2002: 32). After a year in which Berlusconi criticised key RAI journalists (Cozens, 2002), the draft legislation placed before Parliament in 2003 aimed to partially privatise RAI from 2004.[6] This also would allow Mediaset to maintain control of its three terrestrial networks, instead of transferring one to satellite in contravention of a 2002 Constitutional Court ruling (Mazzoleni, 2003: 519).[7] However, in December 2003, President Ciampi refused to sign the bill into law and it was returned to Parliament for further deliberation over concerns it would create a dominant position for one media group through changes to media cross-ownership and advertising rules (Hooper, 2003).

In 2002, the market shares of RAI (44.5 per cent) and Mediaset (45.7 per cent) at peak time were fairly evenly balanced, although RAI had been losing share from a high of 49.3 per cent in 1999 (Mazzoleni, 2003: 521). Rai Uno, a general entertainment channel, was the most popular public channel with a 23.8 per cent share in 2002, followed by Rai Due (13 per cent) with a reputation for fiction and a younger audience profile, and the culturally focused Rai Tre (9.7 per cent) (EAO, 2003a: 90).

PUBLIC SERVICE TELEVISION IN THE SMALLER TERRITORIES

Like their larger neighbours, most small countries in Europe run two networks: a mainstream entertainment service alongside a second service placing greater emphasis on cultural programming, information or content targeted at minority interests (see table 1.2). The size of domestic territories means many television companies are unable to support large-scale domestic production, rendering these countries reliant on imports for more expensive forms of programming such as drama and hampering the development of public service television (see Chapter 6). In Scandinavia, there is a substantial degree of collaboration among public service broadcasters sharing cultural and geographic proximity. For example, the Nordvision network, established in 1959, encourages programme exchanges and co-production (Syvertsen and Skogerbø, 1998: 226). Others have tried to reduce their reliance on acquisitions, such as Irish broadcaster RTE for example, which reduced imports from 65 to 50 per cent between 1984 and 1994 by concentrating on cheaper home-grown programming (Kelly and Truetzchler, 1997: 113).

Language is also a factor. Austria, Ireland and Belgium have been affected by overspill broadcasts from same-language neighbours, which can also be received on cable and satellite. In Portugal, Greece, Scandinavia and the Netherlands, languages which are not widely spoken elsewhere have provided a partial barrier to cultural domination by larger neighbours. In the 1980s and 1990s, however, privatisation, deregulation and transnational satellite television altered the television landscape in all of these countries, forcing broadcasters to develop counter-strategies. For example, following reforms in 1994, light entertainment, talk shows and feature films became the focus of ORF-1 in Austria, with 58 per cent of transmissions dedicated to entertainment in 2003 (Trappel, 2004: 8). According to Trine Syvertsen and Eli Skogerbø, however, the key to survival for public broadcasters in small countries is to retain a distinctly national profile by prioritising popular domestic programming, particularly at peak time (1998: 230).

CASE STUDY: NOS AND PSB IN THE NETHERLANDS

One of the smaller Western European nations, the Netherlands, has developed a complex system of public service television with three channels (Nederland 1,

Table 1.2: Free-to-Air Public Service Television Channels in Western Europe

Country	Broadcaster	Channels (Launch Date)	% Market Share in 2002 (Prime Time)
Austria	Österreichischer Rundfunk und Fernsehen (ORF)	ORF-1 (1955)	30.5 (35.8)
		ORF-2 (1967)	22.7 (22.8)
Belgium[1] (Wallonia)	Radio-Télévision Belge de la Communauté Française (RTBF)	La Une (1960)	16.3 (19.5)
		La Deux (1977)	3.4 (2.2)
Belgium[1] (Flanders)	Vlaamse Radio en Televisieomroep (VRT)	TV-1(1960)	26.4 (29.5)
		Canvas (1977)	9.6 (8.2)
Denmark	Danmarks Radio (DR)	DR1 (1953)	28.4 (33.9)
		DR2 (1996)	3.7 (4.1)
	TV-2	TV-2 (1988)	35.2 (37.6)
		TV-2 Zulu (2000)	3.1 (2.9)
Finland	Yleisradio (YLE)	TV-1 (1957)	23.6 (21.6)
		TV-2 (1964)	21.7 (23.1)
France	France-Télévision	France 2 (1964)	20.8 (22.5)
		France 3 (1972)	16.4 (18.2)
		France 5 (1992)	5.1 –
Germany	Zweites Deutsches Fernsehen (ZDF)	ZDF (1963)	13.9 (15.2)
	Arbeitsgemeinshaft der Rundfunkanstalten Deutschlands (ARD)	ARD (1954)	14.3 (15.2)
	Third Channels	Third Channels (1969)	13.4 (15.6)
Greece	Elliniki Radiofonia Teleorasis (ERT)	ET-1 (1966)	5.9 (5.8)
		NET (1974)	5 (5.4)
		ET-3 (Thessaloniki)	
Ireland	Radio Telefís Eireann (RTE)	RTE-1 (1960)	26.6 (32.7)
		Network 2 (1978)	13.9 (11.7)
		Telefís na Gaeilge (1996)	2.5 (2.5)
Italy	Radiotelevisione Italiana (RAI)	Rai Uno (1954)	23.8 (23.1)
		Rai Due (1961)	13 (12.1)
		Rai Tre (1979)	9.7 (10.4)
Netherlands	Nederlandse Omroep Stichting (NOS)	Nederland 1 (1951)	11.1 (12.4)
		Nederland 2 (1965)	17.2 (17)
		Nederland 3 (1988)	7.6 (8.2)
Portugal	Rádiotelevisão Portuguesa (RTP)	RTP-1 (1957)	21.1 (19.7)
		RTP-2 1968)	5.3 (5)
Spain	Televisíon Española (TVE)	La Primera (1956)	24.7 (26.5)
		La 2 (1965)	7.7 (7.4)
	Regional TV Stations		17.8 (17.8)
Sweden	Sveriges Television (SVT)	SVT-1 (1957)	26.5 (32.3)
		SVT-2 (1969)	16.4 (17.7)
United Kingdom	British Broadcasting Corporation (BBC)	BBC1 (1946)	26.2 (28.5)
		BBC2 (1964)	11.4 (10.4)

Sources: EAO, 2003; TBI, 2002; Channel websites.

Note:

1. Television services commenced in Belgium in 1953. As the linguistic divide became more politicised, separate broadcasting organisations were introduced in 1960 – BRT (VRT from 1997) in Flemish-speaking Flanders and RTBF in French-speaking Wallonia.

2 and 3) operating under the umbrella of NOS. In a small market of 16 million people with a large number of commercial and cross-border channels, the scale of competition faced by NOS is intense. Over 90 per cent of households are cabled and therefore receive all that the multichannel universe has to offer. Nevertheless audience share has held and all three NOS channels can still secure a share of over 36 per cent.

Following the model introduced with radio in the 1920s, public service television was established in 1951 with a 'pillarised' social structure based on religious or political allegiances. The original broadcasting corporations included Vara (Socialist), KRO (Roman Catholic), NCRV (Protestant), VPRO (Protestant-Liberal) and AVRO (Liberal), who were each accorded television airtime based on the size of their membership. In 1969, these religious and ideological ties were relaxed because of pressure from commercial interests and other social groups (Syvertsen and Skogerbø, 1998: 224). Under the 1967 Broadcasting Act, which came into force in 1969, NOS was established as an umbrella organisation responsible for coordination and technical services as well as news and sports programming. The same Act also introduced limited amounts of block advertising to be sold by a non-profit organisation (STER), with proceeds going proportionally to the broadcasters and as compensation to the national press (Brants, 2004: 148). Former pirate broadcasters, TROS and Veronica, with no particular social group affiliation, but with a strong emphasis on entertainment, and EO, a society reflecting the interests of evangelical Protestants, were all awarded licences in 1967. In this way, Dutch television became more commercial from within, with TROS and Veronica proving very popular, forcing other broadcasters within NOS to respond (pp. 148–9). By the end of the 1980s, over half of PSB content was devoted to popular entertainment (Humphreys, 1996: 143–4).

In 1988, a third public channel, N3, was launched but from 1989, public television came under increasing pressure from the Dutch-language commercial service, RTL-4, based in Luxembourg, followed by RTL-5 in 1993. Provisional findings between 1986 and 1995 identified little overall change in public service schedules – but informational programming fell from 54 per cent to 48 per cent and shows (quizzes, game shows, talk shows) rose from 9 to 19 per cent (McQuail, 1998: 121). In response to commercial competition, public television was allowed in 1989 to show advertising on Sundays and the number of advertising blocks was increased. Veronica left NOS in 1995 to form a commercial channel with the Holland Media Group (HMG), and after breaking with HMG in 2000, this HMG channel became the youth-orientated Yorin channel.

Within NOS, eight broadcasting associations provide most of the programming for the three public channels. In 2002, Nederland 2, the most popular network, had a 17 per cent peak-time share, targeting young audiences with entertainment and sport with programming from its principal suppliers TROS, EO, BNN and NOS Sport. Nederland 1, a mainstream channel for older audiences with an emphasis on British detective series and magazine shows, had a 12.4 per cent peak-time share, with programming supplied by AVRO, KRO and NCRV. With an 8.2 per cent peak-time share, Nederland 3 is a culturally progressive and more socially orientated channel with an emphasis on culture and arts programming provided primarily by NPS,[8] VPRO, Vara and the educational broadcasting organisations RVU and Teleac/NOT. Since September 2000, its daytime hours have been dedicated to Z@ppelin, an advertising-free block for children established in response to the success of US-owned Fox Kids.

For the broadcasting organisations, access to the airwaves continues to be governed by the size of their membership, measured by those who buy their listings magazines. The responsiveness of this system was shown in 1998 when BNN, an organisation targeting young audiences, managed to secure airtime on N2 on the basis of a public petition (NOS, 2000). NOS was granted a ten-year licence in September 2000, heralding significant organisational changes. Rather than separate licences for each broadcasting association, the system as a whole was awarded a single licence. Channel coordinators were appointed for separate channels and the output of each association was concentrated on particular channels to raise the profile of individual channels, allowing a more focused response to commercial competition. The Media Act of 2000 specified that information and education had to make up 35 per cent of transmissions, with 25 per cent cultural programming and half in the Dutch language. Entertainment is now restricted to a 25 per cent maximum per channel. In 2000, information accounted for 54 per cent of transmissions, followed by entertainment (27 per cent) and education (12 per cent) (Brants, 2004: 149). In comparison, commercial television was dominated by entertainment (59 per cent) followed by information (26 per cent) and education (2 per cent) (p. 150).

Reduced autonomy in scheduling for the broadcasting associations has led to some complaints of marginalisation by those who believe that ratings are being pursued at the expense of the public service mission. According to Syvertsen and Skogerbø, '[t]he unsolved problem is, nevertheless, to what extent the societies can preserve their identities as representatives of social segments, and, simultaneously, appeal to broad audiences' (1998: 231). Associations retain their autonomy and are responsible for the form and content of programmes. They also participate in editorial boards which advise the separate channel coordinators. The relationship is set down in law. However, the distinctive pluralistic (member-based and ideological) contributions of the individual broadcasting organisations have been watered down in favour of a more uniform approach in a competitive marketplace. According to Kees Brants, public television is holding its ground 'but content and programme policies seem more based on how to hold and attract viewers than on the Enlightenment-inspired, cultural-pedagogic mission which, when it still had a monopoly, was more or less its *raison d'être*' (2004: 152).

PUBLIC SERVICE RESPONSES TO COMPETITION

How have public service broadcasters reacted to the challenge of more competition? All have experienced a fall in audience share, and for Greek broadcaster ERT, the decline has been sufficiently serious to push it into a marginal position.[9] Those broadcasters predominantly or partially funded by advertising also suffered a decline in revenues. For TVE, the Spanish public broadcaster funded almost entirely by advertising, this had serious consequences and the station has been on the verge of financial crisis for several years (Del Valle, 2001). However, even stations only partially funded by advertising suffered serious effects. In Germany, ARD and ZDF saw their advertising revenues plummet. During 1988, about 39 per cent of ZDF's income came from advertising (ZDF, 1988: 205). By 2002, ZDF's commercial revenues, of which advertising is only one source, had dropped to 13.2 per cent (EAO, 2004a: 67).

Faced with more competition, public stations also found that their revenues were not growing sufficiently to meet broadcasting inflation. Sports rights, particularly football rights, saw public broadcasters lose out to wealthier commercial rivals as the cost of rights rose (see Chapter 5). Without the 1996 amendment to the EU's Television Without Frontiers Directive, public broadcasters might have seen themselves excluded from major international sporting events like the Olympic Games and World Cup Football Championships. This amendment (drawing on British precedent) allowed Member States to draw up a list of events to be broadcast unencrypted even if pay television has acquired exclusive rights (see Chapter 4).

The reactions of public service broadcasters to their predicament have varied depending on political support and their relative strength. All have had to take a difficult path, balancing the need to be popular with the requirement to remain distinctively different from their commercial counterparts. If deemed too popular in their approach, public broadcasters are viewed to have abandoned their public mission and to be emulating commercial rivals, raising questions about the necessity of public funding. However, if they air programming which commercial broadcasters would not transmit, they run the risk of alienating a large portion of the audience, thereby undermining support for public funding. In practice, most public broadcasters have taken a pragmatic approach, trying to meet the demands of both the mass audience and minority interests (Blumler, 1993: 403–4).

The dangers of pursuing a populist approach are highlighted by the experience of Portuguese broadcaster RTP. Faced with a loss in share to commercial rival SIC, RTP adopted a more populist tone, screening more entertainment, game shows and Brazilian telenovelas, especially in prime time (Nobre-Correia, 1997: 190). But with RTP facing a financial crisis in 2003, the government considered closing it and setting up a new public service company with a single generalist channel (Pinto and Sousa, 2004: 184).

Under pressure to maintain audience share, core terrestrial services have extended their broadcast hours to match the twenty-four-hour schedules of commercial rivals, and changed schedules to allow more populist serial fiction and infotainment (reality shows, magazine formats) to feature in peak-time slots. Karen Siune and Olof Hultén note there is very little systematic empirical research on the extent to which public television 'converges' or 'diverges' from commercial television (1998: 29). In one example of such work, an eight-year quantitative content analysis of VRT's first channel TV-1 in Flemish-speaking Belgium, the proportion of the schedule devoted to entertainment increased from 48.7 per cent in 1988 to 60.6 per cent in 1995, rising to 74.1 per cent in prime time (de Bens, 1998: 29–30). The same study showed a decline in arts programming (from 4.9 to 2.1 per cent) and educational content (from 17.7 to 14.5 per cent) (p. 30). Levels of information remained steady at around 13 per cent, almost the same as commercial rival, VTM (12 per cent in 1995).

There is evidence that public service television does still offer more news, information and cultural content than commercial channels, and that this output is also qualitatively different (Krüger, 1996; McQuail, 1998: 121–3; and German case study below). A survey of thirty-six channels in six countries in 1997 established that levels of information on mainstream public and commercial channels in prime time were broadly similar in Britain (15.2 per cent – public, 17.1 per cent – commercial), the Netherlands (14.6 per cent – public, 13 per cent – commercial) and to a lesser extent, France (32 per cent – public, 24 per cent – commercial). But levels diverged in Germany (30.7 per cent – public, 2.8 per cent – commercial), Italy (27 per cent – public, 9 per cent – commercial), Flanders (23.3 per cent – public, 5 per cent – commercial) and Wallonia (20.1 per cent – public, 9.6 per cent – commercial) (de Bens and de Smaele, 2001: 55).

Other research points to a strong correlation between high levels of entertainment programming, a focus on mass audiences and the degree of dependency by public broadcasters on commercial revenues. In a report for the BBC, the McKinsey consultancy distinguished between three types of public service broadcaster. In the first cluster, distinctiveness was more important than market share, as broadcasters with low levels of public funding and a highly specialised remit made little impact on the market. Examples included the Public Broadcasting System (PBS) in America and the Australian Broadcasting Corporation (ABC). The second cluster focused on market share over distinctiveness, including broadcasters like RAI in Italy and TVE in Spain, who are heavily dependent on advertising and seek to compete aggressively with commercial competitors, thereby undermining their distinctive public service profile (McKinsey, 1999: 21–2). A third cluster achieved a balance between the pressures of market share and distinctiveness, including SVT in Sweden and ARD in Germany. Looking at these cases, McKinsey claimed a strong connection between levels of distinctiveness and funding: while dependency on advertising led to greater pressure to emulate commercial rivals, the licence fee afforded greater funding stability and the opportunity to innovate and take risks in programming.

Yet even public channels predominantly funded by a licence fee are not averse to adopting the scheduling techniques of commercial rivals. For example, in 2000 it was BBC1 which moved its 9pm news to 10pm, thereby pre-empting rival ITV's decision to move its own news back to 10pm. This gave BBC1 greater scope to schedule popular drama after the 9pm watershed when more adult programming can be screened. Moreover, the BBC invested in game-show formats such as *The Weakest Link* and *Dog Eat Dog*, seeking not only to engage the mainstream audience on its core channel, BBC1, but also to open up a lucrative format/co-production business overseas.

CASE STUDY: PROGRAMMING AND SCHEDULING PATTERNS IN GERMANY

The delicate balance between commercial populism and public service responsibilities was a challenge confronting Germany's two leading public broadcasters, ARD and ZDF, during the 1980s and 90s. In the dual system that emerged in Germany, judgments by the Constitutional Court in 1986 and 1987 outlined the role of PSB. Private broadcasting was allowed to pursue lower standards of content diversity and plurality of opinion, provided public broadcasters met higher standards. ARD and ZDF were required to meet the conditions of *Grundversorgung* or the essential provision of those services which contribute to the functioning of democracy and cultural life (Bundesverfassungsgericht, 1986: 19). *Grundversorgung* was not described in detail but it was clear that it applied to entertainment as well as information and cultural programming (Bundesverfassungsgericht, 1986: 19; Berg, 1986: 800). To meet this obligation, ARD and ZDF were given the constitutional right to existence and further development, including appropriate funding (mainly through the licence fee) (Bundesverfassungsgericht, 1986: 20).

Although levels of entertainment, fiction and information have not changed significantly on the public channels, since the 1980s there is some evidence of a shift in emphasis to maintain channel loyalty. For example, greater stress was placed on serial drama (*Lindenstraße* on ARD) and schools' programming was removed from the mainstream channels (Hickethier, 1996: 117). Regional programming, which had aired before 8pm on ARD (the key slot for advertising), was shifted to the regionally based third channels in the early 1990s, so that advertising revenues could be maximised on the first channel (Krüger and Zapf-Schramm, 1997: 638; Peasey, 1990: 318).

Building on earlier surveys, research by Udo Michael Krüger suggests significant differences have remained between public and commercial television. German public television continued to show diverse types of programming and information (news and current affairs), with commercial channels concentrating on more entertainment and fiction (Krüger, 1996 and 2002; Krüger and Zapf-Schramm, 2001, 2002 and 2003). For example, in 2002 free-to-air public television showed more than twice the amount of information programming (42.5 per cent) than commercial rivals, RTL, Sat.1 and ProSieben (17.5 per cent) (Krüger and Zapf-Schramm, 2003: 102). In 2000, at peak time (19.00–23.00) ARD (35.5 per cent) and ZDF (41.3 per cent) also maintained higher shares of information programming than RTL (24 per cent), Sat.1 (16.4 per cent) and ProSieben (18.6 per cent) (Krüger and Zapf-Schramm, 2001:

Tatort

328). ARD and ZDF were also responsible for some of the most popular programming. In 2002, nine out of the top ten dramas[10] came from public
broadcasters, including the long-running cruise-ship drama, *Das Traumschiff*
(ZDF), and the detective series, *Tatort* (ARD), *Polizeiruf 110* (ARD) and *Ein Fall
für Zwei* (ZDF) (Darschin and Gerhard, 2003: 163). Five of the top ten light
entertainment programmes and seventeen out of twenty information programmes also came from PSB (pp. 163–4).

There are also qualitative differences. Where the private channels confine their
information programming to breakfast television and magazine programmes,
ARD and ZDF still schedule major current affairs, natural history and documentary strands at peak time (Krüger and Zapf-Schramm, 2003: 110–11). Research
indicates that commercial channels tend to present information and politics as
'infotainment' with a greater emphasis on individuals, celebrity and human
interest issues, compared to the political, economic and contemporary themes
favoured by public service channels (Krüger, 2002: 514). This is reflected in different audience perceptions of private and public television, with public
television regarded as more information-orientated and trustworthy than its commercial counterparts (Darschin and Zubayr, 2003; Holtz-Bacha, 2003: 112).

RESPONSES TO TECHNOLOGICAL CHANGE
However, the nature of competition is more complex than simply changing the
focus of existing channels. Technological developments in analogue and now
digital delivery have allowed specialist niche channels and today most broadcasters are obliged to have an Internet presence as well. This raises questions
about how far a public service remit should be extended to include specialist
services which are not strictly broadcasting, and how these new services should
be funded. Adoption by some public service broadcasters of expansionary and
commercial strategies in the digital era has not only caused conflicts with their
traditional remits but also with their commercial competitors.

Responses are in large part conditioned by size and status. At an initial level,
all broadcasters have the ability to amend existing schedules and modernise in
terms of efficiency savings, rationalisation and the greater use of independent
programme commissions or co-production financing. At a second level are
broadcasters who are able to embark on new channels and services. However,
only a few have the financial resources to do this, and political support for
necessary investment is crucial. There is also a need to be mindful of the risk
involved, particularly for digital ventures after the failure of some high-profile
commercial platforms (see Chapter 5). Moving into niche channels represents
anticipation of changing audience preferences but adds fuel to the commercial argument that public service broadcasters are unfairly using public funds

to damage the economic survival of commercial competitors without risk to themselves.

Not surprisingly, it is the largest broadcasters in the leading territories who have launched new niche services. In Britain, the BBC provides both licence fee-funded services and commercial channels. The publicly funded digital channels include BBC News 24, BBC Parliament and, since 2002, BBC4 (arts), BBC3 (youth), CBBC for children between six and thirteen, and CBeebies for children under six. A commercial joint venture between the BBC's commercial subsidiary, BBC Worldwide, and Flextech Television, provides a range of subscription channels in Britain (see following case study). With the collapse of the digital terrestrial service ITV Digital in 2002, the BBC, together with BSkyB, is now providing the bulk of the offerings on Freeview, a free digital terrestrial package (see Chapter 5).

Since 1998, ARD and ZDF in Germany have provided free digital packages of repeats/time shift services (ARD Digital and ZDF Vision). They are jointly responsible for the publicly funded satellite channels KiKa (children), Phoenix (documentary), the cultural service 3SAT (together with ORF in Austria and SRG in Switzerland), and the cultural channel Arte (a joint venture with French public broadcasters). Since 1997, Spanish public broadcaster, TVE, has offered niche channels under its TVE Temática bouquet (Nostalgia, Canal Clásico, Canal Grandes Documentales, Canal 24 Horas, TeleDeporte). From 1999, RaiSat, a separate division of RAI, has offered subscription channels on the Sky Italia (formerly Telepiù) digital satellite platform, with Extra, Premium, Cinemaworld, Gambero Rosso (cookery) and Ragazzi (children). In January 2002, French public broadcaster France Télévision sold its 25 per cent share (held jointly with France Télécom) in the digital satellite platform, TPS, to commercial broadcast rival TF1 (Bulkley, 2002: 16). In spite of the promise of digital terrestrial television, possibly with public service involvement, nothing had materialised by 2003 because the French market was already served by two digital satellite platforms (Canal Satellite and TPS). In Finland, digital terrestrial television launched during 2001, and of the nine digital channels on air by May 2002, YLE is responsible for a news service, YLE-24, and a cultural and educational channel, YLE Teema (Österlund-Karinkanta, 2004: 57).

Children's television has always been considered an essential part of a public service remit, and public broadcasters are adapting children's programming to fit a new multichannel environment. ARD/ZDF (KiKa), the BBC (CBeebies, CBBC), NOS (Z@ppelin), VRT (Ketnet, on the second Flemish channel Canvas), and RAI (Raisat Ragazzi and Melevisione on Rai Tre) all started dedicated children's channels or programming blocks from the late 1990s in response to a perceived need for advertising-free programming for children. These developments are almost certainly a reaction to strong commercial competition, particularly from overseas providers with localised services such as Nickelodeon, the Disney Channel, Cartoon Network and Fox Kids.

Targeting niche audiences raised questions about whether certain types of content could be marginalised or removed from mainstream services. When KiKa was launched in 1997, children's programming was reduced to weekends on the mainstream ARD and ZDF services. Dedicated children's channels also provide a useful outlet for screening productions that can prove profitable in other ways. For example, with *Teletubbies*, *Tweenies* and *The Fimbles*, the BBC established major pre-school franchises which have been produced in volume and sell well overseas. However, the attractions of ancillary rights may privilege certain types of children's programmes over others, for example character-based or animation shows over a broader mix including drama and information.

At a third level, some public broadcasters are seeking a wider commercial role allowing them to increase revenues through international programme sales, co-production activity and the exploitation of ancillary rights (publishing, licensing). The BBC stands out here in respect of the global scale of its commercial activities, which also encompass international joint ventures and international channels undertaken by its commercial subsidiary, BBC Worldwide (see next case study). Other European public broadcasters have a smaller global presence because they do not have the 'language of advantage' (Collins, 1989) which benefits Anglophone services in the most lucrative international market, the United States. However, there are other hurdles. For example, in Germany, joint venture channels with the private sector and access to advertising or subscription revenues to fund additional channels are subject to constitutional and legislative barriers, which thus far have restricted collaboration with commercial partners (Steemers, 2001: 78). With the exception of the few broadcasters who do not take advertising, revenues from advertising sales still constitute the most important and lucrative commercial activity of public broadcasting.

Commercial competitors resent what they see as the more commercial and expansionary approach of some public providers who they regard as a source of cross-subsidised and unfair competition. The legitimacy of advertising funding has also been questioned. The EU, which has always had an uneasy relationship with PSB and a bias towards the logic of the market, has acknowledged the continued existence of PSB and the right of individual states to determine the method of funding and remit of public service stations (European Commission, 1997a). However, there are clearly concerns about the abuse of commercial funding and the acceptance of such forms of funding is now contingent on an adequate definition of PSB which does not conflict with rules on state aid. The

EU will use these definitions to assess whether public funding is always necessary for the fulfilment of the public service mission (European Commission, 2001b).

CASE STUDY: BETWEEN COMMERCE AND CULTURE – THE BBC

Although the BBC does not take advertising on its free-to-air television services, it does have an interest in commercial revenues. In 1994, the Conservative government encouraged the corporation to become 'an international multi-media enterprise', capitalising on its brands at home and abroad so that profits could be fed back into core domestic services (Department of National Heritage, 1994: 1). Since 1997, the Labour government has also encouraged the BBC to become more 'commercial'. With the announcement in 2000 that the licence fee would be raised above the Retail Price Index until 2006–7, it was estimated this move would provide £200 million per year to fund new programmes and channels. This was accompanied by expectations that efficiency savings and income from commercial activities would raise a further £1.1 billion in the same period (Department for Culture, Media and Sport, 2000).

In terms of the global scale of its commercial activities, the BBC stands out from other public service broadcasters and is Europe's largest exporter of television programmes (see Chapter 6). In addition to programme sales, international co-production and ancillary rights' exploitation, the BBC is involved in a range of commercial joint ventures and international channels, and arguably has become Britain's only global media brand. The BBC's commercial interests are represented by commercial subsidiary, BBC Worldwide. In 1997, BBC Worldwide was set a target of contributing £210 million to the corporation by 2006–7 on turnover of £1 billion (BBC Worldwide, 2002). This should of course be seen in the context of the BBC's total revenues of over £3.5 billion in 2002–3. In 2003–4, BBC Worldwide contributed £141 million to the BBC on turnover of £657 million (BBC Worldwide, 2004).

Domestically, BBC Worldwide is involved in a commercial joint venture with Flextech Television to supply a number of commercial subscription channels under the UKTV banner. These are UK Horizons (factual), UK Style (lifestyle), UK Drama, UK Gold (archive entertainment), UK Gold 2, UK Food, UK History and UK Bright Ideas, available in 7.9 to 9.3 million homes in 2003 (BBC Worldwide, 2003a). These are separate from the BBC's wholly owned licence fee-funded digital channels such as BBC4 and CBeebies.

Internationally, BBC Worldwide has a global partnership with the US corporation Discovery Communications Inc., encompassing the joint venture international channels, People and Arts in Latin America and Animal Planet in Asia, Japan, Latin America, Europe and North America. The agreement also covers the co-production of factual programming (*The Blue Planet*, *Walking with Dinosaurs*) and the distribution of BBC Worldwide's wholly owned channel, BBC America, available in 34.5 million US homes in 2003. In 2002, the partnership with Discovery was extended for a further ten years. Other joint venture commercial channels operate in Canada (BBC Kids and BBC Canada with Alliance Atlantis Communications Inc.) and Australia (UKTV owned jointly with FOXTEL and FremantleMedia). Wholly owned BBC Worldwide channels include the news service BBC World (available in over 253 million homes worldwide in 2003) and BBC Prime (available to 11.5 million subscribers in Europe).

Although profits from commercial ventures support the publicly funded core of the BBC, there is concern that commercial involvement may undermine public service priorities in the long term, whatever efforts are made to separate public and commercial activities. Some have remarked that emphasis on international partnerships for high-cost fiction and documentaries, for example, could lead to a neglect of programming aimed specifically at domestic audiences (Sparks, 1995: 336). It is significant, for example, that funding pressures have forced the BBC to look more to co-production finance from the US to fund its upscale period and literary dramas (see Alvarado, 2000). Commercial players are suspicious about the levels of transparency and fair trading between the BBC's commercial and public service operations. Independent producers have complained that the BBC has used its powerful position in the programme supply market to secure by unfair means the rights to independent commissions for secondary and international exploitation (see ITC, 2002). New codes of practice introduced for all terrestrial broadcasters at the start of 2004 aim to give independent producers greater control over the secondary exploitation of their programmes. Moreover, growing unease about the BBC's commercial activities suggests that these will be a key and contested issue in the run up towards the renewal of the BBC's Charter in 2006. In June 2004, the BBC launched a comprehensive review of its commercial activities to report by the end of 2004.

CONCLUSION

At the beginning of the twenty-first century public service television in Western Europe is less powerful and more vulnerable because of increased competition and uncertainties about funding. It has survived, however, and some broadcasters have proved highly adept at instigating competitive scheduling and commissioning strategies. It could also be argued that competition was rather a good thing, because many public channels were perhaps too close to the state, unresponsive to audiences, and wasteful in their use of public resources. Channel expansion gave the public access to levels of sport and drama which simply could not have been accommodated on a restricted number of state-owned channels.

Public service television continues to have an important role in offering a broad range of programming and reflecting a plurality of viewpoints. Its future rests on finding a balance between meeting the needs of the mass audience while also providing the minority or innovative content which commercial suppliers are unwilling or unable to provide. Questions remain about whether this balance can be achieved and whether the public service remit should be extended to encompass niche as well as generalised services.

There are undoubted pressures on public service television to conform to commercial norms but in most cases there are still significant differences in programming profiles between the public and commercial sectors. However, funding remains an ever-present weakness. Advertising and other means of commercial funding can upset the ecology of broadcasting finance, bringing indirect influences on programming which can undermine the public service remit and the justification for public funding. The argument concerning market failure in commercial television provides the best case for publicly owned television. Yet the case for market failure is weakened if there is a perception, rightly or wrongly, that public service broadcasters are not sufficiently distinctive in their strategies, objectives and programming output.

NOTES

1. In Finland, a commercial broadcasting company, MTV (Mainos Television), was allowed in 1957 to transmit on airtime acquired from public broadcaster, YLE (Yleisradio), but this too was developed within a public service framework. By 1993, the relationship had ended when MTV migrated to its own commercial channel, MTV-3.

2. Characteristics of this ideal form of public service television have been outlined variously by Jay Blumler (1992: 7–14 and 1993: 404–9), Kees Brants and Karen Siune (1992: 99–104), BRU (1985), McKinsey (1999: 11–12), Mark Raboy (1995: 5–10) and Michael Tracey (1998: 26–9).

3. Channel 5 changed its name to five in September 2002.

4. This programme moved to Channel 4 in 2004.

5. Sixteenth Additional Provision of the Act 24/2001 on Taxation, Administrative Provisions and Social Affairs (available at <www.igsap.map.es/cia/dispo/I24-01.htm>) (downloaded December 2002).

6. This legislation prevented any shareholder from holding more than a 1 per cent share.

7. The same ruling would have led to the removal of advertising from Rai Tre.

8. NPS, which was separated from NOS in 1995, is responsible for arts and multicultural programming.

9. By 2001, the two Greek public channels could only muster a combined share of 10 per cent (Papathanassopoulos, 2004: 95).

10. With audience shares ranging from 17.5 per cent to 23 per cent.

2

The Commercial Sector – The Rise to Dominance?

At the beginning of the 1980s, there were only a few European commercial broadcasting companies (ITV in the UK, MTV in Finland, Compagnie Luxembourgeoise de Télédiffusion (CLT) in Luxembourg and the newly established Canale 5, Rete 4 and Italia 1 in Italy).[1] In the following two decades, there was an exponential growth of free-to-air commercial channels funded through advertising, together with subscription services usually delivered by cable or satellite:

> In 1980 [the] 'large' [European countries of Italy, France, Germany] each on average had 2.75 TV channels, all of them public. ... In 1990, each country had 8.25 channels – a trebling of TV channels in one decade. By 1990 half of the TV channels were public and half were commercial. (Tunstall and Machin, 1999: 193)

The first part of this chapter will delineate the historical 'phases' of commercialisation in European television. The catalyst for these reforms was the liberalisation of national, regulatory instruments in the 1980s designed to facilitate an introduction of commercial channels in Europe. In the 'first phase', between 1980 and 1988, deregulation led to the introduction of private television stations in Italy, France and Germany (Tunstall and Machin, 1999: 190). In a 'second phase', which occurred in the late 1980s and early 90s, other European countries (Spain, Portugal, Greece, Benelux, Scandinavia) opened up their television markets to commercial services. During this second phase, Europe's oldest commercial television network, Britain's Independent Television (ITV), became subject to the market-driven reforms of the Conservative governments of the 1980s and 90s. These reforms were married to technological changes, the latest being the digitisation of television services in the third 'phase' of commercial development.

The second half of the chapter will consider the imperatives affecting commercial television services in Europe. These changes refer to the *convergence* between telecommunications, broadcasting and computing services and changing ownership patterns which have led to media conglomeration. European-based media conglomerates – Vivendi-Universal, Bertelsmann, Fininvest, and until recently Kirch Media – have entered new markets through a *diversification* of their companies' portfolios and protected their assets by forming strategic alliances with one another. This chapter will provide case studies on the merger of Carlton and Granada in Britain to create a single ITV, the collapse of Kirch Media and the restructuring of Vivendi-Universal assets.

THE FIRST PHASE: THE INTRODUCTION OF COMMERCIAL SERVICES IN ITALY, FRANCE AND GERMANY

Several features characterised the first 'phase' of commercialisation: technological change, the growth of commercial opportunities, national policies to create an unfettered marketplace and the introduction of neo-liberal philosophies (Dyson and Humphreys with Negrine and Simon, 1988). Invariably these factors were associated with deregulation, which became a staple principle of Western European government policies throughout the 1980s (Swann, 1988: 24–5).

With Europe looking towards the United States for the economic principles of deregulatory reform, there was an 'Americanisation' of the European television economy (Tunstall and Machin, 1999: 190). Despite claims that the British television industry acted as a 'Trojan horse' for American entry into Europe, it was Italy which led the way to deregulation in Europe (p. 190). In turn, during the mid-1980s, France and Germany followed the Italian example by commercialising their broadcasting systems. It would, however, be an over-simplification to see the ripples of commercialisation simply emerging from the US and spreading to Europe as the commercial impulse within European television was dictated by distinctive national, economic, legal, cultural and political configurations.

Italy

Italian commercial channels were introduced when the Constitutional Court opened up television to allcomers by deregulating local cable television channels in 1976 (Sassoon, 1985). Subsequently, there was an anarchistic 'chaos of the ether' in programming supply and scheduling as over 700 local channels were created (Fenati and Rizza, 1992: 153). By accident rather than design, television became subject to a comprehensive multiplication of channels and providers.

By 1980, however, the small local private companies could no longer compete and were bought out by Silvio Berlusconi who had transformed his Fininvest property empire into a television corporation. In 1980, Berlusconi established his first commercial station, Canale 5, and subsequently bought up two other national channels, Italia 1 and Rete 4 in 1982 and 1983. Fininvest relied upon imported programming and in 1982 became Europe's largest importer of US programmes when it bought 21,000 hours of programmes from America at a cost of 200 billion lira (Petley, 2002a). In terms of content, Berlusconi's channels preferred to show 'infotainment' or what became known in Italy as 'TV-realita' or 'TV-spazzatura' (television garbage) (Andrews, 2003: 3). Fininvest's home production was noted for its populist approach to quiz shows such as *Il Colpo*, which included infamous 'stripping housewife' sequences (Petley, 2002a).

Berlusconi's channels relied on this diet of imported US and Latin American programming including films, talk shows and daytime soap operas (Tunstall and Machin, 1999: 190–1). To this end, Fininvest employed aggressive scheduling practices and massively inflated the salaries of star performers to maximise audiences and attract advertisers (Petley, 2002a). By having all the commercial television channels under its control, Fininvest was able to heavily cross-promote its programming across its networks. Throughout the remainder of the decade and into the 1990s, Fininvest, through its subsidiary holding company, Mediaset, continued to control Italy's private channels. Over time, Mediaset began to produce a larger number of its own entertainment shows and soap operas (Blain and Cere, 1995).

France

The introduction of commercial channels within France was part of François Mitterand's 1981–6 Socialist government's 'grand design' to dismantle the state monopoly in television. This reform was aided by the new cable and satellite systems, which promised a burgeoning multichannel sector. However, despite attempts to provide a smooth transition from a state monopoly to a competitive television environment, economic and political factors intervened.

France's first commercial terrestrial channel, Canal Plus, funded through subscription, was launched in 1984. Yet any demarcation between state and private interest was more blurred than first appeared. While Canal Plus was placed under the control of the commercial French multimedia company, Havas, this parent organisation had a close relationship with the state, which held over half its shares. As Raymond Kuhn (1995: 178) observes, the state authorities pursued a strategy in which Canal Plus represented 'a new, more indirect mode of state intervention rather than real disengagement'.

Canal Plus established itself as France's market leader by becoming a specialist broadcaster, primarily of feature films and sports. As a pay-television company, Canal Plus did not have to maximise its audience share; its business strategy centred around capturing and consolidating a critical mass of subscribers. When subscribers increased their payments for Canal Plus services by either retaining channels (at an increased cost per annum) or by taking on new programme packages, profitability was achieved (Jezequel and Pineau, 1992: 487).

Canal Plus used its monopoly over pay television to transform French television by providing subscribers with first-run movies and exclusive sports coverage. It hired previously ignored creative talent to develop innovative and challenging fiction programming. In exchange for its licence, Canal Plus agreed to spend 20 per cent of its revenues financing movies, funding as much as 80 per cent of all French films. This not only made Canal Plus a key source of programming but also a vital support mechanism for the French film industry (Crumley, 2002).

By April 1998, Canal Plus had over 6 million subscribers and had expanded on a pan-European basis to establish joint ventures in other European countries (see Chapter 4) (Davis, 1998: 99). Through its joint ownership, with Pathé, Lagardère and Time-Warner, of Canal Satellite, it moved into the French digital satellite market and attracted 900,000 subscribers by June 1999. It became an attractive option for takeover and was bought out by Vivendi in 2000 for $12.5 billion after the water utility company (previously entitled Compagnie Générale des Eaux) transformed itself into a major media concern in the liberalised French television environment of the 1990s (Crumley, 2002).

However, the impetus for commercial reform was eventually undermined during the late 1980s due to the haste in which the private channels were set up, Mitterand's political interests and the uneasy political alliance between the Socialists and the Gaullists. Two other commercial channels, TV6 (now M6) and the now defunct La Cinq, were established and funded by advertising revenue. Despite Gaullist opposition, these channels were created in less than a year and Mitterand allowed the Italian media magnate Berlusconi (who had close relations with the French President's ally, Italy's Socialist Premier, Bettino Craxi) to purchase interests in the Lagardère group's La Cinq. Both channels were entertainment-led and relied heavily on game shows and cheap imports from the US.

After the Gaullist parliamentary victory in 1986, the Statute on the Freedom of Communication led to the privatisation of the state-owned Télévision Française 1 (TF1) channel. The TF1 franchise was fought over by Hachette and the Bouygues consortium, which included François Bouygues's construction company and the late Robert Maxwell's Maxwell Media Corporation (MMC). In the event, the Bouygues consortium won the franchise. The sale demonstrated how a public service channel could be privatised (thereby marginalising the other PSB channels) and how new groups, from different sectors of the economy, could enter the television market (Palmer and Tunstall, 1990: 195).

These changes in TF1's ownership were accompanied by aggressively populist reforms in the station's production, programming and scheduling policies, designed to attract advertising. TF1 commissioned research to determine the market share of each one of its transmissions in relation to production costs and advertising revenue: 'This ... process ... for the first time in France ... [sought] to systematically relate revenue to expenditure on the basis of the choice of programmes, thus costing or displacing the "lame ducks" of the sector' (Jezequel and Pineau, 1992: 488).

Consequently, in its first year, TF1 dropped all its documentary and educational programmes (previously accounting for 15 per cent of its output) and replaced them with entertainment and fiction programmes. These included a steady diet of US imports and an increase in home-produced miniseries patterned on the American models, such as soaps and quiz shows.

TF1 found itself in competition with Antenne 2 (the public service channel funded by advertising, now called France 2) and La Cinq for the rights to sports events and star-studded extravaganzas, thereby increasing the prices of these programmes. Due to its competitive stance, it was able to maximise its resources to outspend its rivals for these rights. As TF1 grew dominant and attracted advertising revenue, La Cinq attempted to compete with TF1 for audience share by launching three ambitious variety programmes in 1987. However, these shows failed to attract audiences and advertisers and the channel was required to restructure its programming by relying on imports. These difficulties led La Cinq into a downward spiral and the channel finally ceased broadcasting in 1992 (pp. 488–9).

France's other commercial television channel M6 (originally TV6) was launched in 1987 and was seen to be 'one channel too many' by the then Culture Minister, Catherine Tasca. Unlike La Cinq, M6 did not initially have major commercial backing to support it and for a while suffered as it was only available to 25 per cent of the French population (p. 438). However, it became more widely available and is owned by RTL (46 per cent) and Suez (37 per cent). While constituted as a general channel funded by advertising, M6 has preferred to develop a niche youth audience due to the requirement that it broadcast music programmes to retain its licence. M6 posted its first profits in 1992, the same year La Cinq ceased to operate. It has continued to make profits by providing popular music programmes such as *Culture-Pub* and *E=M6*, alongside US imports such as *The Cosby Show*. In 2001, it produced a French spin-off to Endemol's reality show *Big Brother*, entitled *Loft Story*. In October 2002, it formed a new general interest channel, TF6, with TF1.

Germany

Launched in 1984, Sat.1 marked the introduction of private television channels in Germany. Germany has since become the leading European, commercial television marketplace. This expansion was associated with the explosion of cable and satellite services and the re-unification of Germany in 1990, which established the largest television audience in Europe. However, in contrast to Italy and France, the legalistic approach taken by the German government initially meant that a strong public service element was retained alongside a burgeoning private sector (Humphreys, 1996: 187).

In 1986, the Constitutional Court approved the introduction of a 'dual system' of public and private broadcasting in which the commercial companies were freed up by a significant, yet measured, degree of deregulation. The decision demanded that they transmit diverse and balanced programming across the range of new communication outlets (external pluralism) under the regulatory supervision of new authorities, the Landesmedienanstalten (p. 187). By the 1990s, German television had six major television services (three public – the Arbeitsgemeinschaft der Rundfunkanstalten Deutschlands (ARD), the Zweites Deutsches Fernsehen (ZDF) and the regional ARD channels and three commercial channels – Sat.1, RTL and Tele5), which accounted for about 80 per cent of the total audience for all public and commercial channels. Alongside these channels, German viewers had access to a range of free and subscription cable or satellite channels.

Throughout the 1980s and 90s, Bertelsmann (the print and publishing company) and Kirch Media, headed by media magnate Leo Kirch, were able to acquire companies within the television market. For several years, RTL, the leading commercial channel in Germany, was jointly owned by Bertelsmann and the Luxembourg-based operator, Compagnie Luxembourgeoise de Télédiffusion (CLT). In 2000, Bertelsmann eventually bought out CLT to acquire the majority ownership of RTL and to confirm its place as the leading European media company. Elsewhere, Kirch held control of the renamed ProSiebenSat.1. It also bought the German television language rights to film and television output from Hollywood, enabling it to launch its digital television platform, Premiere World, in 1996.

In terms of production, programming and scheduling, the commercial channels concentrated on populist programmes such as Hollywood films, cheap game shows and soft-core pornography. In 1987, RTL's schedule consisted of 58 per cent movies, compared to 14 per cent factual programming. In the same year, 64 per cent of Sat.1's light entertainment programmes were drawn from American imports (Petley, 2002a).

For a short time, the public service broadcasters (ARD, ZDF) believed that they could withstand commercial competition due to their thirty-year headstart over their rivals (Brants and de Bens, 2000). However, this attitude changed when RTL and Kirch battled for the rights to the German Football Bundesliga throughout the 1980s and 90s, thereby marginalising the public service broadcasters. Overbidding for sports rights would eventually have dramatic consequences for the whole of the Kirch group (see case study below). It also indicated a more populist attitude to German television services from producers and consumers alike.

THE SECOND PHASE: SPAIN, SCANDINAVIA AND THE UNITED KINGDOM

The introduction of commercial channels continued during the latter half of the 1980s and into the 90s within the Mediterranean countries (Spain, Portugal, Greece) and smaller, northern European states (Benelux, Scandinavia).[2] There was a perpetuation of market-liberal policies, alongside an explosion of commercial opportunities for private operators through the expansion of new media services (cable, satellite, digital).

In Scandinavia, despite resistance from national governments, the development of pan-regional, satellite-based, commercial television services meant that viewers were presented with more choice. In Britain, market reforms affected the ITV network and led to the expansion of News Corporation's interests. These developments demonstrated the dichotomy between commercial imperatives and interventionist content regulations. In this second phase of commercialisation, concerns were raised about the implications of cross-media ownership with regard to funding and programming output.

Spain

The political transition from dictatorship to a modern democracy was key to the introduction of commercial channels in Spain. Consequently, Spain dismantled the state's control over television and developed autonomous, regional, television services. Although Spain's public service broadcaster Radio Televisión Española (RTVE) was established in 1956, between 1975 and 1989, it became subject to significant democratic and commercial reforms, resulting in its dependence on advertising revenue. Consequently, as a large portion of income for Spain's commercial channels was removed, these stations (which were introduced in 1990) have remained financially unstable for many years.

Due to the lack of advertising revenue, Spanish commercial television has been characterised by a high degree of concentration. The Spanish government's liberalisation of media ownership rulings (allowing for a 25 per cent ownership of private television companies by foreign investors and for the cross-media ownership of national newspapers and television companies) led to a significant degree of foreign investment (see Chapter 3). The commercial channels (Antena 3, Telecinco and Canal Plus España) attracted the interests of French, British, German and Italian media companies. Telecinco came under the control of Berlusconi's Fininvest corporation and the media tycoon was mysteriously allowed to secure an 83 per cent stake in the company despite ownership regulations (Tunstall and Machin, 1999: 212).

Spain's three major commercial channels have links with the nation's main newspaper groups. For example, Prisa, publisher of the left-supporting daily *El País* newspaper, has entered the television market through its subsidiary company Sogecable. It has also invested in the successful Canal Plus pay-television channel and pursued acquisitions within the digital television marketplace (p. 213). Prisa's expansionary tendencies in the new digital markets would lead to a dispute with the Conservative Aznar government in the mid-1990s concerning live rights for La Liga football matches. This dispute, known as the 'football war', raised concerns about the public's access to subscription-based sports services and, due to political divisions between the right and the left in Spanish politics, the government stopped Prisa gaining control over sports rights.

Spain's commercial channels have provided their audiences with a diet of entertainment-based programming. For instance, Telecinco's schedule followed Berlusconi's Italian formula of US imports, quizzes, extravaganzas and soft-core pornography. In its first year, light entertainment and popular dramas accounted for 76 per cent of its weekly programmes (Villagrasa, 1992: 410). Initially, Antena 3 faced problems concerning its use of radio stars to front talk shows and its failure to acquire foreign titles. However, changes within the network's management led to a more coherent, commercial, programme strategy based on game shows such as *The Wheel of Fortune* and a reliance on repeats of old US series, including *Bewitched* and *Bonanza* (pp. 408–9).

Scandinavia

When commercial channels were introduced in Scandinavia (Sweden, Norway, Denmark, Finland), they had a dramatic impact on the region's television systems. In the first half of the 1980s, Scandinavia was virtually free of commercial channels but by the second half of the decade, private stations had proliferated. Instead of a clear legislative procedure, private television came through the back door as satellite television from outside Scandinavia's borders saw the lifting of the ban on advertising for domestic television services (Petersen, 1992: 618).

Swedish investment company Kinnevik, through the UK-registered company

ScanSat/TV3 based in London, launched TV3 on Intelsat in 1987. This quickly penetrated Scandinavian markets despite national bans on advertising carried on the channel. TV3 became a regional commercial player and provided a programming mix of films, series, entertainment, sports and news, of which only 20 per cent was produced within the region and for which all imports were subtitled into a Scandinavian language (Dahlgren, 2000: 25). It soon became obvious that TV3 was drawing advertising away from the national economies, and to stem this drain on resources, Sweden established TV4 as a national commercial channel (p. 25).

TV3's success led to further regional commercial channels and pay-television ventures (FilmNet, TV1000, TV Norge) which circumvented national regulations and developed a pan-regional approach to content. A pan-regional strategy proved to be a better way of securing profits as the individual domestic television markets were too small, in terms of population and advertising share, to sustain growth. In the mid-1990s, the pan-European Scandinavian Broadcasting System (SBS) was established with US backing to take advantage of the regional market.

Britain

Market reforms within the British television industry occurred in a different manner. Commercial free-to-air channel, ITV, was established in 1955 and consisted of a regional network of franchisees, including Granada, Thames, Central, Yorkshire and London Weekend Television. The system was heavily regulated and the Independent Broadcasting Authority (IBA) exercised content as well as financial regulation (Wheeler, 1997: 89–92). In response to public concern about ITV companies' excess profits, in the early 1960s, a levy on the regional licences was introduced to ensure that the commercial companies would invest in original programming and follow public service remits (p. 93).

Following the 1990 Broadcasting Act, ITV became subject to a franchise auction and this competitive tendering process saw companies including Thames and TV-AM lose their franchises (replaced by Carlton Communications and Good Morning Television [GMTV] respectively). As a result of the amount ITV had to pay to the government for the privilege of a licence, ITV had to cut costs and develop programming schedules which would conform to the interests of the advertisers (pp. 149–55). Consequently, these financial pressures meant that when the Conservative government lifted ownership rules, the larger ITV companies purchased smaller regional licensees thereby enabling two companies, Carlton and Granada, to become dominant (p. 152). Since 2000, these companies have attempted to merge towards creating a unified ITV. These calls were hastened by the two companies failing to sustain ITV Digital as a successful digital subscription channel, which closed down in 2002 (see Chapter 5). With the 2003 Communication Act, Carlton and Granada were allowed to merge, creating a single company to run ITV (see following case study), and the legislation also permitted non-EU companies to purchase free-to-air commercial channels. As a result, fears have been articulated that a single-owned ITV may become subject to a foreign takeover from a major US media corporation (Wheeler, 2003).

The collapse of ITV Digital allowed the satellite monopoly BSkyB to consolidate its dominance in the digital subscription market (see Chapter 5). It is controlled by Rupert Murdoch's News Corporation, which owns 35.4 per cent of the company since BSkyB went public in 1994 (Horsman, 1998: 133). Murdoch also sought to gain a foothold in UK terrestrial television, and despite Lord David Puttnam's 'public voice' amendments (see Chapter 3) to be administered by the unitary regulatory body Ofcom, the 2003 Act may still enable News Corporation to buy terrestrial channel 5, in which RTL holds a 65 per cent share (see Chapter 3).[3]

Following major structural reforms in Britain's terrestrial, commercial television sector, advertisers gained a greater say in programme schedules and ITV has produced more populist programming including game shows, popular dramas and sports programming. After the 1990 Broadcasting Act, ITV reduced

News at Ten

V Graham Norton

the peak-time provision of religious programming and replaced current affairs programmes such as *World in Action* with infotainment programmes like *Tonight*, hosted by Trevor McDonald (Wheeler, 1997: 154). During the late 1990s, ITV moved its flagship news bulletin, *News at Ten*, to a later time, although Ofcom content regulations still require the network to schedule news and factual content in peak periods.

There are still relatively strong content regulations (including quotas determining the levels of home-produced content) governing ITV (see Chapter 3). Channel 4, a publicly owned corporation funded by advertising revenue, is legally required to produce minority and informational programming (e.g. *Channel 4 News*) at peak times. Since its launch in 1982, the channel has been required to commission original programming from independent producers and to maintain innovation in its output, while pursuing an ever-diminishing share of advertising revenue. This has led to more popular domestic productions including the daily *Richard and Judy* and *V Graham Norton* celebrity talk shows, alongside the purchase of US imports (usually produced by Home Box Office) such as *The Sopranos* and *Six Feet Under*. Yet Channel 4 has been dogged by its failure to attract subscribers for its digital channels (E4 and FilmFour) and in 2002, it endured the collapse of its film production and distribution company, FilmFour.

From the start, Channel 5, the most recently launched terrestrial service, was an explicitly commercial channel engaged in populist scheduling. In terms of programming, the policy of its executives, most notably Programme Director, Dawn Airey, was to base the schedule on cheap productions, US imports and soft-core pornography. More recently, with Airey's departure to BSkyB, the channel has adapted its policy to some degree and has invested in documentaries produced by independent production companies for peak-time transmissions.

As satellite broadcaster BSkyB is technically a Luxembourg-based service, it has been able to successfully circumvent British content regulations. While it has produced more home programming and has a rolling news channel, Sky News, the satellite monopoly has developed entertainment programmes such as *Soccer AM*, *Gamezville* and *Kirsty's Home Videos*, alongside first-run US imports such as *The Simpsons* and *Friends*. Moreover, as a subscription package, BSkyB has followed Canal Plus's model of capturing and consolidating subscribers through rights control over sports (particularly football) and feature films.

CASE STUDY: ITV PLC – THE MERGER OF CARLTON AND GRANADA

Consolidation in the British commercial television sector peaked with the merger of the two largest ITV companies, Granada and Carlton. The 2002 Communications Bill (and 2003 Act) allowed Granada and Carlton (who owned eleven out of the fifteen regional franchises) to create a single ITV. In the climate of the 2001–2 advertising recession, such consolidation was seen as vital by Carlton and Granada. Hurt by the failure of their jointly backed, digital, terrestrial, pay-television venture, ITV Digital, both companies were not only left with a huge hole in their finances, but faced a loss of City confidence in their respective managements. Due to the Bill's proposed removal of restrictions governing non-EU foreign ownership, both companies were also vulnerable to takeover bids.

Faced with this crisis, on 16 October 2002, Carlton and Granada agreed to engage in a £2.6 billion merger. To effect this merger, Carlton's broadcasting licences (London and London News Network [LNN], Central, West Country, Harlech Television [HTV] West and HTV Wales) and its 20 per cent share in the ITN news service would be set aside to form a separate company, which in turn would merge with Granada, which controlled the rest of the licences (Granada, LWT, Yorkshire, Tyne-Tees, Meridian, Anglia and Border) within a newly created broadcaster to be called ITV plc. In terms of ownership, Carlton's shareholders would receive 32 per cent of equity in ITV plc, with Granada shareholders retaining the remainder. Finally, both companies argued the merger would generate about £35 million in savings and that economies of scale could be made through removing duplication in the infrastructure and administration of broadcasting, content and services.

However, while Carlton and Granada's executives restructured their businesses in preparation for the proposed merger, a major obstacle emerged concerning the new company's potentially anti-competitive control over the sale of advertising. Although ITV only achieves a 24 per cent share of the British television audience, as the leading supplier of mass audiences it holds onto a hefty 54 per cent share of the total expenditure on television advertising. Advertisers feared this control would give a combined ITV sales house the power to set the price for advertising slots.

Any merger that exceeded a 25 per cent market share needed to be referred to the competition authorities (*The Economist*, 2002). In the event, Patricia Hewitt, the Secretary of State for Trade and Industry, allowed the merger to go ahead in autumn 2003 after seeking assurances from ITV to stem market dominance over advertising sales (Tryhorn, 2003b). It was announced that Carlton's Chairman, Michael Green, would become the new company's Chairman and that Charles Allen, Granada's Chairman, would act as its Chief Executive (p. 24). However, due to the failure of ITV Digital, the City's confidence in both executives, especially Green, remained low. On 21 October 2003, at the behest of its investors, Michael Green was removed as the Chairman of the merged company, and emerging in a period of instability, the unified ITV could still be seen to be vulnerable to foreign takeover in the future (Deans, 2003).

THE THIRD PHASE OF COMMERCIALISATION: THE DIGITAL REVOLUTION

Since the late 1990s, the development of digital channels and the broadband delivery of services have effected major changes in Europe's commercial television market. It has been predicted that these digital television platforms and technologies may allow for a combination of new or different information services, including an expansion of choice in television channels and interactive possibilities including email, access to the Internet and home shopping. Thus, the major broadcasting organisations and companies have invested in the technology believing that digital convergence would increase economic opportunity and consumer demand. These developments are discussed at greater length in Chapter 5.

MEDIA CONGLOMERATION: ECONOMIC OPPORTUNITIES

For media conglomerates, the commercial television industries hold several attractions. The television business lends itself to consolidation, as there are enormous economies of scale that come from enlarging the footprints of television services both at national and, to a lesser degree, international levels. For instance, in partnership with Albert Frère's GBL group, the German media giant Bertelsmann took control of CLT-UFA, reinforcing its dominant position in the European media economy. Through such linkages Bertelsmann has become active in all of the media content industries: television, radio, book publishing, magazines, newspapers, recorded music, professional information, print and media services, book and music clubs and the Internet. Further, through such means it has been able to expand across national territories and now derives one-third of its revenues from Germany, another third from the rest of Europe, and the remainder from the US market. Thus, by 2000, Bertelsmann belonged to the top ten world media groups with an annual turnover of $6.873 billion (EAO, 2001a: 52).

Simultaneously, the communications marketplace has seen the major media organisations expanding through cross-media ownership and a proliferation of complex alliances between national, transnational and global media corporations across the commercial European television sector. Diversification allows conglomerates to take advantage, if not control, of several stakes in the communications industry, wielding their power through the vertical integration of content production and distribution. Thus, as cross-media ownership opportunities have grown, these organisations have developed a wide variety of business strategies including the pursuit of economies of scale, greater synergies, joint ventures, branding, segmentation and specialisation, and corporate diversification (Murdock, 2000: 38).

Finally, the European commercial television economy has been characterised by movements towards corporate expansion, including takeovers and mergers of media companies. For example, Vivendi, through acquisition from Seagram of the US film, television and music company, Universal, established Vivendi-Universal in 2000, becoming the first European company to enter the top five worldwide media groups. On 3 October 2003, however, it was announced that, due to the financial and corporate difficulties facing the French corporation, Vivendi-Universal had merged its US assets with the US media conglomerate General Electric (GE) (see case study below).

Corporate Expansion within the European Television and Audiovisual Industries

The strongest factor leading to the growth of European media corporations has been the increasing power of American media conglomerates. In the latter half of the 1990s, European media companies viewed developments across the Atlantic with growing concern as a series of mergers within the US media turned a once-fragmented economy into an industry dominated by giants.

Major US companies sought to diversify their interests across content and entertainment businesses. With the US conglomerates benefiting from the size of their domestic market, these companies also moved to test the international market, including European territories. For example, in 2000, Time-Warner entered the European television market through its $896 million backing of French company Lagardère's 34 per cent investment in Canal Plus's satellite platform, Canal Satellite (Lagardère, 2000). To compete, European companies had to grow, for it was through the scale of their enterprise that the American companies had been able to amortise their costs at home, sell programmes cheaply to foreign markets, distribute movies globally and build programming libraries to launch new channels around the world.

However, despite their arguments for corporate expansion and mergers, European media firms were subject to a large number of restrictions when pursuing such business ambitions. Legal controls over the television spectrum of airwaves limited the number of channels that could be owned by commercial broadcasters as they often hit ceilings set by ordinary competition law, precluding mergers between them. Even where deals were possible, media businesses tended to be constrained by national ownership regulations and legislation as governments sought to preserve public service obligations and maintain equity in national media economies (see Chapter 3).

Competition Rulings Concerning Mergers

Those mergers that were sanctioned by national regulators had to be considered by the European Commission (EC). In particular, the EC's Competition Directorate was concerned that too much content may be held in the hands of dominant 'gatekeepers' and that consumer choice would thereby be undermined. With regard to the digital economy, the directorate sought to employ its merger regulations to investigate any proposed cross-communications alliance or merger before it proceeded rather than consider such cases retrospectively. In interpreting these complex merger rules, the EU understood that rapid technological change may enhance the opportunities to increase market concentration, rather than reduce them (Van Miert, 1997). To this end, the EU Competition Directorate has determined to preserve rivalry in the pay-television business within Europe's separate national markets.

In 1994, for example, Germany's commercial television owners, Bertelsmann and Kirch, proposed a joint venture with the German telecommunications monopoly Deutsche Telekom (DT) to be called Media Services Gesellschaft (MSG). They intended that the MSG conglomerate should deliver pay-television and broadband interactive services such as video-on-demand through conditional access and decoder systems. However, the directorate vetoed the merger for three reasons. As Kirch had dominant control over German television programme rights and libraries, MSG would have become the dominant supplier of programmes in the pay-television market. Second, the joint venture would have produced a 'durable dominant position' by controlling the provision of conditional access and subscriber management systems to viewers. Finally, DT's dominance of the German cable market would be enhanced rather than challenged if MSG had been established (Levy, 1999: 88–9).

During 1998, Kirch again sought to merge its digital television interests with Bertelsmann and DT in a second strategic alliance dubbed 'MSGII' (Levy, 1999: 92–3). When the Competition Directorate investigated MSGII, it raised concerns about the formation of a pay-television monopoly in a single, national market, control over programming rights, access to the German cable network, and the proprietary nature of the proposed set-top box. With these concerns in mind, the directorate decided to prohibit the deal to prevent the creation of a monopoly of supply and distribution.

As a consequence, media companies have had to look elsewhere for growth. To some degree they have taken advantage of the EU's 1989 Television Without Frontiers Directive which allowed corporations to invest in transnational joint ventures. For example, in smaller European countries (e.g. Belgium, the Netherlands) richer foreign broadcasters such as the French Canal Plus have entered local markets. Broadcasters have also used EU harmonisation principles to circumvent local controls. For instance, as Swedish television regulations ban advertising to children, the Scandinavian pan-regional channel TV3 broadcasts from Britain where there are no such restrictions. However, these forms of consolidation have remained marginal as there has been little in the way of transnational trade between the major markets due to language barriers, cultural peculiarities and the large-scale reliance on imported US product. Thus, as an alternative they have sought to establish complex corporate alliances with one another.

Proliferation of Corporate Alliances

The complexity of these alliances resulted from both the pressures to consolidate media businesses (e.g. fear of corporate raiding by US corporations or the convergence of audiovisual with telecommunications and information services), alongside those forces peculiar to the European media's political economy (e.g. competition policies, national cultures and political composition) which kept them apart. Within the business environment of the late 1990s, the media corporations purchased minority stakes in one another's companies to enhance their profits and diversify their interests.

For example, in 1999 Murdoch and Kirch negotiated a deal whereby BSkyB bought 24 per cent of KirchPayTV (the holding company for the Premiere World digital platform) from the German media mogul's Kirch Media Group. Kirch was not, however, Murdoch's first choice of partner. He had originally tried to buy interests in Berlusconi's Mediaset television channels but the deal fell through. Simultaneously, Berlusconi's Fininvest also tried to delicately manoeuvre towards an alliance with Kirch aimed at what was then described as the first European television network. Meanwhile, Murdoch invested in the Italian pay-television platform, Stream, in partnership with Berlusconi's Mediaset, Telecom Italia and a number of Italian football teams, while seeking to negotiate a merger with the biggest power in European pay television, Canal Plus. In the event, the competition authorities did not sanction the deal between News Corporation and Canal Plus. In turn, Canal Plus energetically expanded abroad in the 1990s, moving originally into Belgium, then Spain, Germany and Poland. It bought Nethold, a Dutch pay-television operator, in 1996, and acquired Kirch's and Berlusconi's stakes in Telepiù, Italy's main pay-television platform in 1998 (see Chapter 4). However, in 2000 Vivendi eventually bought out Canal Plus.

It would, however, be misleading to suggest that these alliances have been wholly successful (e.g. Canal Plus sold its interest in Telepiù to News Corporation), and in 2003, it appeared that the European commercial television market was entering a period of strategic disentanglement as the media companies weighed up their competitors' assets in preparation for corporate raids and hostile takeovers. Moreover, the failure of digital, pay-television services to attract sufficient subscribers to meet their business objectives and the accompanying decline in advertising expenditures sent the European commercial television market into a tailspin (see Chapter 5).

THE FINANCIAL CRISIS IN EUROPEAN COMMERCIAL TELEVISION

Despite the apparent benefits for corporate expansion in a converging communications marketplace, there are considerable dangers in pursuing these business policies. Invariably, European media corporations have become victims of their own attempts to develop into vertically integrated organisations through their rapacious purchasing of media companies, together with investment in digital pay television and their failure to address declining consumer demand resulting in declining share prices.

CASE STUDY: PAY TELEVISION AND THE FALL OF KIRCH MEDIA

The collapse of the German media giant, Kirch Media, in 2002 reflected many of the challenges facing Europe's major media groups in the television marketplace. These include the consequences of overstretching corporate resources to establish a vertically integrated media empire and the inherent dangers associated with the tangled web of alliances existing between media corporations.

In 1996, Leo Kirch risked his media empire on the success of a very expensive pay-television platform, Premiere World. This corporate plan would see Kirch produce, distribute and sell products across a number of platforms including free-to-air and subscription-based television channels. To realise these opportunities, Kirch took a calculated but expensive risk by paying for exclusive film and sports rights, funded through excessive bank loans and the partial selling of the Kirch Group's assets to other media corporations, most notably News Corporation. Kirch paid for a costly set of ten-year output deals with the Hollywood studios, which, according to its administrators, left a hole of €800 million in Kirch Media's books (Hooper, 2002a). In addition, at great cost, Kirch bought the worldwide broadcasting rights to football's 2002 and 2006 World Cups and Formula One motor racing, together with the rights to top-flight German football (Hooper, 2002b). Unfortunately, in pursuing this list of entertainment and sports rights, Kirch Media owed the banks alone around €5.5 billion (£4.8 billion) (Hooper, 2002c).

Despite Kirch's power as a purchaser of rights and as a marketer, Premiere failed to attract subscribers. Therefore, to sustain its investment, Kirch entered into an alliance with Rupert Murdoch's BSkyB. Murdoch, however, took care to include a contractual clause to drop out if Premiere did not achieve the subscription rates to match its business plans. As Premiere subscribers numbered fewer than 2.4 million in 2001, considerably less than the projected 3.5 million, the resulting gap represented a cash-burn rate of €2 million (£1.2 million) per day. In the financial year 2000–1, Premiere ultimately posted a net loss of €1.9 billion (£1.2 billion) (Hooper and Cassy, 2002).

In total, Kirch invested approximately €5 billion (£3.1 billion) into the pay-television venture and this strain infected the healthier sections of its operations, including its film library and the free-to-air television operation, ProSiebenSat.1. Due to the Hollywood companies and sports right-holders' insistence on selling their rights to Kirch Media rather than the subsidiary, KirchPayTV, the parent company was forced to sell the rights to its own subsidiary. This complex internal arrangement created a fatal division in the business arms of the empire and the full plight of Kirch Media's predicament became clear in December 2001 when the company failed to repay a sum of €500 million (£306 million) to the Dresdner Bank (Clark, 2002).

Leo Kirch resigned from Kirch Media in April 2002 and the four German banks who were each owed around €1.4 billion determined its future. In 2002, they put Kirch Media into 'self-administration', an unusual form of insolvency allowing the existing management to remain in office and assist Wolfgang van Betteray, an insolvency specialist, who was put in place by the banks to run the company. In turn, van Betteray promised major cost-cutting and a return to core competences (Hooper, 2002c).

Kirch Media's insolvency has been Germany's most spectacular post-war corporate failure. In 2002, there was the possibility that a foreign company could purchase Premiere for a 'firesale' price and secure a major foothold in the German media economy. As a consequence, German politicians became concerned about the implications for foreign ownership regulations if either Murdoch or Berlusconi attained a controlling interest within Kirch's television assets (Milmo, 2002). In August 2003, Kirch's most successful asset, ProSiebenSat.1, was sold to the holding company PS71, owned by Israeli-American Haim Saban, who had built his fortune through popular children's television programming (e.g. *Power Rangers*) (Milmo, 2003a).

Bertelsmann

Other vertically integrated media corporations have faced severe difficulties in the depressed European television market. In 2002, Bertelsmann returned the focus of its corporate strategy to its primary assets such as the television company, RTL. This change in corporate strategy was signified by the resignation of Chief Executive Thomas Middelhoff in the summer of 2002 after his acquisitional tendencies had fallen foul of the corporation's board in the climate of uncertainty. Thus, RTL made it clear that it would not seek to expand into the British television market through a rumoured takeover of ITV. Middelhoff's replacement as CEO, Gunter Thielen, informed Germany's DPA news agency: 'We will focus less on wheeling and dealing and more on building and creating' (Burt, 2002).

In the wake of this retrenchment, RTL Head Didier Bellens's decision to resign in February 2003 was seen to mark further a division between Bertelsmann's modernisers and its patriarch, Reinhard Mohn. Against the wishes of so-called Gütersloh 'Bertelsmen', Mohn has rejected global expansion and sought to return Bertelsmann to its core publishing activities and corporate dynastic structure (Cassy, 2003).

CASE STUDY: THE FAILURE OF VIVENDI-UNIVERSAL AND THE CREATION OF NBC-UNIVERSAL

In 2002, as it became clear that France's Vivendi-Universal had been labouring under a €17 billion (£10.6 billion) debt burden, speculation grew that the company would become subject to a hostile break-up bid (Milner, 2002). Responsibility for this crisis was associated with Vivendi's dynamic Chief Executive, Jean-Marie Messier, who had transformed the French water utility company into one of Europe's major media conglomerates. Rumour circulated that Messier would be removed and his position worsened after a misjudged speech in which he favourably compared US culture and business practices with French traditions. This pronouncement lost Messier the support of the French political and business establishment at a crucial period during the company's share slump.

Simultaneously, Messier's sacking of Canal Plus founder, Pierre Lescure, and replacement of him with Xavier Couture, Director of Canal Plus's chief rival TF1, led to criticisms of Messier at Vivendi's 2002 shareholders' meeting. Other objections were raised with demonstrations by the Canal Plus staff against job cuts, denouncements from French film stars such as Juliette Binoche, and a boardroom battle ensued (Milner, 2002). Consequently, Messier resigned in July 2002 to be replaced by Jean-René Fourtou (previously the Vice-Chairman of Franco-German drugs company, Aventis) in preparation for the divestment of Vivendi-Universal's American-based assets towards refocusing the company on its European operations, including Canal Plus (Teather, 2002: 19).

With the arrival of Fourtou, Vivendi's investors and credit-rating agencies were determined to see a drastic reduction in the company's debt through dismantling the portfolio of media companies. However, while Vivendi's music, film, television, telecommunications and Internet interests would obviously attract buyers, the breaking up of the corporation's assets had a significant downside. Messier, like Kirch, had sold his investors the vision of an integrated media machine, seamlessly incorporating media production and distribution systems. Vivendi's spending had been funded through the selling of shares rather than through the sale of its assets, which proved to be a very risky strategy dependent on the maintenance of a high share price. Yet, the slump in Vivendi's share price between 2001 and 2002 meant instead that there was an accumulation of debts, indicating to investors that the holding company was worth considerably less than the sum of its parts.

Throughout 2003, Vivendi's new management sought to restructure the group and reduce debt by selling off a large number of companies. Finally, in October 2003, Fourtou concluded the $43 billion merger of Vivendi-Universal's US entertainment arm with US media conglomerate, General Electric (GE), as the junior partner in a new venture, NBC-Universal (Milmo, 2003b). This deal saw GE owning 80 per cent of NBC-Universal and Vivendi retaining a 20 per cent stake and a payment of $3.3 billion (p. 23). For Fourtou, the merger enabled him to slash Vivendi's debt to less than €5 billion while NBC-Universal took on the remaining debt of $1.7 billion (p. 23). The two companies predicted they would achieve a cost saving of between $400 million and $500 million from combining resources, including Universal Pictures, cable television network USA and NBC's broadcast and cable channels (p. 23).

European Media Conglomerates in a Declining Advertising Market

With the collapse of Kirch, Bertelsmann's strategic retrenchment and Vivendi's merger with GE, the future is by no means clear for some of Europe's largest media and communications corporations. The deposing of executives has resulted in corporate inconsistency and the European television market has seen successive withdrawals of capital from digital platforms by television corporations, such as the RTL Group, Carlton and Granada and telecommunications companies, including France Télécom and Telecom Italia (see Chapter 5).

Concurrently, there has been a spectacular decline in advertising revenues. In part this downturn reflected the general recession in the global economy after the events of 11 September 2001. Yet, most of the troubles faced by European television were in place long before the terrorist attacks, owing to an overall collapse in advertising expenditures. This decline has been exacerbated by the continued cannibalising of advertising spending with the multiplication of television channels and popular adoption of information communication technologies such as the Internet. According to a report produced by Schroder Salomon Smith Barney in 2000–1, dotcom advertising left European commercial television facing a decline in advertising revenues. For instance, in 2001, the German television channel, ProSiebenSat.1, saw a reduction of 2.3 per cent in advertising income during the first quarter (Milmo, 2003a: 24).

This decline has been especially problematic for the European television marketplace. In December 2001, leading commercial television players issued profit warnings. ProSiebenSat.1 claimed that its net income would fall 10 per cent per annum. France's TF1 forecast a similar fall in its annual earnings and the RTL group released its fourth profit warning of 2001. In Britain that same year, ITV suffered from a 12 per cent fall in television advertising, the worst decline since the advent of British commercial television. While European television companies had previously suffered from advertising recessions, they had never faced a crisis on this scale.

CONCLUSION

From the late 1980s, European deregulators have been attracted to the introduction of advertising-funded or subscription-based commercial television channels. This dynamic occurred in tandem with technological changes inaugurated by the growth of cable and satellite channels. These changes promised to expand advertising markets and pay-television services. At an ideological level, reformers provided public choice arguments for the introduction of these services, contending that broadcasting was no different from any commercial enterprise and that open markets would allow for a greater plurality of providers, thereby encouraging consumer sovereignty.

However, the result of these commercial reforms and the increased demand for television programmes was 'not … [a] rapid expansion in European television production, but [an] increased [reliance on] import and a decline in the European production' (de Bens, Kelly and Bakke, 1992: 76). Increasingly, commercial television production, programming and scheduling practices have reflected the demand to appease advertisers by chasing mass audiences leading to a decrease in diversity and a greater degree of homogenised, entertainment-led content over information and education programmes (Dahlgren, 2000: 30).

A further effect of commercialisation has been to open up European television systems to various forms of media concentration as cross-media monopolies consolidate their assets and diversify their interests (Petley, 2002a; Murdock, 1990: 10–11). European media corporations have expanded to offset the growth of US media giants through a variety of strategies, including attempted corporate marriages. However, since the media business is defined by political and regulatory factors as well as economic opportunities, national regulators and the EU Competition Directorate have been concerned that too much content may be in the hands of dominant gatekeepers. A division has therefore occurred in the European television economy between media corporations seeking competitive advantage to protect themselves from US media firms, and the need to ensure a commercial environment that promotes openness, fairness and diversity in the provision of services.

In response, European media corporations have formed complex alliances to match their competitors' strengths. Despite these alliances, the European television marketplace has entered a period of strategic re-alignment as the finances of media companies have declined in the wake of misguided vertical integration strategies. The collapse of Kirch Media reflected these trends as it diversified with a risky but apparently sustainable move from free-to-air to subscription-based services. Alongside Kirch's demise, other vertically integrated media corporations like Bertelsmann have faced difficulties in the depressed European television market. Vivendi-Universal's merger with GE represented an end to its ambitions in the US market and a humiliation for French cultural and business practices.

These problems have been accompanied by a downturn in the European television industries due to the failure of digital pay-television services to attract subscribers, leading to the collapse of a number of DTV platforms. In turn, greater financial pressures have been placed on the major European television companies through declining advertising revenues. Consequently, European commercial television is exhibiting the contradictory but equally powerful imperatives of corporate consolidation and collapse.

NOTES

1. Luxembourg has always had a commercial television system.
2. A similar commercialisation of services occurred in the smaller European states of Portugal, Greece, Belgium and Holland (see Siune and Truetzchler [Eds], 1992).
3. According to Puttnam, the 2003 Act amendment meant that Ofcom would have the power to determine the extent to which a media owner or conglomerate has an unfair or majority share of the public voice across the diverse range of their portfolio of interests. He felt that this would ensure a significant bulwark in the deregulatory thrust of the legislation. Yet the Liberal Democrat Culture and Media spokesman Lord McNally remained sceptical about the potency of this amendment and warned:

> Our media is not defenceless now, but it is still exposed.... The bill should be re-drafted to rule out ... [the] purchase of Channel 5 by Mr Murdoch. Believe me, these forces are out there, [and] in the words of the Terminator, they'll be back. (O.Carroll, 2003)

3

The Legal and Regulatory Context – National Approaches

Technological advances such as cable, satellite and digital compression, together with liberalised regulation, are reshaping the European broadcasting landscape. During the course of history, most Western European states created a politically and culturally protected broadcasting (particularly for television) regulatory environment. This was because of television's opinion-forming power, the scarcity of available frequencies, as well as the high initial investment in technology and infrastructure which prevented a multiplicity of players. This is all changing. On the one hand, we are witnessing a determination by governments to encourage new competitive enterprises in television. On the other, we are seeing the politics of re-regulation (or 'light touch' regulation) and commercialisation, justified politically by the process of globalisation and technological change. Digital technology, in particular, has changed the number, type and relationship of players in the media sector and has brought about a proliferation of new networks and channels. It is also facilitating technological, market and industry convergence.[1]

Technological and market changes associated with digitisation and convergence, ideological shifts as well as changes in society, lifestyles and consumption, call for regulatory reform. The first part of this chapter briefly deals with the traditional basis for television regulation and explains the rationale for establishing a tight policy framework in the sector. The second part looks at the technological, political, economic, legal and socio-cultural factors which altered traditional perceptions of television regulation. It then assesses whether the emerging shape of the television landscape can be best characterised as deregulation, i.e. total dismantling of rules, or re-regulation, i.e. adjustment towards a more relaxed regulatory framework. Despite regulatory differences between countries, the analysis shows restructuring of television systems has resulted in regulatory relaxation rather than complete abandonment of rules. The analysis then considers both the ownership and content regulatory regime which still applies to most European countries. The final part assesses future regulatory attitudes in view of digitisation and the trend towards technological convergence.

THE TRADITIONAL BASIS FOR TELEVISION REGULATION

Until the 1980s, broadcasting in Western Europe contrasted with the US by considering television services as a 'public good', and was therefore highly regulated in terms of both access and content. Television was considered to be an important contributor to the social and political life of nations, through the provision of information, culture and education, and therefore specific rules were needed to protect those objectives. Most governments adopted sector-specific regulation rather than generic regulation. While telecommunications regulation was directed at influencing the behaviour of the dominant incumbent and creating the conditions of a competitive market, television regulation was more directly linked to concerns regarding content. Licence conditions were (and, to a certain extent, still are) generally aimed at encouraging pluralism, impartiality, consumer protection and the promotion of national heritage. Restrictions on media ownership were intended to achieve non-economic objectives, such as plurality of voices and diversity of content.[2]

As outlined in Chapter 1, the establishment of public service broadcasting (PSB) systems across Europe provided for internal pluralism – catering for all interests in a particular society, with universal access free at the point of reception. Of course, the way broadcasting systems were organised and controlled differed from country to country, reflecting the different national, political contexts in which they were embedded. Some countries, like Britain, Finland and Sweden, developed independent public broadcasters, while a partisan public broadcasting tradition prevailed in countries such as Italy and Greece. Belgium developed a decentralised broadcasting system catering to linguistic and cultural fragmentation, while a highly centralised broadcasting system prevailed in countries like France (Humphreys, 1996: 123). Despite these national differences, television broadcasting was subject to content and structural regulation in most Western European countries.

Frequency scarcity determined the traditional arguments for the regulation of television broadcasting: the broadcasting spectrum is limited and if broadcasting is unrestricted, this might result in a chaos in which no signals can be retrieved. Governments regulated to allocate frequencies and signal strength efficiently, intervening to ration access to the medium and thus achieve service quality. In addition to issues related to technical interference, national governments regulated either because they did not want to see private interests occupy all or a large part of that limited public resource, or simply because they wanted to retain control of television. The political influence of broadcasting in creating the conditions for political debate and forming political views motivated governments to initiate and apply broadcasting law and policy. As Levy (1999: 20) points out, the political rationale for regulation has been expressed most clearly in Germany, where concerns to avoid any repeat of the Nazis' abusive use of broadcasting for propaganda weighed heavily on those involved in constructing the new post-war West German state. Greece was another European country which became aware of the political importance of television as the medium was openly used for propaganda purposes under the military dictatorship (1967–74). Even after the restoration of democracy, successive governments intervened directly in the content of television news of public broadcaster ERT (Hellenic Radio and Television) (Katsoudas, 1985).

In practice, many EU countries justified, in one way or another, government involvement in broadcasting on political grounds. In France, public broadcasting for decades did the bidding of mainly conservative governments (Tunstall and Machin, 1999: 92). In post-war Germany, Chancellor Adenauer and the Christian Democrat Party (CDU) spent years trying to undermine the public service broadcasting system imposed by the British and American occupying forces, because they thought it did not serve their political interests. The Italian public broadcaster, RAI (Radiotelevisione Italiana), was close to the Roman Catholic Church and to a succession of corrupt Christian Democrat-led governments. Contrary to the highly politicised broadcasting systems in Italy, France and Greece, in countries like Britain and Sweden, public broadcasters gained a reputation for political neutrality from their inception.

Another reason for regulating television was to ensure quality and diversity of programmes. It was thought that the market alone could not necessarily deliver or achieve impartiality, information diversity, cultural and political pluralism, and thus a minimum of content regulation was required. Advertisers, for example, can influence and restrict the diversity of what is broadcast in the search for the largest possible audiences. Therefore, governments applied both negative content regulation (or consumer protection regulation) – restricting diffusion of certain types of information, text, sound and images, and positive – promoting access to content, guaranteeing quality and diversity of programmes (Forgan and Tambini, 2001: 45). The positive objectives of content regulation were to be secured partly by the maintenance of public broadcasters, who were required by statute to deliver high-quality programmes accessible to all and satisfying all interests, and partly by the establishment of broadcast quotas (see below).

An additional rationale for public intervention in broadcasting is the belief that an unregulated market can result in high levels of concentration. As high-quality audiovisual content is expensive to produce but relatively cheap to replicate, there is a strong incentive for operators to reach a large number of people (exploit economies of scale) and/or use the same product in a variety of different formats (exploit economies of scope) (Graham and Davies, 1997; Graham, 1999). However, economies of scale and scope imply concentration of

Table 3.1: Television Ownership and Cross-media Ownership Rules in Europe (2001)

Country	Limits on Television Ownership	Limits on Cross-media Ownership
Austria	✓	✓
Belgium (Flemish and Francophone)	✓	✓
Denmark	✓	–
Finland	–	–
France	✓	✓
Germany	✓	✓
Greece	✓	✓
Ireland	–	✓
Italy	✓	✓
Luxembourg	–	–
Netherlands	–	✓
Portugal	–	–
Spain	✓	–
Sweden	–	–
United Kingdom	✓	✓

Sources: Author's analysis of data from Department of Trade and Industry/Department for Culture, Media and Sport (2001) and EAO (2001d)

ownership, and most EU television markets are characterised by a high degree of media and cross-media concentration between a few companies (Iosifidis, 1997a and 1997b; Doyle, 2002).

National governments across Europe have established media and cross-media ownership regulation with the aim of safeguarding both 'workable' competition and public interest objectives, such as plurality of viewpoints and diversity of content. Table 3.1 shows that in 2001, limits on television ownership as well as limits on cross-media ownership were in place in most of the fifteen EU Member States. However, different indicators and thresholds are used in different countries to monitor and control media ownership. Across the EU, the criteria used to determine excessive levels of media and cross-media ownership vary from limits on the number of licences which can be held by operators, to turnover, audience share or equity. For example, in France and Greece there are limits on the number of broadcasting licences held, whereas the Italian cross-ownership regime is based on the maximum financial resources, which an operator can accumulate. There are no cross-ownership restrictions in Spain, but there are limits on the number of licences held. Germany has adopted a 'share of voice' model, that is, limiting media ownership by total voice rather than specific media market.

CASE STUDY: THE 'SHARE OF VOICE' MODEL

In Britain there has also been much debate over introducing a share of voice model. Prior to the passing of the 2003 Communications Act, replacing sector-specific regulation, designed to limit the interests that publishers might have in the television or radio services and vice versa, with a simpler, more sophisticated and certainly more liberated model based on the so-called 'share of voice' across all media, was considered. Proponents of the model emphasised that limiting media ownership by total voice rather than specific media market makes more sense today for two reasons: digitisation and the convergence of technologies have blurred the boundaries between different media and communications sectors; as a result of these developments, in recent years the information and communications sectors have been subject to high-profile mergers and acquisitions involving companies operating in diverse sectors, such as print, telecommunications, broadcasting and the Internet. With these developments in mind, share of voice is aimed at regulating and measuring concentration levels across media and communication sectors.

Certainly the share of voice scheme has become more prominent in the digital, converged era, characterised by the emergence of complex, vertically integrated media empires. The model also seems to have considerable intellectual attractions, providing the clarity and certainty needed for media markets to function effectively, while also reflecting the true influence of all media. Still there are some philosophical and practical difficulties when attempting to impose this model to measure cross-media concentration levels. The philosophical issues have to do with the fact that there is no direct correlation between share of voice (an audience-based measure) and the influence exerted by a particular media owner/controller. End-use-based indicators, such as share of voice, cannot directly measure media firms' impact on public opinion. Influence over the audience cannot be assessed by using audience-based criteria, whether that is readership, audience reach, viewing or listenership share, etc. *Audience exposure* to mass media is certainly not the same as *influence over the audience*. The media's impact depends to a large extent on the content of the channel/title, which is not taken into account by this method.

There are also a number of practical problems with adopting the model. In Britain, the Department of Trade and Industry/Department for Culture, Media and Sport *Consultation on Media Ownership Rules* from November 2001 rightly identified weaknesses in implementing the model, not least because of the 'media exchange rate' concept, incorporating the extent to which different media vary in their influence. Attempting to develop a 'media exchange rate' by weighting the influence of different media and capping the total allowable influence across media can be arbitrary and subjective. For example, how would the regulator weigh a newspaper reader against a television viewer? These concerns are touched upon in the paper's own discussion of how a share of voice system might operate (see paragraph 6.5.8). It would indeed be difficult to devise a way of calculating the relative influence of the different media that is universally acceptable. There is a danger that a system that establishes a set of limits on all forms of cross-media ownership would set arbitrary limits and thus be discriminatory in its effect. It was precisely due to these concerns that the British government finally decided not to adopt this model.[3]

Common Rationale for Regulating Market Share

Despite national variations in media and cross-media ownership regulation, there is a common rationale for the overall policy framework. By placing limits on market share, countries seek to promote effective competition in their media markets. They also aim to promote dissemination of a wide range of independent views. For instance, in Germany regulations on media concentration are designed to ensure diversity of opinions and prevent the creation of dominant, opinion-forming, media moguls. In this context, upholding diversity is a principle which goes back to judgments on matters of broadcasting law by the Bundesverfassungsgericht (Federal Constitutional Court) (see Häussermann and Scheuer, 2001: 10). Similarly, the complex French media ownership regime aims to secure diversity of views and the free communication of thought and opinions. In its decision of 18 September 1986, prior to promulgating the Freedom of Communication Act of 30 September 1986, the Constitutional Council considered that

> the diversity of currents of socio-cultural expression is in itself an objective having
> constitutional value; respect for this diversity is one of the conditions of
> democracy; the free communication of thoughts and opinions, guaranteed by
> Article 11 of the 1789 Declaration of the Rights of Man and of the Citizen, would
> not be effective if the public addressed by means of audiovisual communication
> that did not have at its disposal (...) programmes guaranteeing the expression of
> trends of different natures. (quoted in Giudicelli and Derieux, 2001: 56)

In short, governments in Europe placed a social significance upon broadcasting because of objectives relating to technical and economic issues (spectrum scarcity and hence limited competition in the television market), cultural issues (preservation of national identity/culture) and political issues (guaranteeing diverse political views and eliminating the use of television for propaganda purposes). In order to preserve these objectives national governments retained public service broadcasting and imposed tight regulation of media content, including rules on the protection of minors, taste and decency, and broadcast quotas, as well as strong structural controls, such as restrictions on market entry, media concentration and cross-media ownership.

FACTORS AFFECTING TRADITIONAL TELEVISION REGULATION

Since the 1980s, in most EU countries, traditional governmental regulatory concepts have increasingly come to be seen as an obstacle to the economic development of a rapidly changing television industry. On the one hand, this could be attributed to the introduction of new media technologies, ideological shifts and the push from private interests for a more favourable investment environment. On another, changes in society, the decreasing role of the state, and the international dimension also need to be considered when examining regulatory reform. This part of the chapter looks at what have been the distinct technological, political, economic and social factors affecting traditional television regulation.

Technological Advances

It has been argued that with cable and satellite introducing alternative methods of delivery, scarce resources such as frequencies no longer require regulation. Cable, in particular, developed rapidly in the Netherlands and Belgium, where cable connections became almost universal from as early as 1990. In Denmark and Germany, 80.9 per cent and 60.2 per cent of households respectively had cable connections in 2000. Penetration rates of satellite dishes in 2000 were particularly high in Austria (40 per cent) and Denmark (37 per cent) (EAO, 2001a: 36–43).

However, the advent of new distribution technologies is not equal across Europe. In Britain and France, cable and satellite developed at a slower rate than predicted. In 2000, only 14.3 per cent of British households and 13.2 of French homes were connected to cable. In the Mediterranean countries of Italy and Greece, cable and satellite technologies were underdeveloped mainly because of the numerous free-to-air terrestrial channels available. Nevertheless, the average penetration rate of cable connections in the EU for the fifteen Member States increased from 22 per cent in 1992 to 30 per cent in 2000, whereas the average penetration rate of satellite dishes increased from just 8 per cent in 1992 to 20 per cent in 2000. In mid-2000, approximately 70 million of the EU's 145 million households had access to cable and/or satellite (pp. 36–43).

These technological developments have influenced the traditional structure and dynamics of the television industry. While in the past television services were largely confined to domestic markets, the new transmission networks of cable and satellite have brought television into the transnational arena. In particular,

satellites capable of beaming signals across borders have made it difficult to justify nationally based regulation. Europe's tight regulatory regime, which had
supported a limited number of (mostly public) channels, began to erode. This
was particularly evident in countries with a long tradition of government interference in the television sector. Through direct political intervention, the French
state had always played a leading role in the statutory and organisational control of television (Lamizet, 1996: 79–80). However, as early as the 1970s, the
centralised nature of the television system and its output was being openly questioned. During the 1980s there were calls for regional diversity in television
production and programming decentralisation (Kuhn, 1985: 50–4). In part, this
was due to the development of new communications technologies in the early
1980s, particularly direct broadcast by satellite (DBS) and fibre-optic cable.

Across Western Europe, the introduction of these new delivery methods led
to an unprecedented proliferation of channels, undermining the spectrum
scarcity argument for regulation. This has become more apparent in recent years
with the development of digital television (DTV), which has allowed many more
channels (see Chapter 5). DTV, together with the development of the Internet,
has had another, more profound impact on television regulation. Digital technologies allow for the combination of different types of information
representation, such as text, audio, images and video, thereby making the distinctions between different types of information production and distribution
less apparent (Wheeler, 2001: 28). As the sources of television programming
have multiplied and the boundaries between different sectors have become
blurred, it has been argued that regulatory approaches originally established for
terrestrially based, mass audience channels have become more difficult to maintain (Tambini and Verhulst, 2001: 9). There has been discussion both at a
national and EU level of whether technological convergence should result in
regulatory convergence (McQuail and Siune, 1998; Marsden and Verhulst,
1999; Iosifidis, 2002a). In addition, there is debate over whether it is acceptable
to rely more on competition law rather than sector-specific regulation to deliver
economic and public policy objectives (OECD, 2000b; Hardy, 2001; Iosifidis,
2002b). These issues are considered in greater length in the final part of this
chapter.

Economic and Political Trends

In the 1980s across Western Europe, there arose a 'dual' system: private commercial and public broadcasters existing side by side. This was later challenged
by the proliferation of new channels of communication and delivery networks.
As Chapter 2 shows, greater commercialisation of television was allowed in
Western Europe and many more companies entered the market. Competition

became fierce in terms of supply in all communication sectors: public and commercial broadcasting, telecommunications networks and the Internet. In terms of demand, the development of separate markets for free-to-air terrestrial channels and new types of communication services, such as analogue and digital pay television, Near Video on Demand (NVOD),[4] etc. led to price variations for the different services offered. The introduction of subscription television, associated with cable and satellite delivery platforms, allowed viewers to pay directly for services, and the digital business model involves greater customisation of services to meet the specific requests of users.

New opportunities emerged from the changing nature of production and consumption. Cable networks, for instance, offer both telephony and video at competitive prices. An increasing number of traditional telecommunications companies are attempting to provide audiovisual services, such as NVOD and other content services. In the new environment, the various players are seeking a set of laws and institutions that provide them with legitimacy, continued power or the opportunity to profit from technological advantage (Price, 2002: 4–5). In Britain, the moderately re-regulatory Broadcasting Act of 1990 (the main target of which was the 'comfortable duopoly' of the BBC and ITV/Channel 4) handed an effective monopoly of direct satellite broadcasting to Murdoch's BSkyB. Strong controls on concentration and cross-media ownership were eventually relaxed in the 1996 Broadcasting Act and ownership controls were weakened even further with the passing of the 2003 Communications Act (see case study below).

In 1990, the Greek government was lobbied hard by press barons who argued persuasively that an expansion of their activities in the field of broadcasting would improve television's production base and have a positive economic impact. Levels of cross-media concentration increased considerably, with potential to harm pluralism and diversity. For example, the shareholders of the main commercial, terrestrial television channel, Mega Channel, were the traditional publishers Tegopoulos and Lambrakis groups, together with new publishers, Alafouzos, Bobolas and Vardinoyiannis. The German television market is also characterised by high levels of concentration and was, in fact, dominated by two politically opposed media 'families'. Kirch Media was created by Leo Kirch, a media mogul with right-wing political views, before becoming insolvent in 2002 (see Chapter 2), while Bertelsmann is headed by a media family with close ties to the Social Democrats (SPD). Knut Hickethier (1996: 102) argues that in Germany there appears to be a lack of political will to oppose the process of media concentration.

Other concerns arise from the close relations between some media companies and political personalities or government contracts. This close political-industrial relationship is evident in France, where former state company, Havas, became the main shareholder in Canal Plus (later acquired by Vivendi-Universal) and construction company Bouygues owned 39 per cent of the most popular commercial television channel, TF1 (Levy, 1999: 26). Construction mogul Bouygues also enjoyed dominance in television advertising, as TF1 was (and still is) the main recipient of advertising revenues. In Italy, Silvio Berlusconi built his television empire with the backing of his large real estate and construction business.

In all, commercial media interests have managed to influence political decision-making. They succeeded in persuading politicians to allow them both to expand across sectors and develop new media technologies. In part, this was because most governments during the 1980s had become aware of the information technology revolution and were keen to adopt new communication technologies. There were some differences of emphasis, with the French stressing the role for generous state support, the British favouring an industry-led policy and the Germans exploring the social consequences of the new media (Humphreys, 1996: 171). Generally though, the diffusion of new communication technologies had political blessing. In addition, a number of politicians (for example, Mitterrand in France and Thatcher in Britain) hoped to improve their chances of favourable coverage by introducing more flexible broadcasting rules (Hoffmann-Riem, 1992: 152). Those factors provided the basis for an ideological shift away from the traditional model of the welfare state and towards an emphasis on market forces as the key mechanism for societal development.

Social Changes

The shift towards market forces can also be attributed to changes in society, such as greater individualism, or, in Eric Hobsbawm's words, 'the triumph of the individual over society' (1994: 334). Other important social transformations have occurred in lifestyles, aspirations and consumption patterns, and cultural diversification. Cultural differentiation, in some cases resulting from the multi-ethnicity of European nationals, suggests a massive growth in the diversification of leisure and lifestyles. As markets expand, the cultural unity of the past has been replaced by diversified consumer leisure activities (Dahlgren, 2000: 27–8).

Broadcast media have both influenced, and been influenced by, social and cultural change (Weymouth, 1996: 16). Cultural heterogeneity has provided opportunities for greater choice among television viewers, which private consortia have attempted to meet by offering niche channels covering different interests and tastes, or by making offerings on an international scale. For example, transborder television channels, such as CNN, MTV and Bloomberg (global players in the news, music and financial markets respectively), have adapted to the emerging lifestyles of people living in different countries eager to have access to information and/or entertainment on a twenty-four-hour basis. Traditional terrestrial broadcasters, including public broadcasters, who offered a limited number of general interest channels focusing mostly on national events could not satisfy the interests of a large and diverse population and eventually lost some of their appeal. Still, some large public broadcasters, like the BBC, have taken advantage of new digital technologies and succeeded in launching special interest channels to satisfy specific audience needs, both at a national and international level (see Chapter 1).

The Decreasing Role of the State?

In Europe, the rise of transnational television, the shift towards market forces and changes in society have all led to fundamental alterations in statutory instruments and supervisory concepts. The opening up of media markets has made traditional government regulation less effective, and while the state has not completely relinquished its role, its administrative authority is now more than ever to moderate and mediate rather than to control. As Wolfgang Hoffmann-Riem (1992: 169) argues, although the state continues to affect broadcasting systems through specific broadcasting laws and the creation of supervisory bodies, media companies and the market have become factors shaping those systems. Similarly, Monroe E. Price (2002: 3) suggests that in a global environment, the ability of any state to fully control the images that permeate its territory is questioned, while Wolfgang Schulz and Thorsten Held (2001: 6) go further to argue that the 'sovereign state' is changing into a 'corporate bargaining state'.

International organisations have also affected national law. It is fair to say that the scope of possible national action in the EU is now determined, to a large extent, by developments in European (and international) law. In view of the principle of the free flow of information within the EU, it is politically difficult to protect national markets and the domestic broadcasting order from external influences (Hoffmann-Riem, 1992: 155). The emerging international dimension of regulation is a matter of concern for countries like France, which is keen to preserve domestic provision of television content in order to promote French culture and language. However, the continued emphasis on content quotas, applied to both commercial and public television channels, is seen by some other countries, most notably the US, as impeding the free flow of content (see Chapter 4).

Still, the opening of the markets requires regulation in order to protect economic goals, such as healthy competition or guard against abuses of dominant positions. National regulation is also needed to attain specific social goals that continue to remain valid, such as safeguarding diversity of content and protect-

Table 3.2: Broadcasting Regulatory Institutions in Europe (2000)

Country	Carriage Regulation	Content Regulation
Austria	Federal Ministry of Science and Transport, Regional Radio and Cable Broadcasting Authority	Commission for the Observance of the Broadcasting Act, Regional Radio Act, Cable and Satellite Broadcasting Act
Belgium	Flemish Government, Government of the French Community, Government of the German Community	Flemish Government, Government of the French Community, Government of the German Community
Denmark	Ministry of Culture, Local Radio and Television Board, NTA	Ministry of Culture, Local Radio and Television Board, Satellite and Cable Board
Finland	Ministry of Transport and Communications	Council of State, Ministry of Transport and Communications
France	Conseil supérieur de l'audiovisuel (CSA)	CSA
Germany	Direktorenkonferenz der Landesmedienanstalten (DLM), Reg TP	DLM
Greece	Ministry of Press and Mass Media, Ministry of Transport and Communications	Ministry of Press and Mass Media, National Radio and Television Council
Ireland	ODTR	Independent Radio and Television Commission
Italy	Ministry of Communications, AGC	Ministry of Communications, AGC
Luxembourg	-	-
Netherlands	Ministry of Transport, Public Works and Water Management, OPTA	Ministry of Education, Culture and Science, Media Commission
Portugal	Secretary of State for the Mass Media, Institute for the Media, Mass Media Authority, ICP	Secretary of State for the Mass Media, Institute for the Media, Mass Media Authority
Spain	Ministry for Development, Secretariat-General for Communications	Secretariat-General for Communications, Autonomous Communities
Sweden	Ministry of Culture, Radio and Television Authority	Swedish Broadcasting Commission
United Kingdom	Department for Culture, Media and Sport, Independent Television Commission	Independent Television Commission

Source: OECD (2000b)

ing minors. In fact, in most countries, the state has managed to keep a certain degree of control over the de/re-regulated television landscape. This was the case in France, where the state has traditionally been actively involved in setting television rules, but also in Britain, where for many years, the competitive pace was set by independent regulatory authorities. Table 3.2 provides a picture of the level of state intervention in broadcasting. As can be seen, state presence in broadcasting carriage[5] regulation in 2000 (through ministerial or other government bodies) is evident in all EU countries. The table shows that these bodies are also involved in broadcasting content regulation, together with independent regulators.

In general, most regulatory institutions responsible for broadcasting policy across Western Europe are required to report to the relevant ministry. In certain cases, government ministries retain the power to control independent regulators. The independence of regulatory bodies varies from country to country according to the institutional arrangements put in place by laws and regulations. For example, the state in France still commands considerable institutional resources and authority to underpin its agenda-structuring role for television output, particularly news (Kuhn and Stanyer, 1999: 12–14). In Greece, attempts to provide the regulator with a certain degree of independence from the government and the relevant Ministry of Press and Mass Media only began in 2000. Greece was inexperienced in setting up an appropriate regulatory framework in a competitive television environment. It took considerable time to come to terms with the establishment of a regulatory authority in the field of television and when that occurred (the National Radio and Television Council was set up in the early 1990s) it was not really independent from the government. Law 2863 (2000) attempted to provide a degree of independence from the government and the relevant Ministry of Press and Mass Media. In contrast, with Britain and the Nordic countries, there is little evidence of political reprisals or attempts to take control of broadcasting.

The degree of independence is also influenced by factors such as the personality of the head of the regulatory body, but mostly by political traditions (OECD, 2000b). For instance, the German television regulatory structure is fragmented because it is based on a model of decentralised regional regulation.

DEREGULATION OR RE-REGULATION?

The preceding discussion has shown that, since the mid-1980s, European broadcasting has witnessed a shift from tight regulation of public service or state-dominated television to a relaxation of regulatory controls. But how can this process be best characterised? Various terms have been used to describe the emerging shape of the television landscape – deregulation, re-regulation, light touch regulation, etc. Perhaps 're-regulation' or 'light touch regulation' most appropriately describe today's broadcasting landscape, because what is being witnessed, as Graham Murdock (2000: 41) has pointed out, is not a total dismantling of rules but a shift of emphasis towards relaxation. In an earlier study, Murdock (1990: 12–13) also advocated the term re-regulation to describe changes in media and communications policy in the late 1980s and early 90s.

Humphreys (1996: 191–4) suggests that the term re-regulation actually refers to 'a lighter touch' approach, that is, the creation of a more competitive and less hidebound regulatory broadcasting environment. He nevertheless observes that, sometimes, paradoxically, re-regulation may result in more rather than less regulation. He illustrates his point by giving the example of Britain, where, by the 1990s, a confusing system of five regulatory bodies was in operation (Independent Broadcasting Authority, Broadcasting Complaints Commission, Cable Authority, Radio Authority and Office of Telecommunications), where two regulators were previously deemed sufficient.[6] In Spain, there exists a highly complicated regulatory regime, as there are specific rules for nearly each type of broadcasting service (Gomez, 2002). Similarly, in France and Germany, there has been a quite awesome amount of legislative rule-making relating to broadcasting. German policy-making, in particular, is complicated by the fact that it is dominated by the Länder (Federal States). However, Humphreys (1996: 193) notes that it is important not to confuse the number of rules with their scope and substance. In most cases, newly established regulatory bodies were given a 'lighter touch' remit.

For David Hesmondhalgh (2002: 108) the preferred term to describe changes of the period from the 1980s onwards is 'marketisation', reflecting the tendency to produce and exchange cultural goods and services purely for profit. Murdock (2000: 39) also calls this process 'marketisation' because private enterprise has become the dominant model of cultural activity, and also because the market criteria of success, such as market share and return on investment, have become the main yardsticks against which the performance of all cultural institutions is judged. Murdock argues that marketisation is made up of five separate trends: privatisation; liberalisation; the reorientation of regulation; corporatisation; and commodification (p. 39).

Despite the different terminology, in one way or another, all EU countries have embarked upon a process of regulatory adjustment. As previously argued, upheavals in television broadcasting largely began in the mid-1980s, with the dismantling of public ownership and the huge growth of the commercial television sector. However, the process of re-regulation differed between countries. Some (Italy and France) were eager to restructure their television system and introduce commercial television, while others (Germany and Spain) delayed the opening up of the system. In some countries (Britain) the re-regulatory process was gradual and media policy reached a consensus, which lasted until the mid-1980s, whereas in others (Greece) television re-regulation actually occurred without any meaningful debate about its potential impact on the market and existing public channels. Thus different EU countries adopted distinct re-regulatory approaches.

Despite this fragmentation, there are some common trends in re-regulation. The first is the recognition by policy-makers of the impact of new media technologies and the growing internationalisation of television, leading to the application of more relaxed and flexible rules. Second, there has been some consensus among both left- and right-wing political parties about the need to adopt re-regulatory policies. For instance, Mitterrand's Socialist Party in France and Thatcher's Conservative Party in Britain both undertook programmes of privatisation and regulatory change. Mitterrand's presidency even coincided with the sale of public channel TF1 in 1987. Finally, while relaxing their television regulatory regimes, EU countries did not completely abandon but simply adjusted their television regulation.

TOWARDS RELAXING TELEVISION OWNERSHIP RULES

The adjusted regime is evident when one considers the substantial body of regulation relating both to television ownership and content. Following re-regulation, several EU countries relaxed their rules on television ownership and cross-media ownership, thus allowing consolidation in the sector. However, television and cross-media ownership rules still apply in most EU countries (see table 3.1), along with regulation of content. The following section outlines the limits on television ownership in certain EU countries and the next deals with regulation of television content.

Britain

In Britain, there has been a considerable degree of concentration within the main commercial terrestrial broadcaster, ITV. Throughout the 1990s, responding to strong industry pressure to relax ownership rules, successive governments allowed consolidation of television ownership. The 1996 Broadcasting Act substantially relaxed media-ownership rules, previously enforced by the 1990 Broadcasting Act. However, the 1996 Act still prohibited the holding of two or more commercial television licences where the licensee had 15 per cent or more of total television audience share. In addition, the Act disqualified the holding of more than one licence for the same region. This restriction prevented any person or company from holding both the ITV licences for London, and therefore from dominating the London television advertising market.

CASE STUDY: THE UK COMMUNICATIONS ACT 2003

With the Communications Act of 2003, British broadcasting saw the introduction of new legislation abolishing much of the complex web of regulations regarding ownership. During November 2002, the British government published a Communications Bill paving the way for the establishment of a single communications regulator, Ofcom (replacing the existing regulators), and the relaxation of media-ownership rules. With respect to media-ownership rules, the Bill freed up the communications industry far more than was expected, removing the mass of ownership regulations that characterised British broadcasting as it was thought these deprived companies of the economies of scale and scope required to expand into foreign markets.

The Bill resulted in the Communications Act, which received Royal Assent on 17 July 2003. This provided for the removal of rules preventing:

- joint ownership of television and radio stations
- large newspaper groups (e.g. Rupert Murdoch's News Corporation) acquiring the minor commercial terrestrial broadcaster, Channel 5 (controlled by pan-European broadcaster, RTL)
- non-European ownership of broadcasting assets, effectively clearing the field for takeovers by the world's corporate media giants like Viacom and Disney
- single ownership of the main commercial terrestrial broadcaster ITV, opening the way for the creation of a single ITV company, which allowed Carlton and Granada to merge and form ITV plc (see Chapter 2)

In short, the Act liberated media markets, extended 'light touch' regulation and allowed further consolidation of ITV ownership. It allowed non-European companies to buy British companies, thereby giving a chance to US and other media giants to bid for commercial, free-to-air networks. This may result in a media system dominated by powerful, commercial operators, such as now exists in the US. Tessa Jowell, Secretary of the Department for Culture, Media and Sport, has stated: 'allowing a British media asset to accept investment in euros, but not in dollars or yen, makes no sense in a modern market. Why should (French) Vivendi be able to buy in the UK, but not (US) Viacom?' (Jowell, 2002: 5). However, this stance ignored the point that, within the EU, these rights are reciprocal, but in 2003, foreign companies could only buy up to 20 per cent of a US television-network channel.

The probable future scenario of unrestricted foreign ownership, a combined ITV and the creation of vertically integrated media giants, has raised concerns about both sustaining healthy competition and safeguarding the public interest. Precisely because of these concerns, the Act (with a final amendment in summer 2003) stated that any merger or acquisition must pass a 'public interest plurality test', meaning that it will have to show that the proposed consolidation will add to the plurality of voices. By agreeing to a plurality test, the British government acknowledged the concerns of those who fear for pluralism and free speech in an era dominated by global media conglomerates. Thus, although Britain now has one of the most liberalised television markets in Europe, the Act maintains minimum safeguards for plurality.

Germany

Changes in German law during the 1990s led to upheavals in television market structure. In particular, the criterion used to assess concentration and domination in the past was the number of television channels held by a person or company as well as the share of capital and voting rights. However, during the 1990s, owing to the introduction of digital technology, regulators felt that the model was too complicated and outdated. As already mentioned, in 1997 a 'share of voice' model (an audience share model) was adopted, limiting the ownership of commercial television companies to 30 per cent of the German television audience. These revisions were followed by higher levels of concentrated ownership in the television sector and the 30 per cent threshold allowed a few big players (most notably Bertelsmann and the now insolvent Kirch) further opportunities for expansion.

Italy

In Italy, the Media Act of 6 August 1990 stipulated that no person or company may own more than two national television channels, or hold licences to control up to three commercial channels. However, the Communication Act 249/97 (1997) permitted a person or a company to control up to two commercial channels. Also the Act introduced for the first time thresholds based on revenue shares, ruling that no television company may earn revenue greater than 30 per cent of the total resources (including public money, advertising and pay-television revenue) in the national television sector (see Mastrojanni and Cappello, 2001: 47; also Department of Trade and Industry/Department for Culture, Media and Sport, 2001: 39). The alternative method of measuring media concentration based on audience share (as adopted in Germany) was rejected during the parliamentary discussion prior to the passing of the Act. However, in late 2003, the Berlusconi government proposed a controversial new Bill which, if passed, would allow the media tycoon to increase his power.

France

French television has in place a complex and detailed set of ownership restrictions in order to secure diversity of views and the free communication of thought and opinions. The 1986 Freedom of Communication Act (as amended by the Acts of 1 February 1994 and 1 August 2000) stipulates that the maximum holding in national terrestrial television channels (reaching more than 6 million inhabitants) is limited to 49 per cent of the capital. It is worth noting that prior to the amendment made to the Act on 1 February 1994, the limit was 25 per cent. Thus France seems to have followed the same trend towards relaxing television ownership rules observed in Germany, Italy and Britain. The maximum holding in local or regional television channels (reaching fewer than 6 million inhabitants) is limited to 50 per cent of the capital. Other provisions relating to multiple television ownership provide that if a person owns more than a 15 per cent share of a television channel, then the holding of a second channel is limited to 15 per cent, and the holding of the third to just 5 per cent. For digital services, the 49 per cent limit only applies if the channel has a share of the total television audience exceeding 2.5 per cent. Satellite television ownership is limited to a maximum holding in a single channel of 50 per cent, maximum holdings in two channels of 50 per cent in the first and 33.3 per cent in the second, and maximum holdings in three channels of 50 per cent in the first, 33.3 per cent in the second and 5 per cent in the third (see Giudicelli and Derieux, 2001: 55–7; also Department of Trade and Industry/Department for Culture, Media and Sport, 2001: 38).

Spain

In Spain, the Private Television Act 1988 established two types of television ownership limits. First, the Act prohibits one person or company from holding more than one national, terrestrial, television channel, whether analogue or digital. Second, it prohibits a person or company from owning more than a 49 per cent share of a television station (Gomez, 2001: 29).

Small EU Countries

The disparity in national policies on television ownership becomes more striking if one considers the situation in smaller EU countries. These can broadly be divided into those who have set up and retained television-ownership rules for the purposes of guaranteeing pluralism and diversity, and those who have relied solely on competition law for protecting these objectives. In Greece, for example, there exists a strict television-ownership policy framework, in which a person or a legal entity may own no more than one licence to operate a television channel, and may control no more than a 25 per cent share of that channel. Similarly in Austria, no one is allowed more than one analogue or two digital television licences in any given area. However, no restrictions exist beyond normal competition law in countries such as Sweden, Finland and Luxembourg (Department of Trade and Industry/Department for Culture, Media and Sport, 2001: 36–42).

Most modern democracies in Europe have designed television ownership regulation to ensure that a significant number of impartial media voices can be heard (plurality of voices) and that the viewer has access to a highly diverse television output (diversity of content). Undoubtedly, different indicators and thresholds are used in different countries to monitor and control television ownership. One can also detect a trend towards relaxing television-ownership rules. However, specific regulation on television ownership, based on the recognition that television contributes to pluralism and diversity, continues to be essential, yet countries such as Sweden, Finland and Luxembourg have left the regulation of television up to the competition authorities alone.

THE CONTINUING RELEVANCE OF CONTENT REGULATION

Ownership restrictions are not the only method of ensuring pluralism and diversity in European television. Content regulation is also used to safeguard these objectives. Television-content regulation has traditionally been justified because of the pervasiveness, invasiveness and influence of the medium (Tambini and Verhulst, 2001: 6–8). A 2002 McKinsey report for the Independent Television Commission in Britain identified at least three principal objectives in content regulation.

The first is to ensure access to networks and services. Traditionally, this has meant promoting widespread (universal) access to basic content. In Britain, for instance, television policies in the 1980s were developed to ensure that political, ethnic and other minorities had more presence on television (p. 7). The principle of universal access is firmly established in relation to terrestrial television channels. However, since the growth of pay television and the Internet, some countries are increasingly evaluating the relative importance of access to new services. Some countries, such as Germany, are taking the view that access to subscription television is not a regulatory objective, while others (the Netherlands) believe that pay television should be included in the definition of 'access' (McKinsey, 2002: 5).

The second objective of content regulation is to set editorial standards. Most countries are concerned that citizens should be protected from harmful content, with the definition of 'harmful' varying from country to country. For example, the French regulatory agency, Conseil supérieur de l'audiovisuel (CSA) aims to 'safeguard fundamental principles such as respect, human dignity and public order' (p. 5). Another focus of these standards is the desire to maintain impartial, accurate news and current affairs reporting. In Britain, 'due accuracy and impartiality' has always been required of broadcast news, while in Germany, the regulator requires broadcasters 'to distinguish between information and comment' (p. 5).

Promoting quality is the third objective, taking various dimensions, ranging from supporting a shared sense of national identity, to encouraging investment in high-quality programming or upholding diversity and plurality of programming to satisfy all interests. According to McKinsey (2002: 5), most countries pursue one or more of these dimensions simultaneously. The need to encourage and support content quality and domestic production through regulatory intervention is felt most acutely in countries like France, which retains an intense commitment to some form of 'cultural exception' (Lovegrove and Enriquez, 2002: 108). Most countries have introduced positive domestic content regulation that takes the form of broadcast quotas. Sweden, for instance, has set a 70 per cent domestic broadcast quota, France follows with a 60 per cent quota, and Britain and Italy are just behind with a 50 per cent domestic broadcast quota each (p. 109). Finally, in most countries, promotion of content quality and diversity still occurs through the licensing of public service channels (see Chapter 1).

REGULATION IN THE ERA OF DIGITAL CONVERGENCE

As already outlined, most EU countries have maintained a liberal television ownership regulatory regime with the dual aim of protecting effective competition while promoting pluralism and diversity. Similarly, regulation of television content has retained its relevance in the re-regulatory era. However, the latest technological and market changes have created renewed pressure to relax even further, or even abolish, these sector-specific structural and content rules. This is because technological convergence makes it increasingly difficult to differentiate between different media platforms, while content can be delivered across many television channels or websites. Digital content, in particular, can be easily manipulated, altered and stored, independent of delivery platform. As technological change increases the ability to stream video to a personal computer or a third-generation mobile receiver, it may become irrelevant which platform is used to view which content. Ownership and content restrictions that are tied to vertically integrated sectors, which link programme production and dissemination to the audiences, might not make sense if the same programming can be provided by methods that include terrestrial and satellite broadcasting, cable and telecommunications. In view of these developments, there is growing pressure for a common approach to regulation across media.

Some countries have started to examine and revise their existing regulatory structures in the context of convergence. In Britain, the Communications Act 2003 provided for the merging of existing regulatory bodies into one Ofcom with overall responsibility for the regulation of broadcasting and telecommunications. By establishing a centralised regulatory body to cover all communications sectors, the Act attempted to reflect technological convergence in laws, policy initiatives and regulations. Unified communications regulatory bodies already exist in Italy and Finland, but some functions, such as licensing and spectrum allocation, remain outside the merged regulators (McKinsey, 2002: 19). In the Netherlands, the independent regulator OPTA took responsibility for regulating the cable television industry from the Media Commission. In particular, OPTA has the authority to make decisions in disputes between cable-television companies and programme providers (OECD, 2000b: 11).

A study by Anders Henten, Rohan Samarajiva and William H. Melody (2003: 33–5) identifies the potential advantages of establishing a unified regulatory institution, which include:

- being able to apply the same provisions across converged communication areas
- building on a greater knowledge of corporations with activities in different areas
- taking advantage of the economics of regulation
- creating possibilities for a greater political independence for the regulator in relation to implementing policy decisions

However, the study also highlighted the potential problems associated with a unified regulatory organisation. These include more bureaucratic working procedures leading to slower processes, and less clarity in respect of principles and decisions because of the unification of different regulatory rationales (pp. 33–5).

Indeed, the convergence of telecommunications and broadcasting is bringing together two industries with different regulatory rationales. Telecommunications regulation has concentrated on opening monopoly markets to competition, whereas broadcasting regulation has focused on varying degrees of content control, from limitations on certain types of programmes to ownership controls. While technological convergence has certainly provided the rationale to review institutional structures and procedures governing communications sectors, bringing together previously distinct laws and regulatory frameworks could prove a difficult task. It will not be easy for a unified regulatory organisation to adhere to different regulatory principles governing diverse sectors. In Britain, the centralised character of the new regulator, Ofcom, and the emphasis on the promotion of economic competition may result in reduced public service obligations and reduced quality, accountability and diversity.

This inclination to converge regulation at an institutional level is combined with a growing trend towards relying more on competition law rather than sector-specific regulation to deliver economic and public policy objectives (McGougan, 1999; Tambini, 2001; Iosifidis, 2002b). This is particularly evident in Britain, where the Communications Act 2003 puts faith in competition law both to provide sufficient protection from market abuses and to attain social objectives. The advantage of allocating sole regulatory power to the competition authority to oversee communications sectors is that under this model, consistent regulatory supervision across sectors can be ensured. However, the application of competition rules to the television industry cannot always safeguard other values and objectives, such as plurality of sources and diversity of content, which are threatened by undue market concentration (Iosifidis, 1997a and 1997b; Hardy, 2001). While effective competition is a necessary component of a healthy media industry, its purpose is to remedy the effects of anti-competitive behaviour rather than to ensure a pluralistic and diverse media sector. Precisely because competition rules cannot provide the certainty that a significant number of different media voices are heard and that real choice of media products and services exists, other policy instruments have to be enacted and enforced. As previously argued, those instruments range from enforcing production quotas or maintaining public service channels, to setting up media and cross-media ownership rules. These policy instruments should continue to apply to enable citizens to choose from a wide range of ideas (plurality of viewpoints) delivered from a wide range of sources (diversity of supply).

CASE STUDY: ALTERNATIVE FORMS OF REGULATION – CO-REGULATION AND SELF-REGULATION

As centralised regulation is difficult to sustain in the new media environment, alternative forms of regulation have been developed to protect economic (fair competition) and social objectives (pluralism and diversity). These include co-regulation and self-regulation.

Co-regulation is a variable term, describing cooperation between state supervision agencies and self-regulatory bodies, also known as the 'partnership between the public authorities and the industry' (Oreja, 1999), or the 'sharing of responsibilities through agreements between public and private partners' (Liikanen, 2000). In the British Communication White Paper, co-regulation is used in a broader context; that is, to indicate situations in which the regulator would be actively involved in securing that an acceptable and effective solution is achieved. The regulator may for example set objectives which are to be achieved, or provide support for the sanctions available, while still leaving space for self-regulatory initiatives by industry, taking due account of the interests and views of other shareholders, to meet the objectives in the most effective way. The regulator will in any such case have scope to impose more formal regulation if the response of industry is ineffective or not forthcoming in a sufficiently timely manner.[7]

The former British communications regulator, Oftel, calls co-regulation the process when the state is 'encouraging progress and providing assistance in areas where the market is not delivering desired outcomes' (Oftel, 2001).

A second alternative is self-regulation or self-control between senders and users. Price (2002: 102–3) argues that self-regulation can be a plea for more effective cooperation, or it can be a means for avoiding regulation (or a combination).

> Self-regulation of media becomes a kind of dance among media, government, and the public, sensitive to swings in opinion, perceived consequences of the conduct to be regulated (such as violence on television), and the responsiveness by the public to political grandstanding (p. 103).

Schulz and Held (2001: 7) identify two broad variations of self-regulation: 'pure self-regulation' and 'regulated self-regulation'. The former implies a process of self-regulation where the state has no role to play, while the latter is a form of self-regulation that fits in with a legal framework or has a basis laid down in law. The term 'regulated self-regulation' may be somewhat awkward in itself, but describes precisely what is meant, focusing on the instruments the state can use to regulate a self-regulatory process (p. 7). Of course, the emergence of self-regulation should be sensitive to the different social demands, constitutional structures and traditions of industry–government cooperation in the media fields that exist in different states (Price, 2002: 102).

Co-regulation and self-regulation have gained momentum against traditional government regulation in the contemporary media environment because such mechanisms transcend sector differences and substitute uniform transnational patterns. With respect to the Internet and digital television, self-regulation means substituting for government the administration of standards by large transnational corporations that have a stake in harmonising and unifying standards across national boundaries (p. 103). Matters which cannot be subject to state regulation at all, and hence are subject only to voluntary self-regulation, include issues of good taste in television programmes. However, Schulz and Held (2001: 8) argue that some matters, like the protection of human dignity, cannot be subject to self-regulation.

Tambini and Verhulst (2001: 5–20) provide a good account of the role and limitations of self-regulation. They argue that effective self-regulation requires active consumer and citizen consultation based upon shared responsibility at all stages of development and implementation. If the public is to bear more responsibility it has to be aware of the role of self-regulation (p. 15). The problem is that we do not yet have the required levels of public awareness. Public authorities, consumer organisations and the industry itself should take appropriate measures to inform the public about the advantages and disadvantages of self-regulation and therefore minimise confusion.

CONCLUSION

In the past, television broadcasting was regulated in terms of both access and content. A tight regulatory regime applied to television in order to protect common values and preferences, such as freedom of expression, cultural diversity, political pluralism, universality, quality, accessibility, supply of informative and educational programmes along with entertainment material. It was thought that the market would be unable to meet these objectives, values and interests, and consequently would be ineffective in securing them. Indeed, the market's primary objective is to satisfy consumer preferences and not collectively agreed social values.

However, European television broadcasting has been subject to many upheavals in the past two decades due to technological, political, economic and social changes. These have resulted in fundamental changes in regulatory concepts, supervisory re-regulatory arrangements and the role of the state in initiating and implementing regulation. This chapter argued that the new regulatory television environment could best be described as re-regulatory, that is, a shift of emphasis towards more relaxed rules. It also argued that there were different re-regulatory waves and that European countries followed distinct approaches to regulatory reform. Despite national variations in the handling of competition issues, supervisory bodies or the role of the state, the common parameter of the re-regulatory process was the necessity of imposing a minimum of regulatory constraints. Evidence for this is provided in the substantial body of legislation that still applies to television ownership and content. In fact, television remains one of the most tightly regulated industries, even after re-regulation. In no Western European country have television rules been relaxed so as to resemble those applied to the press or telecommunications, for television is still considered too important to be left completely to the rules of the market.

Yet in the future a different regulatory framework may emerge. There are already signs that technological convergence has changed regulatory attitudes. Beliefs in the need to intervene to encourage certain types of output or to prevent concentration have gradually lost ground. There are growing trends towards relying on competition law to achieve economic and social objectives, and towards applying a unified regulatory regime across all communications sectors. No doubt the current regulatory system needs restructuring and modernisation to allow both market players and consumer-citizens to take advantage of the new opportunities. However, technological convergence does not necessarily mean that all media must share the same level of regulation. Television is still more pervasive and invasive than other media and therefore sector-specific regulation is justified to guarantee economic and social objectives, especially in the transitional period until full convergence is realised. Convergence arrives slowly and therefore broadcasting and telecommunications sectors have a long way to go before they are fully indistinguishable. Only when the boundaries between previously separated sectors are completely blurred can alternative forms of regulation, such as self-regulation and co-regulation, perhaps be considered alongside traditional regulatory instruments.

NOTES

1. Convergence – the delivery of similar, existing or new, media, telephony and Internet services via the same transmission platform – can be present at three different, although interrelated, levels: the technological level (mainly due to digitisation of broadcasting, information technology and telecommunications networks), the structural level (as a consequence of corporate alliances across different sectors), and the services and markets level (here reference is made to new value-added and multimedia services) (Noam, 1998).

2. Plurality of viewpoints refers to the media's ability to express diverse opinions, whereas diversity of content concerns the meeting of different needs, including minority content, special-interest programming and regional programming. Plurality of voices can only make sense if there is assurance of diversity of supply, that is, availability of a range of content (Andersen, 2002: 5).

3. For further discussion concerning the 'share of voice' model, see Iosifidis (1997b, 2001 and 2003).

4. NVOD, the forerunner of VOD (Video on Demand is not yet available), allows viewers to make viewing choices from home at times which suit their lifestyles by ordering films or other categories of programmes which commence at fifteen-minute intervals.

5. 'Carriage' refers to the wires, cables, satellite dishes etc., and the information carried across them. 'Content' is the pictures, text etc., that the information

represents. Carriage and content have traditionally been regulated separately, the former related mostly to economic efficiency and the latter to social issues such as freedom of expression and diversity of opinion. However, technological change is generating strong pressures towards regulatory convergence.

6. However, the 2002 Communications Act provided for a new super-regulatory body, Ofcom, to replace these five regulatory bodies.

7. Available at <www.communicationswhitepaper.gov.uk/by_chapter/ch8/8_11.htm> (downloaded April 2002).

4

Pan-European Contexts – Markets and Regulation

Fragmentation of the market into national territories with companies defined by local regulations has been seen to undermine the economic stability of Europe's television industries. Consequently, the stratified European television market has been perceived as ripe for takeovers by US-based corporations. European players have therefore felt they need to establish pan-European television (PETV) businesses that will allow them to overcome national restrictions and protect themselves from potentially hostile foreign takeovers.

This chapter will investigate the economic imperatives that have determined the structure of the PETV industry. For some, these reforms have encouraged profitability so that they may withstand hostile takeovers from US corporations (Davis, 1998: 80). Thus, opportunities for market change occurred with regard to:

- pan-European investment by major television players into a variety of television channels to extend their corporate growth
- the establishment of generic PETV channels (news, sport, music, children's, adult), usually available on cable, satellite or digital television channels, aimed at local and European audiences
- the development of pan-European production companies who have expanded through the international exploitation of their programming rights and formats

To expand the European television market, the EU has undertaken policy responses designed to liberalise the rules governing Europe's television industries. Liberalisation, the Commission felt, would improve the competitiveness of European media companies against the challenges of foreign broadcasters, allowing those companies to establish a sustainable worldwide presence. This chapter will therefore investigate tools such as the Television Without Frontiers (TWF) Directive, aimed at facilitating a dynamic European television market.

Simultaneously, the EU's audiovisual policies have sought to preserve the social, cultural and political priorities associated with the provision of pluralism through diverse and 'high-quality' television services in democratic societies.

Cultural protectionism has been a contradictory, but equally important, imperative underpinning the EU's response to the global media market. There will be an investigation of the EU's quotas and support measures, alongside an analysis of how the EU has defined its position with regard to the General Agreement on Trade and Services (GATS) multilateral negotiations.

The chapter is divided into two parts. The first tracks those factors (cross-media investment, generic channels, production entities) which have contributed to the creation of a pan-European television industry. The second considers the regulatory principles that have led the EU to facilitate a sustainable PETV industry. It will include case studies on Music Television Europe (MTVE), the franchising of adult entertainment channels by the US publishing empire, Playboy, and the deliberations concerning the amendment of the TWF Directive.

INVESTMENT

The European television business has lent itself to *consolidation* due to the economies of scale derived from enlarging the footprint of television services. PETV strategies have also been employed to concentrate television production practices to achieve savings. For example, the Scandinavian Broadcasting System (SBS) has shown how production costs can be cut through the simultaneous production of a variety of its programming formats, which are targeted at different national markets but made from within the same production base.

PETV cross-investment has been offered as a solution to the relative weakness of European television industries within the global marketplace. Although in terms of revenues from advertising and licence fees, national television industries have a dominant position in their domestic markets, there has been a concern that European television companies are too small to compete internationally. The European television industry has become characterised by the disjuncture between a few well-capitalised broadcasters and a larger number of small and more fragmented broadcasters and producers (Davis, 1998: 80).

These difficulties have meant that European television markets stood at a considerable disadvantage against oligopolistic US producers who were more efficient in distributing their product to large international audiences. This led to an imbalance between the demand for programmes (reflected in the growth of channels and airtime to fill) and the limitations governing European production capacity. Thus, several companies have consolidated PETV investment to create producers of sufficient size and scale to effectively offset US companies, while developing their own European-wide levels of production.

Radiodiffusion-Télévision Luxembourg

The Radiodiffusion-Télévision Luxembourg (RTL) Group was created in spring 2000 in the merger between Compagnie Luxembourgeoise de Télédiffusion (CLT), Bertelsmann's audiovisual arm UFA, Pearson Television and Audiofina. RTL is the market leader in concentrating its interests across Europe. As former RTL Chief Executive, Didier Bellens, commented:

> The creation of the ... RTL Group brings together a powerful portfolio of broadcast platforms with leading pan-European content. The strength of our businesses combined with our financial firepower puts us at the forefront of a rapidly consolidating European media industry (Bellens, 2000).

RTL's PETV corporate policy intensified when the German media giant, Bertelsmann, became the majority shareholder (90 per cent) in July 2001. Bertelsmann sought to increase its international share by buying out the British media group, Pearson's 22 per cent stake in RTL, therein taking full control of Britain's Channel 5 and the content producer, FremantleMedia.

The RTL Group owns twenty-three television and twenty-two radio stations in eight countries including Germany, France, Belgium, the Netherlands,

The Bill

Britain, Luxembourg, Spain and Hungary. The majority of its television stations have been start-ups, usually launched in league with local partners, including RTL, RTL II, Super RTL, n-tv and Vox in Germany, M6 in France, Channel 5 in Britain, RTL4, RTL5 and Yorin in the Netherlands, RTL-TVI and Club RTL in Belgium, and RTL Klub in Hungary. However, in Spain, RTL bought into Antena 3 TV when it was already well established. In total, RTL television channels reach an audience of over 140 million European viewers on a daily basis (RTL, 2003: 1).

From this base, RTL has become a leading producer and distributor of television content within Europe. As the owner of FremantleMedia, the group produces over 10,000 hours of programming, including entertainment (e.g. *Pop Idol*), game shows (e.g. *Family Feud*) and soaps (e.g. *The Bill* and *Good Times, Bad Times*). Similarly, it holds control of over 17,500 hours of programming rights and remains the world's leading independent distributor of programming outside the US. By pursuing a PETV investment strategy, RTL believes that as an integrated broadcast and production company, it may further its growth as it develops strong European-wide brands (p. 1). This will enable it to gain entrance into new markets and to access non-advertising-based revenue streams:

> As [a] truly Pan-European ... broadcast and production company ...
> entrepreneurial goals are to strengthen the company's top position in Europe and
> develop [the] RTL Group in key markets and countries (p. 1).

Canal Plus

Owned by Vivendi, which merged its US assets with General Electric (GE) in October 2003, France's Canal Plus has established international arms by engaging in the co-financing of channels with local players in various national territories. Canal Plus has enjoyed certain advantages as a pay-television channel by successfully exporting its business practices across Europe. In 1993, it partnered the Spanish newspaper group Prisa to create Canal Plus España in Spain. As a subscription-funded broadcaster, Canal Plus España was able to remove itself from the advertising war between Spain's other commercial networks and the public service broadcaster, Radio Televisión Española (RTVE), which is primarily funded by advertising. Subsequently, Canal Plus España made substantial profits by providing a mix of generic sport and movie channels to Spanish subscribers (Tunstall and Machin, 1999: 213–14).

Elsewhere, Canal Plus has diversified into Belgium with Canal Plus TVCF. In Germany it also held an interest in Premiere and bought into Telepiù, Italy's main pay-television platform in 1998, before selling its interest in 2003 as News Corporation sought to create Sky Italia (Tryhorn, 2003a). In 1996, it acquired

Nethold (Filmnet) channels, which had been thinly stretched across Italy, Scandinavia, Holland and Belgium, and through this takeover it was able to target 8.5 million European subscribers (Tunstall and Machin, 1999: 196). In May 2000, it bought a 49.5 per cent share in the pan-European sports channel, Eurosport.

As digital services have expanded in Europe, Canal Plus and its international partners have increased the scope of their generic channels to include interactive and pay-per-view-based services. Moreover, as Canal Plus expanded its interests into foreign territories, it became a key patron of several national film industries and a significant European film producer. However, due to Vivendi's divestment of companies, many of Canal Plus's international subsidiaries were sold in 2003–4.

The Scandinavian Broadcasting System

SBS operates a smaller number of commercial television stations in eight European countries. In 1999, it merged with Central European Media Enterprises to own SBS 6 in the Netherlands, Kanal 5 in Sweden, VT4 in Belgium, TVDanmark in Denmark and TVNorge in Norway. This development occurred alongside SBS's continued expansion into Eastern Europe as it formed partnerships with local broadcasters including Nova TV in the Czech Republic, and TV2 in Hungary.

SBS has demonstrated how production costs can be reduced when programme formats are acquired and produced across different territories. For instance, for SBS's version of international format, *Temptation Island*, contestants from different countries were brought in, while the same production crew and sets were used to film one day in Norwegian and another in Danish (Westcott, 2002). SBS argues that it is axiomatic that the greater the proportion of the population that can be reached by a production, the greater the efficiency achieved in making it (p. 5). According to Michael Finkelstein, Vice-Chairman of SBS, this business logic lends itself to the drive for consolidation:

> You have to find a way of doing business to make money. If you say 'I'm going to run this big television station in a big country [where] I'm going to employ six or seven hundred people and produce shows, but at the end of the day you've got a margin of 2 per cent, it's not going to work for the stockholders' (p. 5).

The Limits of Pan-European Investment

While SBS's production model indicates significant economies of scale, there are cultural and linguistic barriers to be overcome. National audiences have proved to be unreceptive to subtitled or dubbed imports from other

European states. There are also business complications concerning PETV investment, not least that most programme rights are sold on a territorial basis. For example, even the rights for the regional club football championship, the European Football Union's (UEFA) Champion's League, are sold nationally. Moreover, despite the relatively low value of broadcasting companies, they often cannot be purchased easily, as broadcasters have kept share prices valued at a premium rate to guard against hostile takeovers (e.g. Carlton and Granada in the UK).

European television companies have found that the complex range of national and regional regulations that exist within different states have proved to be one of the most significant barriers to PETV consolidation. European media companies are presented with a wide range of cross-media ownership, carriageway and content rulings (see Chapter 3). This leads to media corporations buying shares in one another, rather than attempting to merge or invest heavily in foreign companies (see Chapter 2).

The majority of Europe's commercial players prefer to keep the bulk of their interests within national boundaries. For instance, while Berlusconi's Fininvest attempted to invest at the pan-European level, it ultimately removed itself from France and Germany and only operates in Italy and Spain (where it has been trying to offload its stake in Telecinco). Faced with insolvency, Kirch had to refocus its core assets within Germany, while the falling market for media shares has seen Bertelsmann and Vivendi, the parent companies of RTL and Canal Plus, limiting their international investments (sale of US assets) and returning to core competences (publishing, utilities) (Crumley, 2002) (see Chapter 2). According to Jon Watts of Spectrum Strategy Consultants:

> Historically, very few European [television] businesses have ever succeeded in
> growing or achieving significant scale outside their home territory. In other words,
> it's very difficult to replicate the specific circumstances which allow US production
> businesses to achieve scale (Westcott, 2002).

CHANNELS

The development of commercial PETV channels owned by European players has been limited. Several PETV channels have been established by public service broadcasters including Arte, TV5, BBC Prime, BBC World, Euronews and Eurosport (Higham, 2003). More often than not, however, PETV channels have been developed by large US-based corporations seeking entry into foreign markets (Humphreys, 1996: 259). Therefore, in developing a sustainable European television industry, the impact of PETV channels has been mixed (Chalaby, 2002: 190).

Cultural and linguistic barriers have limited the number of PETV channels and several stations are monolingual. Fiction programming such as soap operas, situation comedies and drama remains defined by national demand and cultural interest (de Bens and de Smaele, 2001). Also, the development of PETV channels has been hampered by sales of audiovisual rights on a country-by-country basis, different national advertising regulations and the local catchment areas for cable or satellite pay-television operators (Higham, 2003). Further, as Jean Chalaby has commented, 'the audience for PETV channels is extremely small and their market share rarely passes the 1 per cent mark' (2002: 189).

PETV channels have included generic news, sports, music, children and adult services (Humphreys, 1996: 201).[1] Thematic channels can attract advertising revenue and are, in a number of cases (most especially adult entertainment), determined by the 'niche' services they provide to specialist audiences through subscription. In terms of content, the cultural convergence of pan-European services (Levitt, 1983) has been accompanied by the concurrent move towards *localisation*, with big brands like Fox Kids and the Discovery Channel pushing ahead with local versions of their services (Chalaby, 2002: 191–3; Chalaby, 2003: 458–9). This has been due to the need to attract local advertising windows in which advertisers can ensure their pan-European advertising strategies remain relevant to national markets (Chalaby, 2002: 193). Therefore, despite the regional nature of these channels, they have employed local staff to adapt international content to the national market, produced local programming and engaged in scheduling practices which respond to the demands of national audiences:

> In the competitive environment of twenty-first century European television, broadcasters have realised that … localisation is a strong strategy for survival. In fact there is no channel with an international strategy that has not tailored its content and schedule to cater for local differences. ((Papathanassopoulos, 2002: 161)

News Channels

Several rolling PETV news channels have emerged: Sky News, BBC World, Cable News Network (CNN) International, Cable National Broadcasting Corporation (CNBC), Euronews and Bloomberg. These channels have been targeted at the business community and the top 5 per cent of European households in terms of income (Chalaby, 2002: 191). They have followed local news agendas, employed recognisable newscasters and have established national bureaux. CNN Europe tailored its content to national needs while maintaining an international coverage of events. It also diversified into CNN Deutschland with German-language news programming. Similarly, internationally owned business news channels such as Bloomberg have launched separate local channels in the UK, France, Germany, Italy and Spain.

Euronews, the European news channel, concurrently broadcasts over twenty hours of unbroken daily news in six different languages. While many of the transnational brands are owned by non-European companies, Euronews is backed by all the members of the European Broadcasting Union (EBU), and is run by two organisations, Société Opératrice de la Chaîne Européene Multilingue d'Information (SOCEMIE) (in which Independent Television News [ITN] holds a 49 per cent management share) and Société Éditrice de la Chaîne Européene Multilingue d'Information (SECEMIE) (a consortium of eighteen public service broadcasters including France Télévision, RAI and RTVE) (Papathanassopoulos, 2002: 169; Chalaby, 2002: 190).

As 'Europe is part of its remit' (Chalaby, 2002: 197), Euronews has been uniquely required to provide an international feed for its programming. European issues and politics have featured extensively in its news agenda. In turn, it has sought out an alternative approach to news content by removing onscreen presenters, running news footage without comment and providing unbroken footage alongside different language commentaries (Machill, 1998: 427–50; Euronews, 2003).

Due to the nature of its remit, shortly after its launch, Euronews faced a financial crisis and reformed its editorial practices not only to attract audiences but more importantly to court advertisers (Purvis, 1999). While it refused to introduce presenters, the channel followed more conventional news strands with a stronger human-interest focus and, as far as possible, provided a greater degree of national-based content. However, the failure of Euronews to attract audiences and advertisers may be seen to demonstrate the limits on factual-based PETV programming (Machill, 1998: 435; Chalaby, 2002: 197–8).

Sports Channels

There are several PETV satellite sports channels including Extreme Sports and Eurosport. United Pan-Europe Communications (UPC) and the UK-based programme distributor, the Extreme Group International, jointly own Extreme Sports. This minority channel was founded in 1999 and provides a twenty-four-hour diet of high-risk sports programming specialising in surfing, snowboarding, skateboarding and mountain biking. It is aimed at a youth audience ranging from fourteen to twenty-four and covers Poland, Hungary, Germany, Britain and Estonia (Extreme Sports, 2003).

Eurosport is the more established service, focusing on traditional forms of sports coverage (football, tennis, cricket, rugby, golf) (Rowe, 1996: 570). It was created in 1989 and was originally owned by the EBU and Sky Television. In 1991, Screensport, a rival sports channel, took Eurosport to the European Court of Justice claiming that its dominance over international sports rights was anticompetitive. Shortly after, Sky sold its interest to TF1, and in 1993, the company merged with the European sports network, owned by the Entertainment and Sports Network (ESPN) and Canal Plus. In 2000, Canal Plus bought out ESPN's share, and Eurosport became jointly owned by Canal Plus and TF1 (Eurosport, 2003).

With a footprint covering over 95 million households and reaching approximately 250 million viewers in fifty-four countries, Eurosport is the most widely available sports channel in Europe. It is distributed to subscribers through a variety of means including the European Astra satellite, a basic tier of cable networks, and nearly all the existing digital platforms within Britain, Nordic countries, France, Spain, Italy, Poland, Portugal and Greece. In terms of coverage, Eurosport simultaneously broadcasts its sports coverage in eighteen European languages and has bought highlight rights to the regional football competition, the UEFA Champions League. Alongside the main subscription channel, Eurosport has also established a sports news channel service, which is available to 14 million subscribers.

British Eurosport provides a clear example of how the localisation process works. As a subsidiary, it has a production base in Langley, West London, and employs over fifty collaborators to develop local productions. In terms of programming and marketing, the company produces a national sports news bulletin with content drawn from the European-wide feed. It employs British presenters, buys its own television rights and has removed foreign adverts from its advertising spots. Eurosport's investments in Britain show how heavily competitive markets are unsustainable for pan-regional channels. Audience tastes and interests differ from one country to another, making it impossible for an international feed to be of equal interest everywhere (Chalaby, 2002: 195).

Music Channels

Music stations have been among the most successful of the PETV channels. These channels have been sustained by their appeal to a wide variety of youth and adult audiences as popular and classical forms of music are central to the cultural practices of many different societies (Real, 1996: 5). Moreover, Europe has been particularly attractive to music companies as it is the most mature marketplace in the world after the US. These market dynamics have led to a proliferation of music channels across Europe.

At the forefront of music services has been US company, Music Television (MTV). Established in 1981 and now owned by Viacom, in 1987 MTV sought to diversify within Europe and established a subsidiary organisation, MTV Europe (MTVE), creating several music channels aimed at a Europe-wide audience. MTVE aimed to 'combine a global presence and a single global brand with a product designed for [a] separate regional market' (Papathanassopoulos, 2002: 219). MTVE accounts for one-quarter of MTV's international audience and has been the market leader among PETV music channels.

The success of MTVE led to various business and cultural concerns within the European television market. With the pan-European scope of MTVE, other music channels saw greater potential for tapping into local and nationally defined audiences. There was also the belief that MTVE's international domination of music channels had led to an Americanisation of national forms of musical content. In 1993, Warner Music, Sony, EMI and PolyGram formed a consortium to back the German-based venture, Viva, which was intended to support domestic artists and stem MTVE's Anglo-American-based domination. Throughout the 1990s, other nationally based music channels emerged, including MCM in France, S-Plus in Switzerland, Z-TV in Sweden and the Music Factory in Holland.

CASE STUDY: MUSIC TELEVISION EUROPE

With the launch of new music channels in Europe, by 1994, MTVE faced significant competition and was losing viewers to national services. In response, MTVE localised programming to create services for different European territories. As Chalaby comments:

> The first opportunity presented itself in Italy, where MTV was given access to a channel by a cable operator on condition that it programmed local music. The music channel hired local staff and VJs, opened local production facilities in Milan and launched the first devolved service of its pan-European feed at the end of 1995 (2002: 196).

By the end of the 1990s, MTVE had divided its services into five territories: Britain and Ireland, Central (Austria, Germany and Switzerland), Central Europe (France, Belgium, Greece, Israel and Romania), Southern (Italy) and Nordic (Sweden, Norway, Denmark, Finland) (Chalaby, 2002: 196; Roe and de Meyer, 2000). MTVE subsidiaries were available in thirty-eight European states and reached 85 million households. (Papathanassopoulos, 2002: 220–1). Further localisation occurred in 2000 with services for Spain, Holland and Eastern Europe.

MTVE evolved programming to offset the emergence of new or established business rivals within the most competitive markets – Britain, Germany and

France. Since 2000, it has incorporated a greater amount of localised programming delivered in a range of European languages to accompany the Anglophonic base of its content and to sustain its brand internationally (Chalaby, 2002: 196). For example, in partnership with UPC, MTVE has developed branded MTV and VHI Polska channels in Poland. Such devolution has led to the creation of autonomous managements who maintain their freedom to produce shows and decide schedules (p. 196).

With the development of national competition, MTVE further diversified by offering its viewers a range of stations defined by music genres. In Britain, MTVE took advantage of the satellite monopoly BSkyB's adoption of digital services to provide seven MTV channels (MTV, MTV Hits, MTV2, VHI, VH1Classic, MTV Base, MTV Dance) on this platform (MTVE, 2003). MTV and MTV Hits provide play lists based on the national British singles chart, while VHI and VH1 Classic are aimed at mature audiences who prefer to buy albums. MTV2 is composed from a range of music video styles which have been classified as being nu-metal to alternative. MTV Dance broadcasts dance videos, while MTV Base consists of hip-hop, rap and 'R'n'B' music videos (MTVE, 2003). This segmented approach was defined by the needs of advertisers, who aimed to tap into national audiences, and by the major record labels, which have sought to diversify their product into different territories.

Children's Channels

There are several PETV children's channels including Nickelodeon, Boomerang, the Cartoon Network, Trouble, Disney and Fox Kids. To some degree, these stations have been able to amortise their costs and transmit on a European-wide basis as they rely on certain types of programming (e.g. cartoon shows) which can be easily dubbed for local territories. For example, Fox Kids Europe broadcasts via cable and satellite channels to forty-one countries, in fourteen different languages, reaching more than 23 million households. It also holds one of the largest children's programming libraries and distributes programmes to over 110 European terrestrial, cable and satellite channels (Fox Kids, 2003).

Yet, like other PETV companies, these children's channels have pursued a localised approach in their provision of channels and programming. Some stations have employed opt-outs wherein local presenters are used to introduce programmes to audiences (Nickelodeon), while elsewhere other companies (Disney, Fox Kids) have preferred to develop fully localised channels and information services. Such a strategy enables channels to develop a clear identity and to compete successfully with their national competitors. To this end, between 1999 and 2001, children's channels showed a rapid growth due to the localisation of their brands (*Screen Digest*, 2003).

Adult Channels

Throughout the 1990s, there was a ten-fold escalation of demand for porno-graphic programming among European viewers and several PETV adult entertainment channels have emerged (Papathanassopoulos, 2002: 159).[2] In accordance with other PETV channels, adult programming has followed the principle that local content should drive the evolution of channels aimed at local audiences (Campbell, 2003). However, the wide range of national obscenity laws in Europe makes more specific demands on the development of localised adult programming. For instance, Britain is one of Europe's strictest markets as it prohibits any representation of penetrative sex, while Eastern European countries such as Hungary employ laxer rulings which allow viewers to watch hard-core material on a basic channel at 1.00pm in the afternoon.

CASE STUDY: PLAYBOY TV UK

The American Playboy entertainment group has developed a localised PETV strategy. In the mid-1990s, Playboy pursued several joint ventures with Euro-pean media players in which it owned a minority stake in each locally produced Playboy station. For example, local franchise Playboy TV UK was created in 1995 as a joint venture between Playboy (17 per cent), BSkyB (32 per cent) and Flextech (51 per cent). Playboy was attractive to its British partners as it was able to offer a brand of erotic programming that reflected the 'glossy sheen of [its] famous US magazine' (Papathanassopoulos, 2002: 160). However, between 1999 and 2003, Playboy TV UK faced a series of corporate upheavals and eventually became a 100 per cent subsidiary of the parent US corporation (Campbell, 2003). During this period, Playboy TV UK increased the amount of domestically produced programming to 40 per cent. In this context, the company diversified by providing several British-based adult channels including the soft-core Playboy TV, alongside the development of hard-core pornographic channels including the Adult Channel and Spice Extreme. This drive towards localisation is especially important to Playboy, as it is a producer of adult enter-tainment content whose explicitness (or not) is determined by national obscenity laws.

PRODUCTION COMPANIES

Several PETV production companies, including Endemol and FremantleMedia, own a variety of national, independent producers. Endemol is a subsidiary of European telecommunications company, Telefónica, and FremantleMedia is a subsidiary of the RTL Group. These corporations have increased their prof-itability by developing two major production entities in the European and world television market. As Endemol and FremantleMedia expand, they hope to ensure their products are globally distributed by reaching a sufficient scale of production and maintaining control of a large number of programme formats and libraries.

CASE STUDY: ENDEMOL

In 1994, the Endemol Group of companies was created as a result of the merger between the two major independent Dutch television producers: Joop van den Ende Productions and John de Mol Produkties. Throughout the rest of the decade, the group pursued an aggressive policy of expansion through an acquisitions campaign and by starting production companies outside the Netherlands (Endemol, 2003). For instance, Endemol UK was formed out of existing independent producers such as Bazal, Hawkshead, Brighter Pictures and Zeppotron. Subsequently, Endemol UK was jointly owned by its parent company and the Guardian Media Group (GMG), which was bought out by the Endemol Group in 2000 (Endemol, 2003). Elsewhere, Endemol has been involved in joint ventures in twenty-one countries, including the major European markets, the US, Latin America, South Africa and Australia.

In 2000, Endemol became part of the Telefónica group, the leading provider of telecommunications services in the Spanish and Portuguese-speaking world. With this corporate backing and a greater access to distribution platforms, Endemol expanded further to become a leading developer, producer and distributor of content in the global television marketplace. Endemol sought entry into all the major European and Latin American markets, together with the United States. To achieve its aims, Endemol developed over 500 television-programming formats, which were produced by its local production companies in a range of countries. A few examples of its successful international formats include *Fear Factor*, *Operación Triunfo*, *Big Brother*, *Masterplan*, *1 vs. 100*, *All You Need Is Love*, *Spy TV*, *Changing Rooms*, *Forgive Me*, *DeKok* and *The Soundmix Show*. In 2002, the group enjoyed a combined turnover of €868.8 million and produced more than 18,000 hours of television programmes (Endemol, 2003).

CASE STUDY: FREMANTLEMEDIA

FremantleMedia came into existence when Pearson Television changed its name in October 2001. As Pearson Television, it had been a subsidiary of the international media group, Pearson plc. However, when Pearson merged with CLT-UFA to form the RTL Group in 2000 (see above), the company changed in its name and ownership. In December 2001, Pearson sold its remaining interest in FremantleMedia and it became the solely owned, content-production arm of the RTL Group (Fremantle, 2003).

Men Behaving Badly

FremantleMedia produces more than 260 programming formats in over thirty-nine countries, including Britain, the US, Germany, Australia, France, Italy, Spain, Portugal, Scandinavia, Latin America and Asia. Like Endemol, FremantleMedia has grown internationally through a process of acquisition. It has purchased several well-known creative labels including Grundy in Australia, UFA in Germany, and Thames Television, Talkback and Alomo in Britain. It has production bases in London, Berlin, Cologne, Rome, Madrid, Paris, Los Angeles and Sydney.

In terms of organisation, the international company has been separated into two major divisions: Worldwide Production and FremantleMedia Enterprises. The former is responsible for managing the rights for its game-show, drama and reality formats. The latter is responsible for the exploitation and development of the company's properties offscreen with regard to areas such as the Internet, interactive television and wireless. It also focuses on traditional ancillary rights markets such as licensing, merchandising, home entertainment and music publishing. Finally, FremantleMedia Enterprises incorporates Fremantle's international distribution arm, which distributes 19,000 hours of programmes to broadcasters across 150 countries, including popular shows such as *Baywatch* and *Men Behaving Badly*.

TELEVISION INDUSTRIES AND THE EUROPEAN UNION

While production entities such as Endemol and Fremantle have grown, there is a rather more mixed picture of the development of the whole of the PETV industry. In particular, the limitations on cross-investment and the American-based ownership of several commercial PETV channels have led to concerns being raised about the fragmentation of the European television industries. Thus, the EU has understood that its role should be to facilitate the unification of the under-capitalised European television market. This, it was felt, would create a more sustainable European television economy which could develop the programming infrastructure to compete with the influx of US imports (Davis, 1998: 81).

Competing EU Motives

To aid the rapid growth of the European television market, the deregulatory principles of liberalisation and harmonisation have underpinned the EU's approach to the audiovisual sector through Directives such as Television Without Frontiers. Most especially, Commission officials suggested that through the removal of national forms of protectionism, European companies might compete on a global basis. TWF would allow a Europe-wide liberalisation of broadcasting markets, which was in accord with the EU's overarching goal of an integrated single market enshrined in the 1992 Maastricht Treaty. However, the EU's response to the emergence of trans-frontier satellite television in the 1980s goes beyond the economic considerations of the internal market and the mutual recognition of licensing regimes within the Community. It is also driven by cultural and political considerations, the desire to protect local cultures and the belief that broadcasting is not an industry like any other, because of its contribution to public opinion (Levy, 1999: 39; European Commission, 1999a: 7–8).

These conflicting aims have often led to tensions between those industry interests, European institutions and Member States who favour market liberalisation (Germany, Luxembourg, Britain and Denmark) and those who favour a more interventionist *dirigiste* position, foremost France, but extending to Italy, Belgium and Spain (Levy, 1999: 40–2). Interventionist approaches underpinned the development of national quotas to protect European television industries from US imports, the development of subsidy schemes such as the Mesures pour Encourager le Développement de l'Industrie Audiovisuelle (Measures to Encourage the Development of the European Audiovisual Industry) (MEDIA) programmes, and the EU's position concerning the General Agreement on Tariffs and Trade (GATT) and GATS multilateral negotiations.

CASE STUDY: THE TELEVISION WITHOUT FRONTIERS DIRECTIVE

Adopted on 3 October 1989 by the Council, the TWF Directive (89/552/EEC) remains the liberalising centrepiece of the EU's legal framework for the audio-visual sector (European Council, 1989).3 TWF was subsequently amended on 30 June 1997 by the European Parliament and the Council in Directive 97/36/EC to provide Member States with national measures to protect public access to free-to-air television coverage of major events with societal worth, including the Olympics, the World Cup or the European Football Championship (European Commission, 1997b). In 2000, the Education and Cultural Direc-torate announced that in the light of any potential changes in the European television economy which had accompanied the introduction of digital-based services, there would be a further review of the Directive, from which deliber-ations would be acted upon in 2003–4.

TWF provided a series of rules aimed at encouraging growth within the European television marketplace and stimulating audiovisual production in countries with a small production capacity. Article 2, which stands at the heart of the Directive, effectively abolished the sovereignty of EU Member States over their national systems, thereby facilitating the free movement of television broadcasting services across frontiers within the Union. To this end, the EU employed the Maastricht Treaty's concept of mutual recognition which meant that as long as minimal regulatory rulings were met by the provisions of the originating Member State, the legal justifications for another Member State to impede the reception or retransmission of broadcasts were removed (Collins, 1994: 59–60). Other liberalising recommendations were designed to har-monise the development of a single European market in broadcasting and related activities, such as television advertising, programme sponsorship and the independent production of television programmes (Harcourt and Radaelli, 1997: 8).

The Directive was established to stem any inefficiency resulting from what the EC perceived as unnecessary forms of national regulation, so that a liberalised, single European audiovisual market could flourish. Articles 4 and 6 defined 'European' as referring to 'any legal or natural person domiciled in any of the member states of the Council of Europe' (Collins, 1994: 70). This was clearly a permissive definition, suggesting that US companies based in Europe could be regarded as 'European'. Therefore the original Directive and the 1997 revision conceived of broadcasting as a private service to be determined by consumer demand, ignoring the wider political issues of pluralism and cultural diversity (Radaelli, 1999: 125) and in effect signalled 'a victory for commercial forces and those who favoured anti-protectionist policies' (Negrine and Papathanassopou-los, 1990: 76).

In 2002, the Commission reviewed the TWF Directive to assess its worth in view of technological and market developments inaugurated by the continued digitisation of the European television market. To address these issues, the EC launched three subject reviews (European Commission, 2002a). With the first review, the purpose was to evaluate those measures in TWF designed to promote the distribution and production of European television programmes. In particular, the Education and Culture Directorate wanted to consider how effective the TWF's quotas had been. The second study considered recent technological and market developments in the audiovisual sector and was designed to identify cause-and-effect relationships. Its purpose was to provide the Commission with a series of likely scenarios for the future development of the market. A third study provided an analysis of the growth of new advertising techniques and whether a separation between advertising and other forms of content might be achieved.

To assist these studies, on 6 January 2003 the Commission published the Fourth Report to the Council of Europe and the European Parliament on the application of the TWF Directive (European Commission, 2003). This reviewed the changing European television market and considered how the Directive had been applied. It concluded that the Commission would be required to assess the need to update or adapt TWF taking into account the objective of creating a pro-competitive and growth-orientated environment in the audiovisual sector. The EU adopted the report on 6 June 2003.

From the results of its investigation, the Commission's Communication on the future of European Regulatery Audiovisual policy (European Commission, 2004) has developed new recommendations for the revised TWF Directive in 2003–4. In particular, it feels that TWF must be changed to take into account the technological and economic developments challenging structural arrangements in the European television marketplace. These include the emergence of new forms of consumption as consumers engage with alternative forms of communication and interactive services. Such reforms may have a dramatic impact on traditional forms of advertising as niche audiences develop and television ceases to be a mass medium but one of a range of information services.

Quotas and Support

Simultaneously, the EU has sought to enhance European production through various support measures to subsidise the creation of a single market in television programmes. In terms of non-EU imports, the most important and disputed clause of the TWF Directive is Article 4 which requires broadcasters, 'where practicable' and 'by appropriate means', to reserve a majority of transmission time for European productions, excluding news, sports events, games, advertising, teletext and teleshopping. However, the elastic wording of the clause allows broadcasters to achieve the quotas 'progressively, on the basis of suitable criteria'.

Reports on the fulfilment of the quota have been completed for two-year intervals (1991–2, 1993–4, 1995–6, 1997–8, 1999–2000), and the Commission has generally been satisfied. However, non-compliance has been rife, hampered by poor and inaccurate collection of statistics by governments (Levy, 1999: 44).[4] While the report for 1997–8 confirmed fulfilment of quotas by most mainstream channels, specialist cable and satellite channels still struggle to meet the quota, and data collection remains a problem (European Commission, 2000a: 4, 8). In the latest report for 1999–2000, 62 per cent of transmission time was devoted to European content, and 72.5 per cent of broadcasters complied (European Commission, 2002b). The Directive refers to all output, excluding certain categories, and not surprisingly many channels have met the quota with cheaper domestic entertainment formats rather than more costly fiction.

Quotas have not proved effective in stemming US imports because the introduction of commercial cable and satellite channels in the 1980s created a demand for fiction programming which could not be satisfied in Europe (Dupaigne and Waterman, 1998: 216; Tunstall and Machin, 1999: 200–1). Rather than enhancing European production and forming a European trading bloc to compete with the US, the creation of a single market encouraged an influx of US-owned channels (Galperin, 1999: 55–6). In retrospect, investment quotas rather than transmission quotas may have been more beneficial in increasing levels of EU production (Collins and Murroni, 1996: 125).

Since 1991, the quota stipulations have been supplemented by the MEDIA support programme. MEDIA PLUS, the third phase of the programme, runs from 2001 to 2006, and has a budget of €400 million. It focuses on strengthening the international competitiveness of European audiovisual works through support measures for training, project development, distribution and promotion. It has been argued that the support schemes have only a minimal impact on raising the competitiveness of European producers, and that funding has not only been inadequate and dispersed but also ill-targeted and mismanaged, reducing the effectiveness of the schemes (Galperin, 1999: 58; Levy, 1999: 49).

THE GENERAL AGREEMENT ON TRADE AND SERVICES (GATS)

Although quotas and support schemes have not been particularly effective in raising levels of European production for export or protecting European markets from imports, they have proved a source of heated dispute, particularly with the US, whose stance has always been that television programmes are commercially traded products like any other. This debate on audiovisual trade has taken place within international trade organisations dedicated to the 'higher service of promulgating free trade', but usually on first-world terms (Miller, 1996: 73). The General Agreement on Tariffs and Trade (GATT) negotiations were introduced in 1947 and developed over a series of rounds culminating in the Uruguay Round (1986–94) and the Marrakech Agreement of April 1994. This last round led to the establishment of the more formalised World Trade Organisation (WTO) in January 1995 to administer multilateral trade accords and rule on trade disputes. GATS, which added new sectors to the liberalisation process, is administered by WTO and is relevant to the trade in audiovisual services.

The Uruguay Round and GATS Exemptions

In the final stages of the Uruguay Round in 1993–4, trade in cultural goods and services became an issue because the EU, and France in particular, wanted to exempt the audiovisual sector from GATT and key provisions in GATS, in order to maintain quotas and subsidies. In a dispute between European and US interests that threatened to derail negotiations, a compromise was reached, which secured a cultural exemption and 'an agreement to disagree' (Jeancolas, 1998: 54–9; Wheeler, 2000: 255–6). As a result the Community retains the right to maintain and develop audiovisual policies, particularly in relation to quotas and subsidies.

The 1994 GATS agreement covers the audiovisual sector, but allows countries to exempt audiovisual industries from key provisions. In line with most other members of the WTO, the EU has made no specific commitments on audiovisual services. These are therefore exempt from rules relating to market access and national treatment. Market access (Article XVI) obliges members to open domestic markets to service suppliers from all WTO members, while national treatment (Article XVII) requires that overseas suppliers be treated in the same way as domestic suppliers. The Most Favoured Nation clause (Article II) requires members not to favour certain WTO members above others unless exemptions are specifically listed.[5] The decision to exclude the audiovisual sector from rules on market access and national treatment gave the EU and its members freedom to persist with quotas and subsidies. The lack of agreement within the GATS on what constitutes an audiovisual service also provided flexibility for the Commission to take account of developments such as services based on new technologies whose implications cannot be foreseen (European Commission, 1999b).

GATS 2000 and Audiovisual Services

The Community and its members continue to defend their freedom to formulate audiovisual policy within the WTO/GATS framework because of the perceived importance of the audiovisual sector for cultural and linguistic diversity. It has therefore not submitted a negotiating position on audiovisual services for the GATS 2000 round of negotiations. Vivienne Reding, the EU Commissioner for Education and Culture, summed up the Community's position in 2001:

> While we have a legitimate interest in the success of European works outside the
> European Union, we do not believe that easing restrictions via trade negotiations
> is an appropriate means of promoting trade that respects cultural diversity. We are
> open to trade and cooperation, which are necessary to promote cultural diversity
> in Europe and throughout the world, but we do not regard the tools of
> international trade as an appropriate means of guaranteeing these objectives.
> (Reding, 2001: 2)

Cultural justifications provide an important basis for the EU's stance against global trade rules for the cultural sector, but the US continues to push for the liberalisation of entertainment markets, driven by the priorities of its corporate and entertainment interests (Thussu, 2000: 180; Neil, 2002). Yet the Community's stance also reflects economic concerns. There is little to gain from liberalising a European market, which already imports considerable amounts of US programming but has no significant access to a culturally resistant US market (Reding, 2001: 2; Freedman, 2002: 6).[6] Liberalisation would benefit the US much more than the EU, and the Community's refusal to address cultural policies within the WTO framework also reflects its belief that the WTO is not the correct organisation to address this issue (Reding, 2001: 3).

There are uncertainties about whether the EU can maintain the cultural exemption for audiovisual services in practice. There is no clear definition of what constitutes an audiovisual service in the GATS, leading to uncertainty about which specific rules apply to which services. Confusion about what is a 'good' and what is a 'service' suggests that the obligations of GATT (goods) rather than GATS (services) may apply in some circumstances (Neil, 2002: 2; Freedman, 2002: 2). For the EU, the lack of definition for audiovisual services gave it room to manoeuvre in respect of 'new' services such as online and multimedia content. However, the Commission expected this margin to be questioned in the GATS 2000 negotiations, because Article XIX of the GATS calls for an extension of the liberalisation in services (European Commission, 1999b). The EU maintains that the GATS cultural exemption applies to all electronic deliveries, irrespective of the technology used to deliver services (Reding, 2001: 3; European Commission, 2000b).

Converging Information and Audiovisual Services

Since the Uruguay Round, the parameters of the debate seem to have shifted, reflecting the potential convergence of services and the blurring of distinctions between broadcasting, telecommunications and ecommerce (Wheeler, 2000: 254). The status of the TWF Directive and national treatment for subsidies in relation to traditional broadcasting no longer appear to be such a substantive issue with the Americans (European Commission, 1999b).[7] These issues may have become less important within the EU with the decline of French influence following the end of the Jacques Delors EU presidency and the expansion of the Community in 1995, which have strengthened 'liberal' forces (Humphreys, 1996: 296; Levy, 1999: 47).

In recent years the greater emphasis on market mechanisms, particularly in telecommunications, has also served to undermine 'defensive' interests. Several commentators have pointed out that the possibility of sector convergence may enable the US to bypass current quota restrictions and enter the European audiovisual market through the liberalisation of online services and electronic commerce as 'virtual goods' (Wheeler, 2000: 254; Freedman, 2002: 2; Thussu, 2000: 180). In February 1998, the WTO agreed to a phased liberalisation of basic telecommunications services, and although cable and broadcast distribution were excluded, convergence around digital platforms made it difficult to distinguish effectively between the two (Galperin, 1999: 70). In these circumstances, it would be difficult to apply quotas imposed originally on television services but distributed in future by telephone companies or computer networks, even where such quotas merely replicate those applying to cable and satellite (Neil, 2002: 3).

By the end of 2003, little had been achieved in relation to the audiovisual sector and GATS but negotiations are expected to continue until 2005 or possibly 2007. The US will seek additional commitments on the audiovisual sector and service liberalisation, but the EU continues to resist. The EU does not have substantial 'offensive' interests in the audiovisual sector because it exports very little, but it does in other areas such as agriculture. It has therefore been suggested that there may be a trade-off at a later date involving other sectors (Freedman, 2002: 8; Neil, 2002: 4).

GATS and National Television Markets

While the GATS trade talks provide a forum for discussion and implementation of global free trade, they need to be viewed in terms of what is actually happening in national markets. Here, relaxation of ownership and content rules is proving a potent means of liberalising markets further in line with the GATS principles on global free trade, and with little prospect of any reversal once rules are relaxed. For example, in Britain the 2003 Communications Act allowed non-European companies to acquire the British terrestrial networks (see Chapter 3). Safeguards were taken to prevent the swamping of British commercial television with American programmes, yet concern was expressed about 'a determined and sophisticated attempt [by US companies], backed by enormous marketing expertise, to shift the balance of audience and regulatory expectations away from domestic content produced primarily with a British audience in mind, towards a more US or internationally focused product mix' (Joint Committee on the Draft Communications Bill, 2002). In terms of programme trade and economic efficiency across networks, this might result in:

- more reliance on formats for entertainment and factual output which can be adapted for local markets and branded globally
- the maintenance of locally produced fiction serials, possibly based on formats, but supplemented by 'event' drama produced or co-produced primarily for the US marketplace

However, a particular cause for concern is the possibility that without government commitment to exclude certain key areas of the audiovisual market from the GATS, further negotiations will be used to contest the case for public 'subsidies', such as the licence fee for designated public service broadcasters and all types of content and ownership regulation considered 'burdensome' by commercial interests (Petley, 2002b; Campaign for Press and Broadcasting Freedom, 2002).

CONCLUSION

The pan-European television industry has been characterised by strengths and weaknesses. There has been the development of strong PETV production entities, such as Endemol and FremantleMedia, which have pursued expansionist policies by retaining control over programming rights, libraries and formats, while acquiring well-established national, independent, production companies. However, these developments have to be compared with the relative lack of corporate cross-investment at a PETV level. Of all the major European television companies, only RTL, Canal Plus and SBS have effectively diversified on an international basis. Elsewhere, companies such as the Italian Mediaset, British Granada and German Kirch (before its insolvency) have preferred to consolidate business activities within their own national markets. Further, as RTL's and Canal Plus's parent companies, Bertelsmann and Vivendi, have suffered to varying degrees from the collapse of media share prices and been forced to retrench, the demand for PETV cross-investment has withered.

Moreover, while several successful, thematic PETV channels have been estab-lished, with the exception of public service-backed PETV organisations, these have largely been American in origin. PETV channels have also shown that the European television market has many linguistic, cultural and business barriers to overcome. Thus, in terms of content, different categories of PETV channels have been required to replace their pan-European content with more localised forms of programming. This has led to the division of PETV channels into dif-ferent European regional territories (MTVE), the greater use of local opt-outs (Eurosport) and an increase in the amount of locally produced content (chil-dren's and adult channels). Only the PETV news provider, Euronews, has retained a focus upon European-wide issues and this has been at the expense of audiences, advertisers and revenue.

Consequently, the EU has identified the fundamental problem within the European television markets as being one of fragmentation, which it believes stymied the growth of European television companies when they tried to com-pete within the global market. In attempting to aid the rapid growth of the European television market, the EU employed the principles of *liberalisation* and *harmonisation*. These goals underpinned the TWF Directive, which estab-lished liberal rules aimed at enlarging the European television marketplace and stimulating audiovisual production.

However, the Commission has also sought to *intervene* in the Community's broadcasting markets to redress what it understood as being the undesirable outcomes of an unfettered marketplace relating to the cultural and democratic worth of television services. This market failure imperative has sat unhappily with the demands for liberalisation and has created an inherent tension in the EU policy process between *dirigistes* and liberalisers.

Alongside liberalising tools such as TWF, therefore, the EU has established quotas or support measures, and has been involved in establishing a European position in the GATS multilateral negotiations. These negotiations between the US and Europe concerning audiovisual and communications services represent a battle of ideological will between trade liberalisation and cultural protection. They may well determine the outcome of the flow of cultural product between America and Europe and represent a continuation of the shift in emphasis from cultural and political priorities to economic and industrial ones. Thus, on a more general level, it is to be hoped that as the EU seeks to facilitate a sustainable PETV industry, coherent policies emerge that not only reflect the interests of Europe's television industries but those of its citizens as well.

NOTES

1. While film channels like Turner Classic Movies (TCM) and Canal Plus are pan-regional, many are characteristically defined by national territory, such as Sky Movies in the UK, Cine Cinema in France and Premiere in Germany. PETV documentary channels such as the US Discovery Channel and National Geographic provide local language versions of international programming, and there are also international home-shopping channels such as Quality Value Convenience (QVC).

2. In 2002, it was estimated that the total adult entertainment market stood at $40 billion (Campbell, 2003).

3. Despite the TWF's liberalising nature, it would be incorrect to view all its measures as being market-liberal. For example, EU culturalists ensured that stronger content regulations were to be applied within Member States' national broadcasting systems (Article 3).

4. Compliance in 1991–2 was 74 per cent, but fell in 1993–4 to 61 per cent because of an increase in satellite channels, rising again to 66 per cent in 1995–6.

5. Many countries excluded their film and television co-production treaties from the MFN clause because they favour partner nations, but MFN exemptions are set to expire in 2005 (European Commission, 2000a).

6. Miller (1996: 76) points out that the US too has been guilty of restrictive practices and government financial support.

7. However, Freedman (2002: 8) points out that in 2001 the US still considered quotas as 'a service barrier' that 'hinders the free flow of some programming'.

5

Digital Television in Europe

Technological developments are reshaping the communications and information landscape. The digital revolution allows unlimited uses and applications through compression and the ability to offer text, sound and images in a single format. The Internet has evolved from a support for text-based content to a carrier of multimedia services and may become a true broadcasting medium in the future. Developments in the telecommunications sector support both the digital and Internet revolution, allowing a growing variety of products and services to be accessed via a number of different platforms. The Internet and digital television have emerged as the two major multimedia platforms or distribution forms through which consumer-citizens access various products and services. They are often referred to as 'convergence' technologies – meaning that they blend various features of telecommunications, computing and mass media.

This chapter focuses on the technology, economics, politics and regulation of digital television (DTV) in Europe. The first part considers technical issues, describes current developments in DTV in the EU and offers country-by-country penetration data. The second part looks at the potential of DTV and assesses whether it is simply a continuation of analogue television or the emergence of a new context for broadcasting. It argues that the promise of enhanced programming choice and greater consumer access looks very idealistic. Commercial reality has not allowed certain services to develop and most consumers are reluctant to sign up to them. The chapter also attempts to identify major trends in European DTV, including the consolidation of outlets into a few hands. Despite lower barriers to entry and the proliferation of channels of communication, the European DTV landscape is characterised by the formation of large companies and concentrated power. The final part examines the main drivers for future DTV take-up and assesses the future of the technology.

DTV PLATFORMS

Digital television is a technology for transmitting and receiving broadcast television signals.

A DTV signal is transmitted over the same general set of frequencies used by analogue television broadcasts, but instead of continuous analogue components carrying video and audio information, there is a single, high-speed bit stream. This bit stream is a combination of encoded video, encoded audio and system data (Casey and Aupperle, 1998: 1).

DTV can be received in three ways: satellite dish (Digital Satellite Television – DST), cable line (Digital Cable Television – DCT), or by terrestrial means, using an analogue aerial and television set (Digital Terrestrial Television – DTT).[1] DTT is the cheapest option to install, but the inferior technology does not allow the same number of channels as DST or DCT. This may explain its low levels of development. Strategy Analytics (2002a) found that DTT operators had only 7.4 per cent of the DTV market in 2001, compared to 70.1 per cent for DST operators and 22.5 per cent for DCT operators. Table 5.1 shows that in 2002, DTT was only present in four EU Member States, alongside competing cable and satellite platforms, whereas the availability of DCT and DST was almost universal.

The first EU countries to launch DTT were Sweden, Britain, Finland and Spain. In Sweden, DTT was launched on a commercial basis in April 1999. The initial offer was basically free of charge, but it did not attract many subscribers. The platform did not include TV4, the country's most popular channel, and it was not sufficiently differentiated from the analogue offer. Decoders were expensive (ranging from €300–450) and Sweden is a heavily cabled market, leaving little room for the development of alternative delivery methods. Consequently, the development of DTT was slow and by 2002, around 100,000 households (2 per cent of total Swedish households) had purchased the digital decoder. In Finland, DTT was launched in August 2001, offering a combination of free and pay channels, but has also experienced slow growth for similar reasons (i.e. expensive decoders, high cable penetration). By 2002, only 25,000 decoders had been sold.

The problems of DTT technology were exacerbated in the first half of 2002 after the dramatic failure of two pioneer, digital, pay-television, terrestrial services in Europe – ITV Digital in Britain and Quiero TV in Spain. ITV Digital collapsed in March 2002, and the following month, Quiero TV ceased transmissions. The bankruptcy of these two platforms raised concerns about the future of the technology, but some of these concerns seem to have been lifted thanks to free-to-air DTT initiatives in Britain and Germany towards the end of the year. In Britain, the launch of Freeview altered the direction of DTT by no longer seeking to compete directly with established satellite and cable offerings (see case study on the British context below). In Germany, free-to-air DTT was

Table 5.1: Availability of Digital Television Platforms Across Europe (End 2002)

Country	Satellite	Cable	Terrestrial
Austria	✓	✓	–
Belgium	–	✓	–
Denmark	✓	✓	–
France	✓	–	–
Finland	✓	✓	✓
Germany	✓	✓	✓ [1]
Greece	✓	–	–
Ireland	✓	–	–
Italy	✓	✓	–
Luxembourg	✓	–	–
Netherlands	✓	✓	–
Portugal	✓	–	–
Spain	✓	✓	– [2]
Sweden	✓	✓	✓
United Kingdom	✓	✓	✓ [3]

Sources: Market reports

Notes:
1. In Germany, free-to-view DTT was launched initially in the Berlin and Brandenburg areas in late 2002. Deployment was expected to take place zone by zone, to gradually cover the whole country.
2. In Spain, DTT platform Quiero TV ceased transmissions in April 2002.
3. In Britain, DTT platform, ITV Digital, collapsed in March 2002 but a BBC-led consortium acquired the right to offer DTT free-to-air services in July 2002 and commenced operations in October 2002 under the name Freeview.

launched initially in the Berlin and Brandenburg areas, but it is expected to gradually cover the whole country. In Italy, both public broadcaster RAI and commercial group Mediaset entered the free-to-air DTT arena in early 2004. Across Europe, it seems that the imposition of a free-to-air model has sealed the demise of digital terrestrial television. Strategy Analytics (2002b) sees better prospects for DTT in the longer term as dedicated free-to-air set-top boxes are likely to secure a market niche.

However, DST is leading the way for DTV in Europe and is attracting most commercial interest. Indeed, satellite operators have dominated the European market from the birth of DTV and continue to do so, with 70.1 per cent of viewers by the end of 2001, although their share had fallen from 74.7 per cent a year earlier. While still the preferred choice of viewers, satellite-based, digital television is expected to lose ground to cable in the coming years. In fact, cable increased its share from 18.6 per cent in 2000 to 22.5 per cent in 2001. Strategy Analytics (2002b) predicted 2003 to be the first year that cable television would be the world's fastest growing DTV platform, forecasting that by 2008, 11 per cent of European homes would have DTT, 32 per cent DCT and 29 per cent DST.

EUROPEAN DTV PENETRATION

DTV has developed rapidly since the mid-1990s. Introduced in the US during 1994, by 1996, DTV was present in Japan, Australia, Latin America as well as certain European countries, notably France, Italy and Spain. However, it was in 1999 that DTV established its presence in most EU countries (see table 5.2). The number of DTV European households increased from only 2 million at the end of 1997 to 10 million at the end of 1999 (IDATE, 2000). According to a January 2002 research survey by Strategy Analytics (2002a), the number of European homes acquiring DTV in the year 2001 was 25.8 million, representing a penetration rate of 16.3 per cent. In a follow-up survey in May, Strategy Analytics (2002b) expected continuing consumer demand for DTV and forecast 100 million DTV homes by 2007 (see table 5.3). A survey from consulting firm Jupiter MMXI in March 2002 came up with similar (although more moderate) forecasts (see table 5.4). The reasons seen for such growth were, first, the introduction of new digital technologies and technological convergence, bringing together different media forms, and second, the setting up of new re-regulatory frameworks at both EU and national levels (see Chapter 3). These technological possibilities and the shifting of political perceptions from strict regulation to re-regulatory approaches allowed flexibility for companies to combine their activities and encouraged cross-border and cross-sector strategic alliances. These alliances are considered crucial by the industry in terms of sharing the technical expertise and huge costs involved in developing new digital technologies.

However, by the end of 2003, the European DTV landscape had not reached stability and penetration rates differed substantially among EU Member States. In most of the EU national markets, the availability of DTV remained partial. Whereas the Scandinavian region had successfully developed DTV, with penetration rates in Sweden, Finland and Denmark both above 20 per cent at the end of 2003, in certain countries, particularly the smaller and Mediterranean markets, DTV had not at that time secured a significant share of the television market. Table 5.5 shows that the household penetration of DTV in the small markets of Belgium, Austria and the Netherlands at the end of 2003 was 1 per cent, 8.2 per cent and 3.9 per cent respectively. The small Mediterranean countries of Greece and Portugal had penetration rates of 8.3 per cent and 12.8 per cent respectively.

Table 5.2: Development of Digital Television in Europe (% Households with Access to DTV Packages, 1997–9)

Country	end 1997	end 1998	end 1999
Austria	–	0.4	1.3
Belgium	–	0.6	1.1
Denmark	–	2.2	2.9
Finland	–	0.1	0.2
France	5.5	8.7	10.3
Germany	0.6	1.9	2.3
Greece	–	–	1.4
Ireland	–	–	0.8
Italy	1.1	3.1	3.8
Luxembourg	–	–	0.9
Netherlands	2.4	2.5	2.6
Portugal	–	–	1.5
Spain	3.0	8.1	8.9
Sweden	–	0.8	2.5
United Kingdom	–	0.9	4.1

Source: IDATE (2000)

Note:
All figures are for the three DTV platforms – satellite, terrestrial, cable – combined.

Table 5.3: Forecast for Digital Television Ownership Across Europe

	2000	2001	2002	2003	2004	2005	2006	2007	2008
Household Penetration (%)	12	16	21	27	34	43	53	63	73
Number of Households (m)	18.9	25.8	33.0	42.8	54.9	70.0	87.0	104.8	122.2

Source: Strategy Analytics (2002b)

Note:
Figures are for all DTV platforms combined.

Table 5.4: Forecast for Digital Ownership in Europe

	2001	2002	2003	2004	2005	2006	2007
Household Penetration (%)	15	20	26	35	43	52	59
Number of Households (m)	24.3	32.2	42.2	56.4	71.0	85.5	98.8

Source: Jupiter MMXI (2002)

Note:
Figures are for all DTV platforms combined.

Table 5.5: Digital Television Penetration in Europe (End 2003)

Country	Digital Pay Television Penetration (%)	Digital Television Penetration – Free and Pay (%)
Austria	1.1	8.2
Belgium	0	1.0
Denmark	14.7	20.0
Finland	4.3	20.2
France	18.9	23.3
Germany	3.6	4.3
Greece	4.7	8.3
Ireland	36.1	38.8
Italy	12.3	16.3
Netherlands	2.9	3.9
Portugal	12.6	12.8
Spain	15.6	17.4
Sweden	24.8	27.2
United Kingdom	36.1	48.4
Europe Average	14.7	19.0

Source: *Screen Digest* (2004)

CASE STUDY: BRITAIN – EUROPE'S MOST COMPETITIVE DTV MARKET

In sharp contrast to other European nations, at the end of 2003, 48.4 per cent of British households had DTV. This compared to a European average of 19.0 per cent. Intense competition between operators is widely assumed to explain the success of DTV in Britain, one of the few countries to have had three commercial DTV platforms: satellite, cable and terrestrial. Competition between platforms resulted in operators giving away set-top boxes for free and offering relatively low prices for subscription to basic DTV packages compared to other countries (see table 5.6). Britain's adoption of DTV can partly be explained by the limited number of terrestrial channels (just five) available. The relatively high digital penetration rate, particularly for DST, also stemmed from BSkyB's early conversion from analogue to digital for its satellite customers. This effectively undermined the chances of digital terrestrial and the collapse of DTT platform, ITV Digital, has shown that the DTV market in Britain cannot support a number of competing pay-television platforms.

Indeed, in April 2002 ITV Digital, jointly owned by commercial broadcasters, Carlton Communications and Granada Media Group, filed for bankruptcy. This financial crisis was mainly caused by overbidding for football rights.[2] In 2001, ITV Digital had signed a three-year £315 million deal to show Nationwide

Table 5.6: Cost of Monthly Subscription for Digital Television Services in Europe (€)

Country	GDP per head	Basic Package	Full Package
Austria	23.611	15	45
Belgium	21.990	17.2	67
Denmark	29.379	25	96
France	22.130	20.6	104
Finland	21.899	28	59
Germany	23.674	15	45
Greece	11.351	53	–
Ireland	17.824	19	53
Italy	20.091	17.1	51.3
Netherlands	21.741	29	–
Portugal	8.967	16.2	36
Spain	12.548	21.6	51.6
Sweden	20.330	12.2	54
United Kingdom	20.733	15	45

Source: IDATE (2000)

League (First Division) games, the largest broadcasting contract in the League's history. The intention was to compete with BSkyB, which had previously acquired the rights to show live Premiership matches. The problem was that the Nationwide is a lower league and so ITV Digital attempted to copy BSkyB's strategy by using less appealing football matches, attracting fewer football fans and viewers.[3]

This collapse had a negative effect on the seventy-two English football clubs that depended on ITV Digital for much of their income. It was also a major setback to government plans for an all-digital Britain.[4] ITV Digital only signed 1.23 million subscribers before its closure. Of course, some migrated to satellite or cable packages but the damage was huge. With NTL and Telewest, Britain's largest cable television providers, also facing financial difficulties in 2002,[5] one platform emerged as a clear winner – satellite. Murdoch-controlled BSkyB confirmed its dominance over DTV in Britain as the leading pay-television operator with 6.6 million subscribers in September 2003 (7 million if Irish households included).

Following the collapse of ITV Digital, two main bidders emerged to take over its digital terrestrial licences – a BBC–BSkyB joint service (a free-to-air service including the BBC's digital channels and offerings from BSkyB and other private broadcasters), and an ITV–Channel 4 alliance (a combination of free-to-air and pay-television services).[6] In July 2002, the Independent Television Commission (ITC) decided to opt for a free-to-air service and gave the BBC the go-ahead to run DTT with BSkyB in a twelve-year deal starting in October 2002. The transmission company, Crown Castle, became the new owner of the three digital terrestrial licences abandoned by ITV Digital. With these decisions, the ITC put an end to the uncertainty over the future of digital terrestrial television.

DTT in Britain has turned into a free-to-air only platform. Freeview, the service created through a partnership between the BBC, BSkyB and Crown Castle, enables people to receive up to thirty channels through a set-top box priced at around £80–100 but without paying a monthly subscription fee. Freeview is a 'light' but diverse line-up of free-to-air services, offering a package including the existing five terrestrial channels, all the BBC's digital channels and some BSkyB channels. Although popular pay channels such as Sky Sports, Sky One, Sky Movies, E4 and FilmFour are not included, Freeview showed stronger increase than expected and ended 2003 with 3.28 million users representing a share of 23.7 per cent of the DTV market.

Freeview is aimed at an audience confused by DTV and hostile to subscription services. The service is expected to increase awareness of the advantages of digital services, which is where BSkyB comes in. BSkyB is without doubt one of Britain's foremost DTV providers, with expert knowledge of digital viewers and customer service. It therefore made sense to involve BSkyB, as a channel provider to Freeview, in the marketing and support of the service (Kehoe, 2002). However, the award of the licence to a consortium comprising the two main players in terrestrial and satellite television – the powerful public broadcaster BBC and satellite monopoly BSkyB – raised concerns about competition. The ITC was criticised for supporting the BBC's expansionist policy in the digital era, while at the same time allowing Murdoch-owned BSkyB to become involved in DTT.

Germany

Digital services have faced an even worse situation in Germany, where only 4.3 per cent of German households watched DTV at the end of 2003, leaving doubts over the future of the technology in Europe's largest market. The main obstacle to the rollout of digital has been that German households can access fifteen analogue programmes from public service broadcasters (PSBs) and over thirty free-to-air channels on cable and satellite. Those channels offer a wide range of programming and involve a relatively high cost for viewers (€15.15 per month licence fee for the PSBs and approximately €15 per month for cable), thereby dissuading viewers from subscribing to the additional cost of digital pay-television services. The financial problems that Premiere World faced in 2002, following the insolvency of the parent company Kirch, showed that any pay-television operator would struggle in a free-to-air dominated German television market. However, DTV penetration in Germany is expected to rise, despite the gloom caused by the downfall of the Kirch empire. In September 2003, Premiere, the only broadcaster transmitting exclusively on digital technology, had 2.76 million subscribers, while a year earlier in September 2002 it had 2.44 million subscribers, a net increase of approximately 320,000 subscribers (Christmann, 2003). By the end of 2003, Germany was expected to account for 13 per cent of European DTV households, with Britain accounting for 35 per cent followed by France (15 per cent) and Italy (9 per cent) (Thomas, Groner and Dyson, 2003).

Spain, Greece and Italy

Further questions about the future of DTV in Europe are raised by the Spanish, Greek and Italian markets. In these territories, the closures during 2002 of Spanish DTT platform, Quiero TV, and Greek DST consortium, Alpha Digital Synthesis, together with the merger of Telepiù and Stream in Italy that year, all contributed towards unsettling the early enthusiasm which had greeted the arrival of DTV in Europe.

CASE STUDY: THE FAILURE OF DTT AND CONSOLIDATION OF DST IN SPAIN

In January 1999, the Spanish government, through the Ministry of Science and Technology, invited tenders for national DTT services. The successful company would be allocated three multiplexes of four programme services each and two programme services in another multiplex (totalling fourteen programme services). The sole company to apply for such a licence was Onda Digital (later renamed Quiero TV), making Spain the third country in the world to launch DTT (the other two being Britain and Sweden). The main shareholder in Quiero TV was Retevision, controlled by the Spanish bank Santander Central Hispano and Spanish electric utilities, Endesa and Union Fenosa (Gomez, 2002).

Owing to huge debts, in April 2002, Quiero TV's shareholders decided to close the platform. By that time, Quiero TV had 90,000 subscribers, falling significantly short of the 200,000 for the end of 2000 predicted in earlier estimates. Quiero TV's failure can be attributed to a number of factors. Quiero TV offered a relatively limited number of services, consisting of just fourteen pay-television channels and some interactive services and ecommerce. This compared to sixty television channels, thirty-two radio stations and various interactive services on digital satellite platform, Canal Satellite Digital, along with fifty television channels, several radio stations and interactive services on rival digital satellite platform, Via Digital. Further problems came from the limited geographical reach of Quiero TV, covering only 60 per cent of the Spanish population, together with the failure to acquire any rights for showing Spanish football and the prohibitive cost (€400–500) of the digital decoder.

Following the collapse of Quiero TV, the future of DTT in Spain was left uncertain. In May 2003, the Spanish administration still hoped to resurrect the DTT market with a new free-to-air DTT model, with public broadcaster RTVE as the main driving force. In this context, DST has emerged as the most developed DTV platform in Spain. Until the end of 2002, the DST market was made up of two digital satellite pay-television consortia, Canal Satellite Digital (CSD) and Via Digital. Launched in February 1997, CSD was owned (83 per cent) by pay-television company, Sogecable (controlled by Vivendi-Universal's Canal Plus and the Spanish media group, Prisa), and by the end of 2001, had roughly 1.2 million subscribers. Its conditional access system was Mediaguard and its Application Program Interface (API) Mediahighway. Weaker rival, Via Digital, started broadcasts in September 1997 with the Spanish telecommunications giant, Telefonica (48.6 per cent), being its main shareholder. Via Digital's conditional access system was Nagravision and its API Open TV, making the service incompatible with CSD. Spanish consumers therefore needed to buy two different decoders to have access to all the DST services. By the end of 2001, Via Digital's subscribers totalled 800,000 (Gomez, 2002).

In May 2002, the two rival DST consortia decided to merge in an effort to stem operating losses. Sogecable and Telefonica, the main shareholders in the two platforms, saw that the Spanish market could not sustain rival pay-television services. The agreement created a single satellite pay-television company in Spain with more than 2 million subscribers in 2002 and sales of €1.3 billion. When the Spanish government approved the merger in November 2002, it sought conditions, including a four-year price freeze and limits on cooperation between Sogecable and Telefonica.

As in other Mediterranean countries, DCT is still in its infancy in Spain. DCT services are offered by two cable companies: Madritel (which operates in Madrid) and Euskatel (providing cable services in the Basque country). Once again, the conditional access systems used by the two companies are incompatible (Madritel uses NDS Videoguard, while Euskatel uses Nagravision). The two services do not attract many users and the rollout of cable networks in Spain (both analogue and digital) is well behind schedule. By the end of 2001, approximately 550,000 households subscribed to cable, a very small figure if one takes into account the large size of the market (40 million people). This low take-up is partly due to construction problems and delays in getting planning permission (Gomez, 2002).

CASE STUDY: IS THE GREEK DTV DREAM OVER?

In early 2001, Alpha Digital Synthesis S.A. (ADS) launched a digital satellite package to compete with DST package Nova, which had been introduced in 1999 by pay-television company NetMed Hellas, a subsidiary of Multichoice. To increase its subscriber potential, ADS signed a two-year deal to broadcast live the home matches of ten out of sixteen Greek league football clubs at a cost of €72 million. By Greek standards at least this was an astronomical figure, for in 1996, NetMed Hellas had paid just €44 million to broadcast the matches of all football clubs in the Greek league in a five-year agreement. Like Kirch Media in Germany and ITV Digital in Britain, ADS overpaid for football rights. By mid-2002, ADS had only 40,000 subscribers and revenues were too small to cover the initial investment and running costs. ADS eventually collapsed in September 2002, leaving Nova as the undisputable winner and many football clubs facing financial ruin.

ADS's failure could be attributed to several factors. First, at around 3 million television households, the small size of the Greek market meant that it would have taken a considerable time for ADS to achieve breakeven. Earlier predictions of 200,000–300,000 subscribers in the first two years of operation did not materialise and the offering of sports, movies and children's programming was not enough to convince Greeks to subscribe. A second obstacle was the cost of purchasing the necessary reception equipment (in 2001 the set-top box together with the satellite dish cost €450) as well as the monthly subscription fee of around €50. Third, the limited capacity of Greek producers hampered the ability to offer a great deal of high-quality domestic programming. Finally, Greek viewers could already enjoy eight terrestrial commercial channels with national coverage, together with widely available satellite channels which re-broadcast for free on public broadcaster, ERT.

Considering these factors, it is no surprise that ADS failed to create a large subscriber base. Its closure meant that only one DTV platform could survive in the small and saturated Greek television market. Still, Nova could not flourish, for by the end of 2002, it had around 85,000 subscribers and appeared unlikely to increase this to the 300,000–400,000 needed to break even. As DTT is not considered a valid option and DCT is virtually non-existent due to limited infrastructure, the prospects for the whole DTV market in Greece seem very poor.

CASE STUDY: MERGER TRENDS IN THE ITALIAN DTV MARKET

Within months of the closures of Quiero TV in Spain and ADS in Greece, the DTV market in Italy saw the two previously competing DST consortia, Telepiù and Stream, agreeing to merge in October 2002 in order to overcome huge losses. Losses at Telepiù, the Italian pay-television subsidiary of Canal Plus, had been running at around €1 million per day owing to rampant piracy, the high costs of television football rights and competition from Murdoch's rival and similarly loss-making platform, Stream. Telepiù is estimated to have lost about €350 million in 2001, while Stream lost at least €400 million (Johnson and Harding, 2002). Following several months of bitter negotiations with Jean-René Fourtou, the new President of Telepiù's parent company Vivendi-Universal, Murdoch decided in early October 2002, to buy the rival platform in a €893 million cash and debt deal. The debt-burdened French conglomerate Vivendi-Universal originally hoped to realise €1.5 billion from the sale of Telepiù. However, News Corporation agreed to pay only €470 million in cash to Vivendi-Universal and assume Telepiù's estimated €423 million debt. The deal formed part of a €12 billion disposal programme as Vivendi-Universal struggled to cut net debts of €17 billion.

By taking over Telepiù, Murdoch was gambling that as sole operator of pay television in Italy, the business could become as profitable as BSkyB in Britain (Kapner, 2002). Murdoch's monopoly could perhaps change the economics of pay television in Italy, for with no competition for football match rights, he would be in a position to re-negotiate contracts signed with Italy's leading teams. Also, News Corporation had developed technology with greater security, hoping to eliminate piracy, which was estimated to account for 2.5 million homes watching Telepiù and Stream in 2001 (p. 31).

Sky Italia, the new merged platform, was 80.1 per cent owned by News Corporation and 19.9 per cent by Telecom Italia. It went on air on 31 July 2003 with a basic package containing fifty channels, including the country's first twenty-four-hour news service, Tg24. Subscribers could supplement this line-up with sports and film channels. In April 2003, the EC Competition Directorate allowed the merger, but with a number of conditions, including the following: exclusive rights for non-satellite transmission would be waived; News Corporation would offer non-satellite competitors wholesale prices on a 'retail minus principle' and any content would be unbundled and non-exclusive; rights holders could halt current contracts with Stream and Telepiù with no penalties; future contracts would be limited to two years for football and three years for film; access to the satellite platform would be offered on 'fair and reasonable' terms; and licences for conditional access technology would be granted on 'a fair and non-discriminatory basis' (*New Media Markets*, 2003). By the end of 2003, Sky Italia had 2.7 million subscribers and expected it would break even in the first half of 2005 with 4 million users.

THE PROMISE OF DTV

As the above examples demonstrate, DTV in Europe has seen various national contexts witnessing greater concentration, putting pluralism, diversity and choice in danger. However, things were regarded differently in the 1990s, when it was anticipated that the brilliance of digital technology would promise more choice and make diverse content accessible to all. Indeed, DTV offers the potential to overcome some of the limitations of analogue television, such as spectrum scarcity and picture interference. It delivers better and sharper pictures and sound, and uses the broadcast spectrum more efficiently than analogue television, thus allowing many more channels. The availability of bandwidth allows viewers access to hundreds of channels, each aiming at specific market segments and each catering for specific interests. Some commentators (e.g. Gilder, 1992; Negroponte, 1995) believe that digital networks will bring about vast opportunities for specialised production and distribution that will eventually end the dominance of centralised broadcasting systems. In the future, people will not share the same viewing experiences, as is currently the case with mass-appeal programming and the provision of 'national moments' offered by free-to-air channels. To quote technology guru, Nicholas Negroponte, 'digital television is really like downloading to a computer' (1995: 48), because programmes and information can be broadcast to an individual viewer at the specific time he/she chooses to watch it. Negroponte adds, 'the key to the future of television is to stop thinking about television as television' (p. 45). Viewed this way, DTV would fundamentally change the nature and structure of the television industry, representing a new technological infrastructure and competitive paradigm.

More crucially, DTV would change the economics of the television business. DTV has largely developed as pay television and has introduced new methods of financing such as pay-per-view and NVOD (Near Video on Demand). Subscription charges allow television firms to raise revenues directly from the viewers, thus freeing the industry from its traditional dependence on advertising (Papathanassopoulos, 2002: 38). DTV also comes with the promise to lower entry costs for new broadcasters, creating an ideal scenario in which it is possible to imagine a proliferation of channels with the entry of new, small and talented broadcasters creating fresh ideas, contributing to innovation, choice and diversity. DTV can also offer full Internet access and bring broadband to a large number of potentially excluded households. Viewers can also access an array of interactive services based on the television set, including email, news on demand, television shopping, betting, access to Internet sites and other enhanced services, such as the ability to follow individual football players and look at different camera angles or statistics during a football match.

In this way, DTV can be seen as a catalyst for convergence between telecommunications, computing and mass media. As technologies rapidly converge, they create shared interests between companies operating on different platforms, thereby resulting in additional revenue streams. There are also potential benefits from a citizenship point of view. By allowing broadband access through a familiar screen terminal already present in 97 per cent of EU households, DTV enables those who may be reluctant to buy a computer to become networked through a significantly cheaper investment (Liikanen, 2001). That is why the EC has argued that Member States should cooperate to facilitate the introduction of digital television services with Internet capabilities (European Commission, 2001a).

THE REALITY OF DTV

The scenario outlined would portray rather a new digital utopia for television in Europe. For other commentators, however, DTV symbolises just another technological innovation, such as the change from black-and-white to colour television, representing simply an extension of analogue television provided by the traditional suppliers of television content. Several trends would appear to challenge the utopian vision of DTV.

Consolidation

Graham Murdock (2000) assessed whether DTV is television as usual or a revolution. In doing so, he distinguished two broad currents of change: replacement and convergence. He identified replacement as 'the uneven transmission from analogue to digital forms of production and transmission that is currently taking place in the three established television "platforms", terrestrial, satellite and cable, at different speeds in different European countries' (p. 43). Convergence referred to 'the rapid growth of new broadcasting platforms based on wired and mobile telephone networks and the Internet, together with the development of systems convergence and multifunction television sets' (p. 44). Murdock then identified five basic dimensions of these transitions – enhancement; compression; consolidation; interactivity; and access. He concluded that, while enhancement and compression appeared primarily as forces ensuring continuity, consolidation provided real obstacles to interactivity and access potential as interlocking corporate interests hinder the liberatory potential of interactivity (pp. 45–54). Similar concerns about the ability of DTV to enhance access and offer greater choice for the viewer have also been raised by Allen (1998), Humphreys and Lang (1998), Hesmondhalgh (2002) and Papathanassopoulos (2002).

Indeed, many of the DTV opportunities described look very idealistic. As the examples discussed would indicate, commercial reality and low consumer take-up have not allowed much scope for the development of certain DTV services. While the provision of more channels and improved picture quality has become a reality, the interactive potential of DTV has been slow to materialise. Television, including DTV, is still considered a mass-entertainment medium, rather than an information or educational tool. Most online activity revolves around

communications, emails and chat, but these activities have not been traditionally associated with television. For most people, television is still mostly regarded
as a medium for entertainment and relaxation.

Audience Fragmentation?
When it comes to the matter of choice and the disintegration of shared mass
viewing, it is true that the explosion of television choice has led to some changes
in consumer attitudes and behaviour. However, in many EU countries the established terrestrial channels still get the lion's share of television viewing. People
still settle down to just eight to ten channels and search out shared television
experiences – *The World Cup*, *Who Wants to Be a Millionaire?*, *Big Brother*
(Ewington, 2002: 36). In 2002, the advanced multichannel Dutch television
market saw the top ten channels holding more than 86 per cent audience share.

Pop Idol

Also the success in 2002 of television formats like *Pop Idol* in Britain (shown on the main, commercial, terrestrial broadcaster ITV1), and of *The Bar* and *The Farm* in Greece (shown on the private terrestrial channels, Mega Channel and Antenna TV), demonstrated how mainstream channels can still unite big, broad audiences and create a national obsession despite the wide availability of alternative media choices.

Overbidding

Another problem with DTV is that revenues are not sufficient to justify investment in original production or the acquisition of popular programming. Only a handful of large incumbent channels can afford to bid for premium content that mostly takes the form of exclusive sports rights and the latest movies.

The cost of acquiring such content has increased considerably in recent years. The rising costs of broadcasting rights can be attributed to the liberalisation of the market, which allowed more channels and generated fierce competition between players with deep pockets. For example, the German conglomerate, Kirch, acquired broadcasting rights to the 2002 and 2006 Football World Cups for the astronomical fee of $2.36 billion. By comparison, Fifa sold the broadcasting rights for the 1998 World Cup to the European Broadcasting Union, the body representing public broadcasters, for just $134 million. In Britain, BSkyB paid £1.1 billion (about a third of its total programme budget) in 2000 for the live coverage of sixty-six Premiership matches in a three-year deal (2001–4). The previous four-year deal had cost BSkyB £670 million and the five-year contract before that cost even less (£191.5 million).[7]

Smaller broadcasters may not be able to acquire the rights to those programmes that would enable them to build large subscriber bases, and would be reluctant to enter the market, leaving the incumbents to pursue their own interests unchallenged and expand even further. A related, worrying situation is that the big commercial DTV channels have the ability to outbid free-to-air channels, including public service broadcasters, for premium content including major sporting events and new Hollywood films. As a result, universal access for such content can disappear, with audiences divided according to the ability to pay and leaving many excluded from the benefits of DTV services.

However, experience shows that even major broadcasters like Kirch, Carlton and Granada can be damaged by overbidding for rights. Similarly the downfall of operators like ADS in Greece and Quiero TV in Spain could partly be attributed to overpayment for programme rights. A lesson to be drawn from this turmoil is that there are limits to how far consumers are prepared to pay for premium content such as football.

National Monopolies and the Major Players in European DTV
It seems that only further consolidation – the formation of industrial alliances between players – can provide a viable alternative to closing down operations. As already mentioned, faced with financial difficulties in Spain and Italy, DTV consortia have been involved in mergers and takeovers.

The trend towards consolidation in the media and communications industries, and the increasing number of industrial alliances in particular, has prompted some analysts to describe the new emerging pattern as 'co-opetition', reflecting the increased cooperation rather than competition between companies (Harding cited in Murdock, 2000: 48). These developments also signal that more than one player (in certain cases two) cannot co-exist in the same market. Direct competition between platforms reduces the slice of income going to the channels. As Oliver (2002: 53) argues, perhaps small pay-television channels need to adopt a complementary strategy to established operators rather than engage in head-to-head competition.

With the whole DTV market in Europe struggling to establish a commercially viable foundation, different national markets have witnessed the same trends: after the rollout of several platforms, satellite comes to displace other means of digital delivery, with single companies establishing strong national monopolies for digital television. Experience shows that the key companies in pay television are those with deep pockets who enter their markets first, leaving no room for new competitors, and acquire premium content (the latest film releases and sports rights). The result is that Europe's pay-television map is now dominated by a few players. At the forefront is Rupert Murdoch's News Corporation, a vertically integrated, global media company involved in newspaper publishing as well as the production and distribution of films and television. In the field of digital television, News Corporation has a controlling stake in BSkyB (35.4 per cent) and also owns Sky Italia. By the end of 2003, BSkyB had more than 7 million subscribers in Britain and Ireland, while the takeover and re-launch of Sky Italia established Murdoch as a significant DST player in continental Europe. Murdoch's partnership with the BBC for the Freeview DTT service means that News Corporation will also have some presence in terrestrial television in the digital era.

The second main player is NBC-Universal (formerly Vivendi-Universal), whose audiovisual activities are primarily concentrated in its 49 per cent controlling interest in the French pay-television operator, Canal Plus, and the 19.74 per cent stake in the leading Spanish pay-television group Sogecable. Canal Plus is Europe's largest pay-television operator, with subsidiaries in Belgium, Italy, the Netherlands, Spain and the Nordic countries. Founded in 1989, Sogecable pioneered the introduction of DTV and interactive services in Spain, and following the merger between the company's CSD and rival Via Digital DST platforms in May 2002 (see above), Sogecable reached 2.5 million DTV Spanish subscribers by the end of 2002, enhancing its leading position in the Spanish pay-television market.

John Malone's Liberty Media is the third main player in European DTV, controlling United Pan-Europe Communications (UPC – Europe's largest cable operator) and part of cable network, Telewest. UPC is a major provider of broadband communication and entertainment in Europe. Its services, which include analogue and digital cable television, are offered in seventeen countries. Liberty Media has stakes in a wide variety of cable channels, such as the Discovery Channel, and owns 98 per cent of home-shopping network, QVC. In addition, it is one of the largest shareholders in News Corporation, with an 18 per cent stake. It has twice tried to seize control of NTL – Britain's largest cable company – in a bid to merge it with Telewest, in which it has a 25 per cent stake.

All the three main players were already established companies in the analogue cable (Liberty Media) and satellite (News Corporation and Vivendi) pay-television environment of the late 1980s and early 1990s. It is from this foundation that they have been able to remain dominant in the digital era too.[8]

DRIVERS FOR DTV TAKE-UP

Commercial forces have hindered the utopian promises of DTV. Opportunities for increased programming choice, the launch of enhanced services and even a reduction of the 'digital divide' have not yet come true. Consequently, much of the early excitement that centred around DTV has disappeared. DTV in 2002–3 was in a 'shake-out' phase as some companies failed and others consolidated their activities. Free access, the termination of analogue services, programming, Internet connectivity, affordability, awareness and regulation are just some of the issues and factors which are currently driving the future prospects and potential for DTV in Europe.

Free-to-Air DTV

So far, the economic model for DTV has been largely based on pay-television services offered by private consortia. These consortia have acquired exclusive popular programming and require subscribers to buy a set-top box (and, in the case of satellite, a dish) to access it. While pay television has driven the initial uptake of DTV in Europe, saturation of the pay-television market in terms of penetration may occur. Already the market may have arrived at a situation in which those consumers prepared to sign up to digital pay-television services have already done so. In the highly competitive British digital pay-television market, about 40 per cent of homes had taken up digital television by the end of 2002, leaving 60 per cent of homes unconvinced. Attention is therefore likely to focus on the free-to-view markets. As the earlier discussion of the British context showed, the re-direction of DTT towards a primarily free-to-air system may prove compelling to many households which are negative about pay television. RAI in Italy also launched free-to-air DTV bouquets in early 2004, while the French public broadcaster was planning for a free-to-air DTT platform for 2005 to offer some thirty channels for a €100–150 initial investment in the set-top box and the ability to upgrade to subscription channels.

Analogue Switch-off

Another driver for DTV take-up could be the setting of a firm date for analogue switch-off. So far, a few countries have committed to a prompt date for analogue switch-off. Italy has asserted that it expects to switch off the analogue frequency in 2007 and to speed the changeover, the government is offering a €150 subsidy to buyers of the first 700,000 set-top boxes required to receive digital signals. In Spain, the Minister of Science and Technology, Josep Pique, announced his government's determination to switch off analogue in 2007 too, five years earlier than initially scheduled (Digital Television Group, 2003). Sweden plans to switch off analogue in February 2008, while in Germany the phasing out of analogue terrestrial transmission is expected to take place in 2010. The British government have timetabled switch-off to occur in 2012.

At an EU level, in September 2003, the European Commission published a communication on the transition to digital broadcasting aimed at assisting Member States in making that transition. This provides a guide on how best to migrate from analogue to digital radio and television broadcasting in a consumer-friendly fashion. Erkki Liikanen, Commissioner for Enterprise and the Information Society, emphasised that the EU was not considering 'intrusive measures' like prescribing deadlines for digital switchover, since progress varies widely across the Union. However, the Commission is actively monitoring national processes and will continue to run benchmarking exercises. The Commission's aim is to elicit voluntary switchovers through a series of incentives. Under the eEurope 2005 Action Plan, Member States were expected to publish their digital switchover plans by the end of 2003, but very few had done so by mid-2004.

The transition to digital broadcasting has pros and cons. Selling off a scarce commodity like the spectrum involves tremendous economic benefits for both broadcasters and governments. The switch-off could be advantageous to the television industry as the free spectrum could be used for more powerful, digital channels. Until switch-off, the national coverage of digital terrestrial television cannot go beyond 70 to 75 per cent because analogue broadcasters have exclusive use of the internationally free channels which are cleared for full power transmission (Smadja, 2003). Prompt analogue switch-off could release frequencies to be sold for other purposes, such as third-generation mobile telephony. However, analogue switch-off may result in social exclusion if DTV is not available to a large part of the population. Therefore governments need to work towards ensuring that full switchover from analogue to digital takes place only when certain criteria of availability, affordability and accessibility are satisfied.

Programming

Digital technology is only a means to deliver entertainment, utility and information services. It is not an end in itself for it is the content and services that aggregate around and support a technology that determine the consumer's willingness to spend time and money on it (Hughes and Marshall, 2002: 31). In the media and communications industry, 'content is king' is a frequently repeated aphorism.

The European experience shows that popular programming, such as movies and sports, is among the main reasons for the take-up of DTV services. Films and football, coupled with a successful marketing and packaging strategy, drove the success of BSkyB in the early to mid-1990s. However, as previously argued, the cost of acquiring exclusive rights for broadcasting such content has risen considerably in recent years. This has in turn led to the closure of a number of DTV operators. On another level, 'the heavy cost of investment in new technology and infrastructure has absorbed funds that might otherwise have gone into content creation' (Lovegrove and Enriquez, 2002: 105). Many operators, particularly new ones, have been forced to seek lower-cost sources of supply, such as easily replicable formats and US imports. Premium content may therefore be a necessary attraction for the take-up of DTV. However the price of such material does not encourage greater programming diversity.

Internet Connectivity

Additional DTV drivers include the provision of interactive services, such as home banking and home shopping, the potential for full Internet and broadband access, possibilities for distance learning and the potential delivery of information services, whereas the Internet is currently the major delivery platform for these services. As television receivers have always been more pervasive than personal computers and are likely to remain so, a case can be made that Internet access via the television set can potentially diminish the so-called 'digital divide'. According to an OECD report (2000a), because of their high levels

of diffusion, low cost, familiarity and ease of use, television sets could potentially bring the Internet to poor, less well-educated, elderly and other low-access
groups, and thus help to bridge the digital divide.[9]

However, this is likely to be slow, and patterns of household television-Internet
use are likely to be different from PC-Internet use. There is little evidence that
DTV is the gateway to mass Internet use in any EU country. The technology might
be there but, as the market struggles with consumer habits, there are no signs that
television and the Internet will converge into a single electronic medium. There
may be a conceptual difficulty with thinking about the television as a window for
Internet access, for, as Ian Hargreaves (2001) suggests, 'digital television offers a
commercially controlled "walled garden" experience of the internet and, in any
case, the TV set is just not the right piece of furniture for online activities'. Yet
future generations who may grow up with digital television could be more willing
to access interactive services via a television set or other devices, such as a mobile
phone.

Affordability

The cost of purchasing the new equipment to receive DTV services has so far
been relatively high. In the case of digital terrestrial and cable television, customers need to purchase either an integrated television set (with a built-in
adapter) or buy a digital set-top box. With digital satellite television, customers
also need to be equipped with a satellite dish. Monthly subscription applies to
all the commercial platforms – whether terrestrial, cable or satellite – although
latest propositions, like the BBC's Freeview, are completely free once consumers
have bought the digital adapter.

Prices charged thus far by most subscription-based commercial operators are
still relatively high. This is evident especially in countries where competition is
virtually non-existent. In Greece, for example, where digital satellite television
is the only option, the subscription price in 2000 for Nova was €53, whereas in
the competitive British market, subscriptions started from as little as €15. The
comparison becomes more striking if one takes into account that the Gross
Domestic Product (GDP) per head in Greece in 2000 was as low as €11,351
while in Britain it was €20,733 (see table 5.6).

During 2003, set-top box prices retailed in Europe for around €100, but
according to Strategy Analytics (2003), supplier competition will lead to rapid
price declines. The research firm predicted that digital terrestrial television
receivers will sell for as little as €36 by 2007 (see table 5.7). As the British experience shows, any commitment by industry to give away set-top boxes boosts the
market. BSkyB built an impressive DTV subscriber base partly by giving away
decoders.

Table 5.7: Digital Terrestrial Television Set-top Boxes – Retail Price Projections

(End of Year)	2003	2004	2005	2006	2007
Retail Price (Euros)	84.00	63.00	50.40	42.84	36.41
Retail Price (£)	61.35	46.01	36.81	31.29	26.60

Source: Strategy Analytics (2003)

Note:
Figures are based on entry-level devices sold in Europe at constant 2003 exchange rates.

Public Awareness

Public awareness of the pros and cons of the new technology can certainly drive the market up. A large part of the European population is confused about the technology of DTV and, as a result, does not seem to be interested in it. Evidence of this is that despite the growth in uptake, by the end of 2002, around 80 per cent of the European population had not signed up to DTV services (see tables 5.3 and 5.4). Public authorities, consumer organisations and the industry itself can play an important role in promoting public awareness and building user trust and confidence in digital technologies (European Commission, 2002c). The launch of a well-designed government campaign may increase awareness of the benefits of DTV. In countries like Britain, where there exist free-to-air DTT channels, such a campaign could combat the common misconception that all DTV channels must be paid for.

Regulation

Setting up of a clear and transparent regulatory regime, providing for interconnection of networks, technical interoperability of services and compatibility of equipment could also speed up the rollout of DTV (European Commission, 2002c). Regulators should be able to reach a delicate balance between the interests of business in making a return on any initial investment in digital technology, and the public interest in having access to a wide range of high-quality services at a minimum cost. As Lovegrove and Enriquez (2002: 107–10) argue, regulators face three challenges: the access challenge, the standards challenge and the investment and content quality challenge.

The first is to ensure the widest possible availability of content by encouraging investment in new networks and services while minimising the risk of market dominance. According to Dransfeld and Jacobs (2000: 145–6), two different forms of monopoly are developing in the area of digital television: gateway provision and content provision. Gateway provision entails a company controlling viewer access to all television programmes on one or more of the three delivery platforms in a given market: satellite, cable or terrestrial transmission. A gateway monopolist owns the interface between the channel bouquet and subscribers, as well as the technology for the reception of television signals. General competition law, rather than specific regulation, is widely used both at a national and an EU level to deal with these issues. But competition law has not proved the most effective means of addressing these challenges, particularly the interoperability challenge. By declining to impose an EU-wide interoperability mandate for digital set-top boxes, the EC effectively allowed the deployment of incompatible standards (Levy, 1997; Galperin, 2002: 7–8). It is fair to say that interoperability of conditional access systems remains a technical possibility, rather than a reality. However, this can slow down the development of DTV. This is particularly evident in countries like Spain, where the incompatibility of proprietary digital set-top boxes from CSD and Via Digital held back the take-up of DTV services.

A monopoly on content provision occurs when the structure of a given market allows a company exclusive control over the choice and timing of programmes to be transmitted over either cable, satellite or terrestrial television. Normally pay-television providers are after lucrative events drawing large audiences (Dransfeld and Jacobs, 2000: 146–7). However, the EC and certain EU countries have taken measures to guard against the acquisition of exclusive rights for premium programming which is regarded as being in the public interest, protecting specific types of programmes for free-to-air channels with the so-called 'listed events' like the Olympic Games and the football championships.

The second regulatory challenge identified by Lovegrove and Enriquez concerns editorial standards and is equally complex in an environment of content proliferation. Regulators have to find ways to segment content sources and to identify those that pose the greatest risk to editorial standards. On the one hand, there is a need to maintain active monitoring of editorial standards across traditional mass-market media, notably the leading free-to-air television channels. On the other, there is perhaps the requirement for a 'lighter touch' approach to new niche channels aimed at an inherently smaller and more self-selecting audience (Lovegrove and Enriquez, 2002: 107). Finally, regulators have to create an environment that encourages investment and quality of content. Regulatory intervention is needed to nurture high-quality, indigenous content creation (pp. 107–9). Measures which could achieve this include the imposition of content requirements on all channels, the establishment of domestic content quotas and the funding of public service broadcasters mandated to deliver key aspects of quality and diversity (see Chapter 3).

CONCLUSION

This chapter started by looking at DTV in the early days of its emergence and outlined the current state of development in Europe. It explored the technical characteristics of the medium, investment strategies and consumer demand (technological and economic analysis). It argued that DTV has been developing rapidly in Europe since the late 1990s, boosted by technological advances like digitisation and convergence, which triggered investments across sectors and brought together different media forms. However, it is becoming clear that in 2002–3, DTV suffered severe reversals of fortune in many parts of Europe. Growth has been uneven and rapid. While DTV is thriving in countries like Britain, where there are only five terrestrial channels available, it has struggled in countries like Germany where there are over thirty free-to-air channels. In Spain, Italy and Greece, there is a strong tendency towards national digital pay-television monopolies. As experience indicates only one digital pay-television platform is likely to survive in any national market (in rare cases two), DTV in Europe is likely to witness further and continuing market consolidation. In these circumstances, the DTV environment in Europe has become dominated by a few national and private players.

Alongside these commercial considerations, the chapter also assessed the social impact of DTV, asking whether digital services offer something entirely new or simply extend the model of broadcasting found with analogue television. It was argued that the early excitement about DTV was overestimated, and that promises to offer more choice and diversity, greater interactivity and even diminish the digital divide have not been realised. Market reality, corporate mergers, the collapse of several DTV platforms and limited consumer demand have together hindered the development of DTV. So far DTV is about more channels, with some serving niche markets, but most recycling existing television material to fill up transmission hours. This has not resulted in an abundance of choice and interactivity for users and has certainly not contributed to the creation of an information-based, all-inclusive society.

Regulation could address this alarming situation and provide a future for the biggest revolution in television since the introduction of colour. Effective regulation could tackle consolidation and guarantee competition, while also encouraging investment and content quality. Finally, steps need to be taken to make DTV more affordable and available to large parts of the population. The role of public service broadcasters is crucial in achieving the objectives of affordability and universality, thus avoiding the emergence of a digital underclass. In which case, the BBC's provision of a portfolio of free digital services could perhaps provide the model for others to follow.

NOTES

1. ADSL (Asymmetric Digital Subscriber Lines) will soon represent another DTV network but it is likely to remain a niche-delivery platform.

2. Other reasons for ITV Digital's failure included extremely poor management policy, technical problems (picture freezing) and the decision to give away free set-top boxes to emulate the strategy of BSkyB.

3. The ITV Digital management did try to bid for the Premier League but were overruled by the Granada-Carlton parent management.

4. The British government believes that the development of DTT will contribute to the dream of a broadband Britain and strengthen the country's role in the e-economy.

5. NTL filed for bankruptcy protection from creditors in New York on 12 May 2002. The company listed £11.5 billion in assets and £16 billion debt in its filing for reorganisation under Chapter 11 of the US Bankruptcy Code in a Manhattan court. In 2002, the company was in the process of restructuring to reduce its debt. Telewest was also under pressure to restructure in order to cover its own £5 billion debt burden.

6. Additional bidders included Apax (a venture capitalist company) and SDN (a small, digital terrestrial operator jointly owned by NTL, United Business Media and S4C).

7. However, sports rights have reduced in worth in more recent years, while the EU Competition Directorate has brought in rules governing the distribution of rights. For example, in autumn 2003, BSkyB signed another £1.024 billion deal with the English Premier League to show live football matches for three years (2004–7), a reduction in price compared to the 2000 deal. In 2003, the deal was under investigation from the EU Competition Commissioner, Mario Monti, who viewed the exclusivity and the duration of the contract as bad for competition in broadcasting markets and bad for consumers. As a result, the pay-television operator was allowed to keep the vast majority of its lucrative TV rights for live Premiership football, but was forced to sub-license one of its four Premiership rights packages to a rival broadcaster.

8. Bertelsmann, another major player in European media and communications, is not mentioned as it is not involved in any DTV activities.

9. Clearly though, the digital divide is much more complex than a mere lack of access to new technology. As argued by Lisa J. Servon (2002: 7), the digital divide has three dimensions. In addition to access, other dimensions include training (the ability to use new technology for a range of purposes), and content, with content meeting the needs and demands of disenfranchised groups or created by these groups.

6

European Television in the Global Marketplace

In spite of the EU's best efforts to create a single market for broadcasting (see Chapter 4), television in Western Europe remains a largely territory-based affair. The historical origins of broadcasting as a national concern, and the enormous cultural and linguistic diversity within Europe, have meant that the vast majority of television is still produced for and targeted at distinct national audiences (see McAnany and Wilkinson, 1996: 16). In 2002, over 1,500 channels were circulating within Western Europe compared to only forty-seven in 1989, but fifty nationally based channels accounted for a 75 per cent audience share in the region (Reding, 2002: 5). Previous efforts to create pan-European satellite television in the 1980s (SuperChannel) were singularly disappointing (Collins, 1989) and even American-owned thematic channels (e.g. Cartoon Network, CNN, MTV, National Geographic, Discovery, Nickelodeon, Fox Kids) have been impelled to localise their offerings in the face of strong local competition (Chalaby, 2002).

Although television is primarily targeted at national audiences, there has always been concern about American imports and about the ability of Western Europe to support the production and circulation of European programming. At an economic level, this concern is reflected in debates about the growing trade imbalance with the US, and the potentially negative impact of imports on growth and jobs. The limited trade in programming between European countries has reinforced these concerns (see Buonanno, 1998: 18–20; Tunstall and Machin, 1999: 9). American imports also raise cultural concerns based on long-standing and deep-rooted fears about the Americanisation of mass culture associated with the discourse of cultural imperialism (see, for example, Hamelink, 1983; Herman and McChesney, 1997; Schiller, 1976, 1991 and 1992). The circulation of programmes and formats therefore constitutes more than a trade issue, and is linked to broader concerns about cultural and political sovereignty.

This chapter concentrates on the trade in television programmes and formats across Europe.[1] The first part considers trade trends and assesses the value and volume of US imports into the EU. A case study on British television programme exports provides an example of the industrial imperatives underpinning the drive to increase exports. The second part looks at the types of programming in circulation, focusing on those categories of content which have most value internationally among fiction, factual and children's programmes. Case studies on drama co-production and the activities of pre-school television specialist, HIT Entertainment, illustrate the strategies that European players have pursued in the face of falling budgets and a declining market for finished programmes. The third part looks at the growing importance of different types of formats which satisfy the demand for local origination in a global marketplace characterised by transnational ownership and the global production of locally originated formats or programming concepts (see Robertson, 1994, 1995).

TRENDS IN PROGRAMME TRADE

The rapid increase in private television channels in Western Europe during the 1980s resulted in a surge of American imports because fledgling commercial stations could not initially afford to invest in domestic production. The need for more programming could not be met within Western Europe because domestic television production continued to be dominated by a small number of vertically integrated public service broadcasters, resulting in a weak independent production sector (see Tunstall and Machin, 1999). By contrast, the large and wealthy American domestic market could support substantial volumes of high-cost fiction, which met demands for long-running series and feature films (Hoskins, McFadyen and Finn, 1997; Hoskins and Mirus, 1988). Acquisitions of American feature films, fiction and game-show formats not only provided a relatively inexpensive route to profitability, but also offered a distinctive alternative to the programmes provided by public service broadcasters, which were then less focused on popular entertainment. US imports sustained the necessary bulk of films to run pay-television services, and on the back of feature films, US suppliers were also able to sell longer-running series and sitcoms to new European channels with large amounts of transmission time to fill.

In 2000, the EU was estimated to have an audiovisual trade deficit with the US of $8.2 billion, 14 per cent higher than in 1999 (table 6.1) (EAO, 2002). Television accounted for just under half of American revenues at $4.38 billion, more than double the revenues of 1995 ($2.06 billion). European audiovisual exports to North America came to a paltry $827 million in 2000. In spite of this growing trade deficit, domestic European programming predominates on EU screens. The European Commission's report on the implementation of the Television Without Frontiers quota stipulations in 1999 and 2000 found that television broadcasters devoted an average of 62 per cent of transmission time to European programming (European Commission, 2002b). 72.5 per cent of

Table 6.1: Estimated Trade in Audiovisual Programmes between European Union and the United States, 1995–2000 (US$m)

Estimated Revenues of US Members of the MPA and AFMA in the EU						
	1995	1996	1997	1998	1999	2000
Theatrical Rental/Sales	1,178	1,392	1,494	1,734	1,721	1,750
Television	2,062	2,645	2,880	3,187	3,781	4,384
Video Rental/Sales	2,092	2,224	2,271	2,392	2,540	2,897
Total	5,331	6,262	6,645	7,313	8,042	9,031

Estimated EU Audiovisual Revenues in the US						
	1995	1996	1997	1998	1999	2000
Total UK Revenues	426	499	536	550	705	691
(of which TV Revenues)	83	77	193	200	197	180
Total EU Revenues	92	115	132	156	148	136
(of which French TV Revenues)	46	84	73	113	87	95
Total	518	614	668	706	853	827

Difference Between EU and US Revenues						
	1995	1996	1997	1998	1999	2000
Deficit US$m	4,813	5,648	5,977	6,607	7,190	8,204

Source: EAO (2002)

broadcasters complied with the quota, with non-compliance restricted largely to the cable and satellite sector.

However, the Commission's findings did not focus on fiction, the most heavily traded and costly genre, constituting two-thirds of global trade by volume (Department for Culture, Media and Sport, 1999a: 35). The trade in fiction is dominated by the US, which was estimated to account for 72 per cent of the global trade in drama, 63 per cent of feature films and 81 per cent of TV movies by volume in 1996–7 (p. 34). Drama constitutes the core of US exports to Western Europe, because fiction takes up a large share of transmission time. A study of thirty-six mainstream channels in six Western European countries during 1997 established that fiction accounted for 37.4 per cent of broadcasts with higher levels on commercial channels (48.9 per cent) and at peak time (44.9 per cent) (de Bens and de Smaele, 2001: 55). Although limited to two two-week surveys, the same research shows how the share of US series and films grew at the expense of domestic fiction between 1988 and 1997 as channels extended their transmission times. The share of US series/serials rose from 36 per cent in 1988 to 64 per cent in 1997, but the share of national series/serials declined from 37 per cent to 20 per cent (p. 65). American sources dominated the share of television movies and feature films both overall (57.5 per cent) and at peak time (67 per cent) in 1997. But it is worth noting that domestically produced series/serials had a greater share at peak time (44 per cent) in 1997 than American imports (39 per cent).

Other research further confirms the growing primacy of domestic fiction in prime time. A Eurofiction survey (10–16 March 2002) of mainstream channels found that domestic fiction (excluding feature films, but including repeats) accounted for 53 per cent of British fiction transmissions, 53 per cent in Germany, 23 per cent in France, 23 per cent in Italy and 35 per cent in Spain. These levels rose in peak time to 93 per cent in Britain, 84 per cent in Germany, 75 per cent in France, 65 per cent in Italy and 100 per cent in Spain (Hallenberger, 2003: 493).

Although Europe's audiovisual deficit with the US appears to be growing in terms of value, the volume of programming being sold appears to have reached a plateau. This is because of increases in domestic production which have pushed US fiction into more marginal daytime or late-night slots on the mainstream channels (Buonanno, 2000; Kapner, 2003; Rouse, 2001). In 2000, US imports accounted for a 68.7 per cent share (213,928 hours) of imported fiction (including films, repeats) transmitted on 101 networks in sixteen Western European countries. This represented a decline from 222,884 hours in 1999, the first drop since 1994 (EAO, 2002). By 2002, the US share of imported fiction had dropped to 65.1 per cent of 216,185 hours (EAO, 2003b: 95). Although the US continues to dominate between 70 and 90 per cent of fiction acquisitions in Western Europe (Steemers, 2002), buyers in the largest territories point to increased domestic production and the declining ability of the Americans to include the most attractive feature films in their packages as contributory factors in the shift of American fiction from more valuable prime-time slots (Grignaffini and Stewart, 2002; Herfurth, 2002; Pugnetti, 2002; Ramos, 2002).

The trend towards higher levels of domestic programming, particularly at peak time on mainstream free-to-air channels, suggests growing market maturity. This maturity is evident in the growth of the independent production sector. According to EU data, independent productions accounted for over 40 per cent of EU transmissions, excluding sport, news, games and advertising in 2000 (European Commission, 2002b). However, with the exception of a limited number of transnational players (for example, the Dutch-based Endemol, owned since 2000 by the Spanish communications giant, Telefónica, and FremantleMedia owned by the RTL Group), very few production companies are active beyond their national boundaries. With the exception of some formats (see below), intra-European exchanges of programming and exports to the US continue to be negligible, suggesting that Western Europe has a long way to go before it can be deemed a player on the global stage. Concerns about underperformance in the global marketplace are an issue for the larger Western European countries and became a particular focus of attention in Britain during 1999.

CASE STUDY: BRITISH TELEVISION EXPORTS AND THE 'WRONG' MODEL OF TELEVISION

After America, Britain is often cited as the world's second largest exporter of television programmes. In 2002 it was estimated that the US accounted for £3 billion of the £4 billion global television export market, followed by Britain with sales worth £430 million, and Australia and France, each with sales worth £50 million (see Appendix 1 of ITC, 2002: 30). This position has been consistent since the earliest studies of international programme flow (Nordenstreng and Varis, 1974; Varis, 1984, 1985), but the gap between first and second place has always remained substantial.

Britain's position as the world's second largest exporter is certainly attributable to the English language, which has given British exporters preferential access to the notoriously difficult but valuable US market. In 2003, trade with the US accounted for almost 43 per cent of British television programme exports ($399 million) (British Television Distributors' Association, 2004). Combined, the Western European territories, led by Germany (7 per cent), accounted for $280 million (30 per cent) of $921 million in revenues. However, the growth of regional production centres in Latin America (Brazil, Mexico) and Asia (Hong Kong, China, India) suggests that Britain's position as the second largest exporter may be under threat, certainly in respect of the volume of exports (see Sinclair, Jacka and Cunningham, 1996).

British exports may have grown, but imports have grown faster. By 1999, imports into Britain, largely by cable and satellite channels, totalled £843 million, and there was a television programme trade deficit of £403 million (Department for Culture, Media and Sport, 2001). Despite concerns over this situation, the debate initiated by the Labour government as part of its Creative Industries initiative focused on exports rather than imports. To include imports in the debate would have impinged on the activities of BSkyB, part of Rupert Murdoch's News Corporation, whose support the Labour government has sought to cultivate (Blanchard, 2001). Public policy on imports also flew in the face of the government's commitment to free trade and international competitiveness (Department of Trade and Industry/Department for Culture, Media and Sport, 2002: 3).

In April 1999, the Department for Culture, Media and Sport (DCMS) published *Building a Global Audience: British Television in Overseas Markets*, a study carried out by David Graham and Associates (Department for Culture, Media and Sport, 1999b). The report concluded that British exporters were underperforming because of Britain's failure to produce programmes which overseas buyers actually wanted to buy. The problem was seen to lie in a public service inspired regulatory culture, which prioritised the domestic audience and therefore made the 'wrong' type of television for international consumption (p. 32). Drawing mainly on interviews with European buyers, British drama was accused of being 'too dark; too slow; unattractive; too gritty or socio-political' (p. 24). British situation comedies were no longer 'funny', and suffered from a lack of team-writing, which worked against the production of longer series (p. 27). Alongside issues of quality, Britain did not produce enough thirteen- or twenty-six-part series and sitcoms or ninety-minute television movies to meet overseas schedule requirements (p. 21). The report also maintained that British producers were failing to take advantage of co-productions with European partners (p. 30). It concluded that the British domestic market would have to adopt a more commercial US model of production if it wanted to appeal to a European television market, which was increasingly adopting US commercial practices (pp. 32–3). Britain's failure to export was used as a platform to propose the dismantling of regulations that inhibited commercial free-to-air broadcasters from commissioning 'genuinely commercial programmes' with international appeal (p. 32).

However, the findings of *Building a Global Audience* were disputed by another DCMS inquiry, *The Report of the Creative Industries Task Force Inquiry into UK Television Exports* (Department for Culture, Media and Sport, 1999a), undertaken by industry representatives. This pointed out that Britain's 9 per cent share of the global market by volume not only outperformed its closest rivals (France and Australia, 3 per cent each), but also exceeded the UK's 4.7 per cent share of global GDP (p. 33). At peak time, Britain's 13 per cent share was more than six times larger than France and Australia (2 per cent each) (p. 33). Although considerably lagging behind the US (68 per cent), Britain still outperformed its nearest rivals. The report's rejection of underperformance was accompanied by a rejection of any drastic changes to the style, scheduling or commissioning of British programmes (p. 42). Any dramatic modification to the style of British programming to increase exports was regarded as not realistic, because with British programmes being still predominantly funded in the domestic marketplace by free-to-air broadcasters, they had to serve British audiences first (p. 39).

The argument about export failure appeared to have been buried. However, the exports debate also needs to be seen within the broader context of the consistent push since the 1980s towards a more commercial model of television and the Labour government's desire to integrate British television more fully into the global marketplace. The 2003 Communications Act opened up commercial free-to-air television (ITV, Channel 5) to US ownership in the belief that harnessing British ideas and content to American finance and distribution muscle would help the British production sector to break out of the protected confines of the domestic market (Department of Trade and Industry/Department for Culture, Media and Sport, 2002; ITC, 2002). What impact this has on domestic television and export performance has yet to be seen. Even if British television is not swamped by American imports, concern has been expressed about a 'determined and sophisticated attempt [by US companies], backed by enormous marketing expertise, to shift the balance of audience and regulatory expectations away from domestic content produced primarily with a British audience in mind, towards a more US or internationally focused product mix' (Joint Committee on the Draft Communications Bill, 2002: 65).

TELEVISION PROGRAMME TRADE

The vast majority of television programmes aired in Europe are local and several commentators have pointed out that audiences prefer locally produced programmes if these are available (see Sinclair, Jacka and Cunningham, 1996: 10; Straubhaar, 1991; Tracey, 1988; Wildman and Siwek, 1988: 41–4). However, countries will import or co-produce programming which they cannot afford to make in volume – drama, animation and more costly factual programmes. News programmes, current affairs, sport (except for international events) and factual programming about local issues have limited appeal in other markets because of their cultural specificity. Equally, locally produced game shows, reality programmes and lifestyle shows have limited international potential, although this does not always apply to the formats on which these programmes are based. Within Western Europe, programme exports are largely the preserve of the larger countries (Britain, France, Germany), whose wealth and population size allow them to finance higher levels of production, including drama, the most costly and most heavily traded genre.

Drama

US fiction may have lost some of its peak-time appeal but continues to dominate the fiction acquisitions of most Western European channels. What are the motivations of buyers who, in their role as gatekeepers, are making decisions based on their understanding of domestic audiences, channel requirements, scheduling practices and the prevailing national television landscape? In the case of mainstream commercial channels, decisions usually boil down to hard-nosed commercial choices and the need to purchase content which will deliver reliable audience ratings.[2] Formulaic American fiction offers that reliability. It may not be the most popular programming but it performs an economic function, for purchasing a US television movie or long-running sitcom is much cheaper than original production and acquisitions are highly likely to recoup their costs in advertising revenues, particularly in off-peak slots.

Among buyers, however, there are some differences between public service broadcasters and commercial channels. Buyers from the commercial mainstream networks place a much stronger emphasis on the need to locate programmes to beat the competition in particular time slots (Huhn, 2002; Lidén, 2002; Stewart, 2002). A buyer's success is linked to their ability to select programmes that will achieve good ratings, regardless of their own personal preferences. By contrast, some but not all buyers for the public service networks emphasise their desire for quality, variety and even personal preference above ratings, which leads them to choose from a wider range of programming sources, including European content. This tendency is strongest at those public service stations which are less reliant on advertising revenues (NOS in the Netherlands, SVT in Sweden, BR, WDR and ZDF in Germany). Some buyers at public broadcasters in the Netherlands and Sweden emphasise the importance of experimentation and buying certain programmes on principle because they satisfy their perception of the public service mission, even if they have no identifiable slot (Windhorst, 2002; Kjellberg, 2002). However, public service stations that are highly dependent on advertising (France 2 and 3, RAI in Italy, TVE in Spain, ERT in Greece) are closer to their commercial counterparts in prioritising ratings over public service considerations in their fiction purchases.

In contrast to US fiction, the circulation of European fiction within Europe and beyond is very limited. In 1999 the US accounted for 71 per cent of imported fiction (including feature films and repeats) into the EU, compared to 11.4 per cent imported from European sources (but excluding European co-productions' 4.1 per cent) (EAO, 2001a: 152–3). In a sample week in March 2000, the Eurofiction Project established that levels of European fiction (excluding feature films) on the major free-to-air networks ranged from 0 per cent in Britain to 4 per cent in Italy, 5 per cent in Germany, 7 per cent in Spain and 15 per cent in France (EAO, 2001b). Quotas for French channels that demand 60 per cent European content and 40 per cent French content dictate higher levels of European fiction, but it is noticeable that levels of European fiction fell to 0 per cent in prime time. In Italy and Spain, transmissions of European fiction fall some way behind imports of more linguistically and culturally proximate Latin American soaps (telenovelas), representing 13 per cent and 17 per cent of television fiction transmissions respectively (see also de Bens and de Smaele, 2001: 56; Bilkereyst and Meers, 2000; Buonanno, 2000: 22).

The small trade in European fiction is limited largely to a narrow range of programming – thrillers, detective series with self-contained episodes, and action-adventure television movies and series – from the larger territories. Subtitled British thrillers and detective series work well on institutionally proximate public service networks in smaller anglophone and geographically close markets like the Netherlands and Sweden, which are too small to support large-scale domestic production. Indeed, the Dutch NOS channel, N1, has developed a weekly 'Detectives' strand in peak time based largely on British imports (e.g. *Inspector Morse* [Carlton], *A Touch of Frost* [Granada] and *Silent Witness* [BBC]). Yet British fiction is less successful on commercial networks in these territories, because these seek to differentiate themselves from public service rivals with more 'mass appeal' American fiction and domestic productions (Easter, 2002).

Occasionally, European fiction works in situations where it can function as a substitute for US imports. Commercial German suppliers found success in the late 1990s with action-oriented series (e.g. *HeliCops* [Kirch], *Kommissar Rex* [Kirch] and *Alarm für Cobra 11* [RTL]) chiefly in France and Italy, but not in Spain or Britain. According to one Italian commercial buyer, the success of German fiction from commercial suppliers could be traced back to basic action-adventure plots and stereotypical characters. This was the sort of programming no longer made by US producers but it was ideally suited to the less demanding daytime schedules of Italian television (Grignaffini and Stewart, 2002). However, the daytime slots available on mainstream French channels like France 2 for long-running German police series such as *Derrick* (ZDF) and *Ein Fall für Zwei* (ZDF) may be more indicative of the need to meet strictly enforced European quotas.

A greater 'cultural discount' (Hoskins and Mirus, 1988) applies to non-US fiction in the larger markets of Germany, France, Spain and Italy, where there are not only issues about language (almost all programmes are dubbed) but also style, pace and content. Buyers in these territories, particularly from the commercial channels, claim their audiences are more familiar with 'lighter' American series and films featuring recognisable casts, settings and storylines (Anan, 2002; Leveaux, 2002; Misert, 2002; Ramos, 2002; Stewart, 2002). This aversion to European drama in the larger territories would seem to corroborate Joseph Straubhaar's views on 'cultural proximity', the idea that audiences 'tend to prefer that programming which is closest or most proximate to their own culture', and will seek substitutes in terms of content, humour, costume and narrative conventions if domestic alternatives are not available (cited in Sinclair, Jacka and Cunningham, 1996: 14).

This resistance to the charms of European fiction within Europe is even more marked in the US, where non-English-language programmes are rarely screened, and European exports account for less than 2 per cent of US transmissions (European Commission, 1999a: 7). Sharing a common language and a degree of cultural proximity, a small number of co-funded British detective series, historical and literary-based dramas that trade on British heritage regularly find a home on PBS (Public Broadcasting System) or the Arts and Entertainment (A&E) cable channel in the US. However, as these channels attract low audiences, the impact of these programmes is marginal. Yet financial contributions from these two outlets have become a key ingredient of British 'quality' or event drama such as *The Lost World* (BBC/A&E, 2001), based on Sir Arthur Conan Doyle's 1912 dinosaur fantasy, and literary adaptations such as *Daniel Deronda* (BBC/WGBH, 2003), based on the novel by George Eliot.

Co-production has been pinpointed as one way of raising levels of European fiction but co-production levels remain low. In 1999, co-productions represented just 6 per cent of first-run television fiction (totalling 536 episodes) in the five largest European countries (Jezequel and Lange, 2000: 4). However, they did account for 14.6 per cent of total production value (€400 million), demonstrating that co-production is used for more expensive productions. France, Germany and Italy were involved in the greatest number of co-productions, with 17 per cent, 10 per cent and 7 per cent of co-produced episodes respectively, trailed by Britain (3 per cent) and Spain (0.5 per cent). However, French and German co-productions with same-language smaller neighbours make up a large proportion of such collaborations (see also Buonanno, 1998: 18; de Bens and de Smaele, 2001: 69), while British drama co-productions occur predominantly with same-language partners in the US. Giovanni Bechelloni points out that in this case co-productions become an extension of national productions, 'heavily rooted in the culture of the dominant country' (1998: xvi).

CASE STUDY: EUROPEAN DRAMA CO-PRODUCTION – *DR ZHIVAGO*

British broadcaster Granada, the ITV franchise holder, embarked on its first European drama co-production in 2001 with a television remake of *Dr Zhivago*. Broadcast on ITV during November 2002, the project was a collaboration between Evision (a joint venture between the German Kirch Group and the Italian commercial broadcaster, Mediaset) and the US public broadcaster, WGBH. Shot in English, it had an Italian director (Giacomo Campiotti), an international cast, Russian literary provenance in Boris Pasternak, and a British writer, Andrew Davies. *Dr Zhivago* came out of Granada's perceived need to broaden its funding sources beyond its usual US backers at WGBH and A&E as a precursor to better access to its partners' markets (Torrance, 2001).

However, such large-scale, literary-based projects are rare for a number of reasons. The need to alter cultural parameters to fit in with the requirements of others constitutes one of the main obstacles of co-production and for this reason they tend to be focused on a small range of high-cost projects with transnational

Dr Zhivago

appeal, which no single territory can afford. There are increased financial costs associated with project coordination, they take a long time to set up, and are dependent on finding compromises on casting, setting and subject matter to satisfy both the domestic and international markets (see Hoskins, McFadyen, Finn and Jäckel, 1995: 240). With the exception of co-productions between same-language territories, co-produced European drama has to exhibit considerable cross-cultural appeal and tends therefore to concentrate on a narrow range of topics based on biblical epics, historic figures (Napoleon, Julius Caesar) or classic literary works (*The Count of Monte Cristo*, *Les Misérables*) (Arata, 2002). There is little call for contemporary drama. In the case of Evision, projects are usually limited to two large-scale peak-time events a year for transmission on Mediaset's Canale 5. For Mediaset, projects like *Dr Zhivago* represent a promotional opportunity to show 'that you can gather a big cast on a project that's yours' (Arata, 2002). However, the drive to secure consistently large audiences, the difficulty of scheduling events, the problem of finding the right projects with international appeal and the popularity of entertainment and reality formats have made such co-productions an increasingly difficult proposition (Arata, 2002; Tettenborn, 2002).

Factual Programming

Most factual programming is inherently local and only certain types of programming have broad international appeal. Ageless 'uncontroversial' programmes dealing with natural history, wildlife and science are in most demand internationally. On mainstream European free-to-air channels, which have the highest licence fees, factual programming is constrained by its low share of transmission time and lack of access to prime-time slots. However, the emergence of the Discovery Channel in the US in 1985 altered industry perceptions about non-fiction programming by establishing a viable business aimed at discrete audience segments, raising global demand for content (Chris, 2002). Alongside localised versions of US channels (Discovery, National Geographic, History Channel, Animal Planet), there are also European non-fiction specialists in Britain (UK Horizons, UK History), France (France 5, Planète, Absat, Histoire, Odyssée), Italy (Planete, RaiSat), Germany (ZDF Doku, Phoenix) and Spain (Odisea, Documania).

Within Western Europe, Britain, and particularly the BBC, has a strong reputation for natural history, wildlife, historical and popular science programming. Britain was estimated to have an 18 per cent share of the factual market globally by volume in 1996–7 behind the US with 37 per cent (Department for Culture, Media and Sport, 1999a: 34–5). However, factual programming only represented 8 per cent of the global trade in television. The BBC's strength in factual programming is partially attributable to a longstanding documentary tradition involving long-term investment in talent and resources, such as the BBC's Natural History Unit. But it also rests on the assiduous development of co-production relationships with the US – foremost with Discovery Communications Inc (DCI) with whom it has had a joint venture partnership since 1997. This has enabled the BBC to attract production budgets which other European broadcasters cannot match. Co-production finance from DCI has allowed the BBC to invest in event properties such as the natural history series *The Blue Planet* (2002) and *Walking with Dinosaurs* (1999), which are not only attractive to public service channels, which share a commitment to factual programming, but also to commercial outlets. For example, in 1999, *Walking with Dinosaurs* was acquired by German commercial channel, ProSieben, and Spanish commercial channel, Telecinco, two channels without any strong commitment to factual programming, particularly in peak time. For both, the shift from the more traditional natural history documentary to the drama and spectacle of bringing dinosaurs to life with computer graphics was a determining factor in the decision to buy (von Hennet, 2002; Misert, 2002).

Unlike most fiction, natural history, wildlife and science programming is not always easily identifiable as the product of a particular country, enhancing its international appeal. In fact, such programming is often adapted in such a way that it is localised, thereby increasing its domestic appeal. As well as the addition of voiceovers, programmes may be edited down to fit particular slots. For example, at Rai Uno in Italy, 'blue chip' science or natural history programmes such as the BBC's *The Blue Planet* are accommodated as one of several items within a two-hour, peak-time magazine programme, *Superquark*, that includes both acquisitions and domestically produced features. These are presented in a studio by a host with a longstanding reputation and connection with this particular series. Studio discussions and commentary reinforce the localising process.

Children's Television

Children's programming, a great amount of which is comprised of the less culturally specific genre of animation, was estimated to account for 13 per cent of global trade by volume in 1996–7. The US took a 60 per cent share followed by Japan (6 per cent), Canada (5 per cent) and Britain (4 per cent), with other European players hardly featuring at all (Department for Culture, Media and Sport, 1999b: 35). In 2001, children's departments spent over two-thirds of their budgets on animation, and 78 per cent of animation budgets were spent on acquisitions, mainly from the US, but increasingly from Japan, whose longrunning animation series, *Pokémon*, emerged as the most popular acquisition in 2001 (Walker and Scott, 2002: 25).

Animation and character-based formats are ideally suited to international exploitation because they can be easily adapted through dubbing. They can also be sold repeatedly as the target audience changes every two or three years. As a consequence, the most successful series have become valuable international brands. By contrast, the trade in children's fiction or information programming, like its adult counterparts, is more limited, because of cultural specificity. However, animation is costly to produce ($150,000–$300,000 per half hour) and cash-strapped children's departments in Western Europe tend to acquire or prebuy animation series.

Within Europe, it is the larger territories of France, Germany, Britain and Spain which are most heavily involved in the production, funding and export of animation. Smaller players are active in Scandinavia (Egmont in Denmark; Happy Life in Sweden), but usually collaborate with partners from larger territories (Fry, 2002). France is the leading animation producer in Europe (370 hours in 2000) because of generous subsidies from the government-backed Centre National de la Cinématographie (CNC), production quotas that demand investment in programming of domestic origination and content quotas that require at least 60 per cent European-originated content including 40 per cent French content (Jeremy, 2002; Pennington, 2001: 40). Subsidies have made co-productions attractive. In 2001, French producers were involved in 241 hours of co-produced animation, with Canada (113 hours) followed by the US (53 hours) as the main co-production partners (Jeremy, 2002). Key players include France Animation (*Titeuf*), Marathon (*Totally Spies*), Alphanim and Millimages (*Pablo The Little Red Fox*, *64 Zoo Lane*), which launched as an IPO (initial public offering) on the Paris Nouveau Marché in June 2000 (Jeremy, 2001: 29).

Germany saw a surge of investment in animation production during the late 1990s because of subsidies and the emergence of dedicated domestic children's channels, KiKa and SuperRTL. The market was flooded by capital raised by the flotation of animation-related companies (EM.TV, RTV Family Entertainment, Igel Media, TV Loonland, BKN International) on the German Neuer Markt stock exchange (Jeremy, 2001: 30). However, by 2002, an economic downturn had reduced the importance of Germany as an investor, and oversupply had forced children's specialists EM.TV and RTV to contract their operations to survive (Fry, 2002).

In Britain, there are no government subsidies or tax incentives, but the BBC and HIT Entertainment have emerged as key players in the pre-school market. The BBC has developed successful, long-running brands (*Teletubbies*, *Tweenies* and *The Fimbles*) which earn substantial revenues, and it has become the major backer of pre-school programming outside the US. The strength of pre-school production in Britain owes much to the public service view that children's television needs to serve a range of age groups. Sales have been strong to other public service channels, which regard British programming as a reliable alternative to what is perceived as the violence inherent in some Japanese animation or low-quality production values from the Far East and Southern Europe (Kuiper, 2002; Müller, 2002). Sales in Western Europe have also been fuelled by sales to the US of successful series, with PBS buying *Teletubbies* and pre-school specialist, Nick Junior, acquiring *Bob the Builder*. These sales have given British children's programmes an entry into the lucrative video and licensed product markets in the US.

However, pre-school programming is not always attractive to commercial channels, because advertisers are not sufficiently interested in this age group. The biggest supporters of pre-school programming tend to be European public service networks who are required to air such content (ZDF, Rai Tre, TVE, Forta, NOS, SVT), along with thematic channels like KiKa and Super RTL in Germany and Tiji in France which target this age group. Older children are more attractive to advertisers because they can express and even act on their consumer preferences (Mozzetti, 2002).

From the mid-1990s, the greatest impact on children's television in Western Europe came from the introduction of localised US-owned transnational channels (Cartoon Network, Nickelodeon, Fox Kids, Disney), which contributed to a fragmentation of the child audience. In response to US competition, European public broadcasters created children's channels of their own, for example the BBC with CBeebies and CBBC, and KiKa from ARD and ZDF in Germany. In the Netherlands, public broadcaster, NOS, developed a dedicated daily block on its third channel (Z@ppelin) in 2000 as an advertising-free counterweight to Fox Kids. Since 1999, Italian public broadcaster, Rai Tre, has aired *Melevisione*, a block of European programming for younger children intended as an alternative to the US and Japanese fare served up by Rai Due and commercial rival, Italia Uno. In Germany, children's television is now dominated by dedicated channels, with Super RTL (established in 1995 as a joint venture between RTL and Disney) and KiKa (established in 1997). In the schedules of public (ARD, ZDF) and commercial (RTL, Sat.1) broadcasters, children's television is now largely reduced to weekend transmissions. Children's television in France is still dominated by the morning blocks of free-to-air broadcasters, TF1 and France 3, while the niche market (Tiji, Canal, J, Teletoon) is less developed than in either Britain or Germany because of low cable and satellite penetration. However, experience suggests that here too, the trend is away from children's blocks on the mainstream channels towards dedicated children's services.

Increased outlets and financial pressures have changed the funding mechanisms of children's television. Mirroring experience in the US, children's television is now often simply a platform for opening up more profitable revenue streams from consumer products (toys, computer games, clothing, food products), publishing and video/DVD, with companies seeking to craft an ancillary rights strategy from the outset. For example, since its launch in 1997, by 2002 *Teletubbies* had sold to 120 countries, including China (BBC Worldwide, 2002: 16). This generated £116 million in programme sales for BBC Worldwide but an estimated £1 billion in retail (BBC Worldwide, 2003c). For exporters with a valuable property, it is therefore crucial to gain access to those channels with the largest audiences and highest market profile. This is a risky strategy if the property is not successful on television and fails to function as a platform for other revenue streams. Moreover, the expectation of ancillary revenues has depressed licence fees and strengthened the position of broadcasters in the larger markets who now often expect to participate in revenues from video and licensed product. Outlets like Super RTL and France 3 will often act as gatekeepers to domestic exploitation activity in ancillary rights by becoming licensing agents in return for handing over airtime.

CASE STUDY: HIT ENTERTAINMENT PLC

The experience of the British pre-school specialist, HIT Entertainment, illustrates the special nature of children's television, which, more than any other type of programming, offers extensive opportunities for ancillary rights exploitation.

HIT was established in 1989 as a distributor of programming owned by other companies. It has since undergone a transformation based on ownership of all rights in enduring character-based children's properties, recognising that programme sales alone offered only limited potential for growth. Instead, HIT has evolved into a specialist in brand management through the funding and development of its own productions (*Bob the Builder*, *Angelina Ballerina*, *Rubbadubbers*) and strategic acquisitions of established properties with a licensing track record in the US, Japan and Western Europe (*Barney*, *Thomas the Tank Engine*, *Pingu*).

The transformation of the company was made possible with a launch on the Alternative Investment Market in 1996 followed by a full British stock market listing in 1997. This and other rights issues allowed the company to establish an animation facility, HOT Animation, in Manchester during 1997, and fully fund the production of the stop-frame animation series, *Bob the Builder*, now seen in over 150 territories (HIT, 2002: 5). Inhouse video and consumer products divisions followed. To broaden the base of its activities, the company acquired the American Lyrick Corporation for £189 million in 2001 (HIT, 2001: 2). Lyrick produced *Barney*, a successful pre-school property about a dinosaur, which had aired on PBS in the US since 1992. The acquisition of Lyrick cemented HIT's US presence and by 2002, it was the fourth largest player in the US children's video market with a 13 per cent market share based on the success of *Barney*, together with airings of *Bob the Builder* on US pre-school channel, Nick Junior, and *Angelina Ballerina* on PBS (HIT, 2002: 9).

HIT's growth has been fuelled by further acquisitions with international potential. In 2001, the company paid £15.9 million for all rights to Pingu, a popular European stop-frame property, which generated £2 million from consumer product royalties in the lucrative Japanese market during 2001 (HIT, 2001: 2–3). In 2002, HIT acquired the British company Gullane Entertainment for £134 million, owner of the pre-school property, *Thomas the Tank Engine*, which is well known in the all-important American and Japanese markets (HIT, 2002: 5).

The key to HIT's growth has been the ownership and development of preschool brands with long-term value, which are driven by television exposure and work across different markets in home entertainment (video/DVD) and consumer products, particularly in North America. As a consequence, the focus of the company has shifted. By 2003, America accounted for 66 per cent of £168.9 million in turnover by origin, and consumer products and publishing accounted for 87 per cent of revenues by activity, with income from television sales generating just 7 per cent of revenues (£12.2 million) (HIT, 2003).

THE RISE OF FORMATS

In the more competitive and fragmented broadcasting environment that emerged in Western Europe during the 1990s, formats made commercial sense. Faced with an expansion of transmission time and the loss of key sporting events and films to pay television, formats provide a cost-effective way of filling schedules with localised productions which proved more popular than imported films and series. Tried and tested in other markets, formats reduce the risk of failure, offer savings on development costs and are usually cheaper to produce than original drama. Yet many of the new breed of entertainment formats are noticeably different from the highly structured quiz and game-show formats (*The Wheel of Fortune, Family Feud*) which previously circulated. New formats are often hybrids, with elements of observational documentary, game shows and soap drama fused to create new variations on old genres that can be exploited on a global scale.

For channels trying to stand out in a crowded marketplace, locally produced formats have greater attractions for audiences than imports, because national adaptations speak to different audiences through the inclusion of local settings, casts, presenters and participants. Moreover, a format adaptation is invariably classed as a domestic production rather than an import, benefiting channels which can then claim that they are supporting local production (Moran, 1998: 22–3). The growth in format sales and local production reinforces the notion that the most successful trade in cultural products involves the suppression of the look and feel of programming concepts which express national origins (Sinclair, 1996: 45–6).

Types of Formats

Within Western Europe, scripted formats proved particularly effective for daily serial drama in a small number of markets which initially had little experience of writing for this type of production. In the early 1990s, Australian company Grundy (now part of the RTL Group's FremantleMedia production arm) recreated local versions with local partners of the Australian soap, *The Restless Years*, in a strategy dubbed 'parochial internationalism' (Cunningham and Jacka, 1996: 82). Reversioned as *Goede Tijden, Slechte Tijden* for the Dutch commercial channel, RTL 4, and as *Gute Zeiten, Schlechte Zeiten* for German commercial channel, RTL, both were still airing in prime-time access in 2003. Other examples of scripted format adaptations include FremantleMedia's loose adaptation of Australian soap, *Neighbours,* as *Un Posto al sole* (*A Place in the Sun*, 1996–) for the Italian public channel, Rai Tre, and IDTV's short-lived adaptation in 1992–3 of the BBC soap opera, *EastEnders*, as *Het Oude Noorden* for the Dutch public broadcaster, Vara.

This trade in scripted formats also extends to the US. In the mid-1990s,

British exporters sought access to American network television in an attempt to replicate earlier successful sitcom adaptations – including *All in the Family* (based on the BBC's *Till Death Us Do Part*, CBS 1971–5) and *Three's Company* (based on Thames's *Man about the House*, ABC 1977–84). However, in the highly competitive US market, most of these adaptations were cancelled at the pilot stage or axed mid-run. ABC dropped *Fitz*, based on Granada's psychological thriller, *Cracker*, after just sixteen episodes in 1998. NBC cancelled an American version of Granada's contemporary relationship drama, *Cold Feet*, shortly after launch because it failed to secure a sufficiently large audience, in an environment where 'it's utterly a numbers and demographics game' (Root, 2001). In October 2003, NBC dropped from its Thursday-night schedule the US version of Hartswood Films' relationship sitcom, *Coupling*, after it failed to attract enough viewers. The only British show to break this pattern is Channel 4's gay drama format, *Queer as Folk*, which during 2003, secured a third season on pay-television outlet, Showtime. However, this lack of success needs to be seen within the context of a broadcasting environment where failure is an accepted part of the annual commissioning cycle, and only one in ten pilots make it into series production (Root, 2001; Hoskins and Mirus, 1988: 505; Waller, 2002a).

In the meantime, other types of formats were making steady progress within Western Europe. Throughout the 1990s, Endemol Entertainment UK (formerly Bazal Productions) sold lifestyle formats with a game-show element revolving

Un Posto al sole

around cookery (*Ready, Steady, Cook*),[3] the home (*Changing Rooms*) and garden makeovers (*Ground Force*) to broadcasters in Northern Europe. In the early 1990s, the consumer affairs series, *That's Life*, became the BBC's most successful format package in Europe, selling to Germany, Norway, Spain, Belgium and the Netherlands (Moran, 1998: 28). Granada's studio-based entertainment format, *Surprise, Surprise*, involving the lives of ordinary people proved a success for Rai Uno in Italy as *Carrambà che sorpresa*, securing a 40 per cent share in January 2002, and entering its seventh season in Holland in 2002 (Mutimer, 2002).

However, the greatest surge in format adaptation came in the late 1990s when big-money game shows and a new breed of reality-based shows emerged as key components in prime-time schedules. American studio-based game-show formats (*The Wheel of Fortune* [King World], *Jeopardy!* [King World], *Family Feud* [FremantleMedia] and *The Price Is Right* [FremantleMedia]) had been traded within Western Europe for many years, but their use was largely restricted to off-peak daytime slots as cost-effective filler. Within the US itself, innovation in entertainment stagnated because mainstream American television prioritised drama at peak time. With US producers paying little attention to the entertainment market, European players began to fill the gap in provision in Europe, where entertainment formats were still popular, innovating with reality-based shows which exploited interactivity and the Internet. The Dutch-based Endemol and Pearson Television (which became FremantleMedia in October 2001, following its incorporation as a wholly owned subsidiary of the RTL Group) became key players in Western Europe, both in terms of the origination and local production of formats.

Three formats from European producers became the catalysts for this change: Celador's big-money quiz show, *Who Wants to Be a Millionaire?* (ITV), originating in Britain from 1998 (see case study below); Endemol's reality elimination format, *Big Brother* (Veronica), in the Netherlands in 1999; and British company Castaway's reality elimination show set on a desert island, *Survivor*, produced for the CBS network in the US in 2000. These formats satisfied demand internationally for cost-effective domestically produced programmes in prime time, with a type of programming defined by Frances Bonner (2003) as 'ordinary television' featuring 'ordinary people', which is rarely imported in its original form.

Ordinary people were combined with CCTV techniques to great effect on *Big Brother*, which incorporated both competition and drama by invoking participants to nominate fellow housemates for eviction. Based on ten people isolated from the outside world in a specially constructed house, whose every move and word is recorded, *Big Brother*'s mixture of docusoap, game show, soap opera and social experiment proved a ratings success throughout Western Europe. In the

Netherlands, the first series garnered an average 14.5 rating in the 18–34 demographic and a 62.1 per cent share over 100 days on air (Johnson, 2000). On 15 September 2000, the final episode of the first series in Britain went out on minority channel, Channel 4, securing a 46.5 per cent share and 9 million viewers (Avis, 2000). In Germany, the first season on RTL2 proved so popular that a second season in autumn 2000 was extended to include a new weekly strand, entitled *Big Brother – Family and Friends* in prime time on the main RTL network (ibid.). With the expulsion of one resident in October 2000, the small Portuguese private channel, TV1, gained a 65 per cent share (ibid.). Spanish commercial channel Telecinco's average 21 per cent share was boosted to 70 per cent for the final show in July 2000 (Hill, 2002: 325). The French version (*Loft Story*) boosted the performance of commercial channel, M6, achieving a 37 per cent share for its final episode in July 2001, making M6 the most popular network for the first time in its history (Fry, 2001: 12). In Sweden, the format failed to deliver similarly strong ratings for commercial channel, Kanal 5, increasing average share from 9.7 per cent to only 10.3 per cent during autumn 2000, possibly because it was scheduled against Swedish company, Strix Television's reality format, *The Bar*, on TV3 (Avis, 2000). While the format only averaged a 12 per cent share when shown in the US on CBS during 2000, it was still re-commissioned for a second series (Hill, 2002). Some have speculated that the 20.00hrs time slot contributed to a weak performance because the voyeuristic factor could not be exploited on a mainstream channel at this time (Avis, 2000). American network audiences also voted out the most interesting and opinionated contestants early on, resulting in less interesting storylines.

Despite the disappointing performance of *Big Brother* in the US, the success of *Who Wants to Be a Millionaire?* and *Survivor* on the lucrative, but previously closed, American networks fuelled further activity, predominantly among British players with successful format sales for BBC Worldwide (*The Weakest Link*, NBC, 2001), Granada (*Boot Camp*, Fox, 2001, and *I'm a Celebrity … Get Me out of Here!*, ABC, 2003), Action Time (*King of the Castle*, CBS, 2002), FremantleMedia (*Pop Idol/American Idol*, Fox, 2002) and Target/Screentime (*Popstars*, WB, 2000). In contrast to the situation with the trade in completed programmes, smaller territories have also made a mark with format sales. *The Mole* (Woestijnvis), a Belgian reality format involving contestants guessing the identity of a saboteur among them, was aired on ABC in 2001 (table 6.2). Swedish company Strix, the first producer of *Survivor/Expedite Robinson* on SVT 2 in 1997, has also been successful with reality formats, *The Bar* and *The Farm* (Scott, 2003).

The success of game/quiz shows and reality formats has boosted interest in other format adaptations focusing on 'real' people in artificial situations, blur-

Table 6.2: Selected Entertainment Formats in European Territories

	Who Wants to Be a Millionaire?	Big Brother	The Weakest Link	Popstars[1]	Survivor/Castaway	The Mole	Fort Boyard	Greed	The Bar
Creator	Celador	Endemol	BBC Worldwide	Target	Carlton	Woestijnvis	Studio Canal	Fremantle	Strix
Origination	UK	Netherlands	UK	UK	UK	Belgium	France	US/UK	Sweden
Austria	ORF 1	–	–	–	ORF 1	–	–	–	–
Belgium	VTM/RTL	K2	VTM	VT 4	VT 4	TV 1	VT 4	–	–
Denmark	TV 2	TV 2	DR 1	TV 2	TV 3	–	TV 3	TV 3	TV 3
Finland	Nelonen 4	–	–	MTV 3	–	–	–	MTV 3	–
France	TF 1	M6	TF 1	M6	TF 1	–	FR 2	M6	–
Germany	RTL	RTL	RTL	RTL 2	RTL 2	Pro 7	Pro 7	ZDF	RTL
Greece	Mega	Antenna	Mega	–	–	–	–	–	Mega
Ireland	RTE 1	–	TV 3	RTE 1	–	–	–	–	–
Italy	Canale 5	Canale 5	Italia 1	Italia 1	Italia 1	Italia 1	–	RAI 2	–
Netherlands	SBS 6	Yorin	RTL 4	–	Net 5	Ned 1	Ned 1	–	Yorin
Portugal	RTP 1	TV 1	–	Sic	TV 1	RTP 1	–	Sic	Sic
Spain	Tele 5	Tele 5	TVE 1	–	Tele 5	–	Tele 5	TVE 1	–
Sweden	TV4	Kanal 5	–	Kanal 5	SVT 2	Kanal 5	TV 4	SVT 2	TV 3
UK	ITV 1	Channel 4	BBC	ITV 1	ITV 1	Five	Five	Five	–

Source: *Television Business International*, April–May 2002, p. 16

Note:
1. *Popstars* was marketed by British distribution company, Target but was devised by Screentime in Australia and Zeal in Britain.

ring the distinction between game shows and factual programming by moving away from studio locations into people's homes and workplaces. The most successful of this new breed of factual entertainment formats originate in Britain. Endemol UK's home-makeover format *Changing Rooms* was transformed into *Trading Spaces* for US cable channel, TLC, in November 2000, becoming the highest rating show in TLC's history in May 2002 (Waller, 2002b). Other factual entertainment formats include *Faking It* and *Wife Swap* from the British company, RDF Media. In the former, which was sold to TLC in 2002, individuals are coached to pass themselves off as professionals in a job at odds with their own experience. *Wife Swap*, which first aired on Channel 4 in 2002, was ordered by US network ABC in 2003, with further orders from M6 in France and TV3 in Denmark.

Selling Formats

Format sales are markedly different from the sale of completed programmes. Drama, situation comedies, quiz/game shows and 'reality' concepts are sold on the basis of scripts or detailed 'bibles', where a show's narrative or distinctive elements (rules, catchphrases, sets, artwork, computer graphics) and production details are set down for adaptation in other markets (Moran, 1998: 14–15; Viljoen, 2002: 79). To succeed internationally, a format needs to have a unique structure or unique elements which distinguish it from other forms of the genre produced around the world.

The growing importance of format sales is reflected in changes to the economics of the business. For the most successful formats the returns are considerable, but format fees based on a percentage of the production budget (5–15 per cent per episode) and limited amounts of consultancy are no longer the lynch-pin of the most successful properties. For increasingly complex reality formats involving ordinary people and prime-time entertainment formats, the value of a format rests on selling production expertise, incorporating casting, filming and editing skills to make a successful show. For hit shows like *Who Wants to Be a Millionaire?* or *The Weakest Link*, broadcasters pay licence fees determined by market demand, and are sold complex packages and computer software with little opportunity to deviate from the format in the interests of maintaining creative control over what are perceived as global brands (see Keighron, 2003a: 18).

Increasingly format-owners are involved as co-producers or producers. For example, the British company RDF Media set up an American production outpost in 2001 to produce its formats (*Wife Swap* [ABC], *Faking It* [TLC], and *Scrapheap Challenge* [TLC]) for US channels, allowing it to benefit from production revenues as well as format fees. On *The Weakest Link*, BBC Worldwide, the commercial subsidiary of the BBC, sought a co-production role, contracting local producers in order to maintain greater creative control and financial benefit from production (Jarvis, 2001).

As global brands, the most successful shows are capable of generating new revenue streams from SMS text messaging, premium phone lines, online applications, licensed merchandise and sponsorship across different platforms on television and the Web. For example, the reality-based talent show, *Pop Idol* (FremantleMedia/19TV), is reputed to have netted $1billion in revenues in the US where it aired as *American Idol* on Fox in 2002. Approximately half of these revenues were generated from third-party deals, including artist management, music licensing and sponsorship from Coca-Cola, Ford and AT&T (Hodgson, 2003).

The Limits of Local Adaptation

However, the desire to control the exploitation of a format across different territories as a distinctive brand stands in tension with the desire by local broadcasters to air programming with local appeal. Highly structured quiz formats like *Who Wants to Be a Millionaire?* or *The Weakest Link* look almost identical to the original with the exception of the local host, local contestants and variations in the questions to reflect local knowledge. In contrast, reality-based game shows (*Big Brother*) and factual formats (*Faking It, Wife Swap*) require scope for adaptation and are less easy to pin down in terms of specific elements. With these formats, interpreting a concept for local preferences is equally as important as the concept itself for success in local markets (Rouse, 2003).

Some formats falter because, regardless of local production, the underlying concept, rooted in one culture, fails to connect with the styles and values to which audiences have become accustomed. *Survivor* was a hit in the US but failed to deliver in Britain, Spain and Italy (Hill, 2002; Mutimer, 2002). In Spain and Italy, its lacklustre performance was attributed to the lack of a studio setting, a key fixture of prime-time entertainment shows in these markets (ibid.). Moreover, Spanish and Italian buyers expressed a preference for shows that demonstrated drama and tapped into emotions such as *Big Brother* and *Surprise, Surprise*, against 'nasty' shows which either pitted contestants against each other or forced them to undergo public humiliation, such as *Fear Factor* (Endemol/NBC), *Temptation Island* (Fox) and *The Chair* (Touchdown/ABC).

CASE STUDY: WHO WANTS TO BE A MILLIONAIRE?

With *Who Wants to Be a Millionaire?*, formats were placed on a new footing with a different approach to exploitation. Recognising that it had a global brand, production company, Celador, dictated the ground rules for the show's adaptation by marketing a complete package, incorporating production expertise and technical know-how. This gave Celador greater control over the end product and its exploitation in related consumer products (board games, quiz books, computer games). In Europe, *Millionaire* was optioned as a complete package by Endemol, whose local production outposts went on to produce the programme in close consultation with Celador (table 6.2). With its elaborately specified set, software, lights, graphics and music, the show was a hit across Western Europe. In September–October 2001, it was rated number one in Sweden (TV4) and Holland (SBS 6), number two in Germany (RTL), number three in Britain (ITV), and in the top ten in France (TF1) and Italy (Canale 5) (Biddiscombe, 2002).

Launched in Italy during 2000 as *Chi vuol essere milionario?* on commercial channel, Canale 5, the format satisfied the Italian preference for studio-based entertainment and signalled 'a big return of the quiz in prime time, with big big prizes. It was an event on its terms, because everybody talked about the show' (Battocchio, 2002). In its first season, the show raised Canale 5's average share from 22 to 30 per cent (Muscara and Zamparutti, 2000). A mix of familiarity and difference heightened its appeal. Viewers could identify with local contestants, studio audiences and hosts, who were already known to them as personalities in the domestic marketplace. Buyers attributed this success to the show's capacity for drama and emotion, with the host as 'your friend' offering the prospect of winning a million (Saló, 2002). The drama was heightened by the tactics employed by contestants to further their progress, including opportunities to phone a friend for advice or poll the audience.

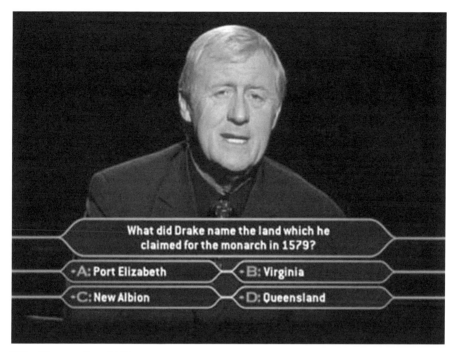

Who Wants to Be a Millionaire?

However, success can be undermined by overexposure. In the US, *Who Wants to Be a Millionaire?* was phenomenally successful for ABC, drawing in audiences of 29 million viewers in 1999–2000 (Winstone, 2002). By scheduling the show up to four times a week in 1999, without using it as a launchpad for new programming, ABC's ratings declined in 2002, resulting in the gradual withdrawal of the show from prime time (Hazelton, 2002). Overexposure also affected the format in Spain, where it launched on commercial channel, Telecinco, during April 1999. Nevertheless, having sold to more than 100 countries by 2003 and generating $750 million in revenues since its British launch on ITV in 1998, the format has become one of Britain's most successful television exports (Keighron, 2003b).

CONCLUSION

The emergence of multichannel commercial television in the 1980s and 1990s made Western Europe an important export destination for US films and series. Western Europe itself, however, has been rather less successful as an exporter, with the qualified exception of Britain where linguistic and cultural proximity has given producers preferential access to a small sector of the wealthy US television market. Within Europe, there is a noticeable preference for US fiction imports over imports from other European countries, but growing maturity among mainstream channels has resulted in a greater emphasis on domestic fiction and entertainment in peak time, the most valuable part of the schedule. Volume exports of European fiction remain elusive because of linguistic and cultural barriers in the global marketplace, but success has been achieved in other areas. British exporters, foremost the BBC, have established a reputation for universally appealing factual entertainment, co-funded by American networks (*Walking with Dinosaurs*, *The Blue Planet*). Some European companies, with British producers again the main players (BBC Worldwide, HIT Entertainment), have become successful in the non-culturally specific area of animation and pre-school television. But this market is overcrowded, underfunded and is too reliant on uncertain success in ancillary markets (consumer products, video). Entertainment and reality formats have emerged as the European export success story of the late 1990s, with European players such as Endemol, FremantleMedia, BBC Worldwide and Celador accessing network television in the US. Whether this success can be sustained has yet to be seen. European players are disadvantaged in the US marketplace because they do not control access to distribution, and the American competitors who do are unlikely to remain dependent on Europe for concepts if they can develop and market their own ideas worldwide, possibly even by incorporating European companies as part of transnational corporations.

NOTES

1. Financial support for this research was provided by the Leverhulme Trust (Research Fellowship), a small grant from the British Academy, and the Arts and Humanities Research Board (AHRB) Research Leave Scheme.

2. This section synthesises comments from interviews with television programme buyers in France, Germany, Italy, Spain, Sweden and the Netherlands between January and July 2002.

3. The rights to *Ready, Steady, Cook* were shared between BBC Worldwide and Endemol Entertainment UK.

Conclusion

It has been the purpose of this volume to chart those trends which have affected the development of the European television industries. To this end, there has been a detailed review of the technological, economic, political and ideological changes which have shaped television markets in Western Europe.

Across Western Europe, the introduction of cable and satellite technologies in the 1980s led to new commercial opportunities for industry players and those governments who preferred a de/re-regulatory approach to television markets. During the 1990s, the pace of change quickened, as the digitisation of television services in national markets across Europe became a major and important trend through the emergence of new services, integration of different platforms and the gradual 'convergence' of broadcasting, telecommunication and information technologies. These technological imperatives had major consequences for the ecology of the European television marketplace. They allowed a rapid commercialisation of television services as many European states sought, at varying levels, to pursue more market-driven policies. Thus, in both the larger territories of France, Germany, Britain, Italy and Spain, and the smaller European territories, successive 'phases' of commercialisation saw new players entering the media and communications markets. In the 1990s, these market conditions suited the development of vertically integrated, transnational media conglomerates, such as Bertelsmann, News Corporation, Vivendi-Universal (reconfigured as NBC-Universal) and the now defunct Kirch Media.

Another characteristic of this corporate growth was the development of pan-European television (PETV) investment strategies and the growth of transnational channels. However, although European television systems became less defined by national boundaries in terms of ownership or transmission, the most successful television channels still targeted national audiences with increasing proportions of locally produced programming. PETV levels of cross-media investment remain in the purview of only a few players (RTL, Canal Plus, SBS) and linguistic and cultural barriers have hampered the development of transnational channels. Most recently, the key trends within PETV channels have referred to the extension of local opt-out clauses or the development of national variations within generic news, music, sport, adult and children's channels.

For policy-makers at both national and supranational levels, market reforms not only opened up television to new entrants but were also seen as vital to establishing a sustainable, European television economy able to withstand competition from US media conglomerates. A major characteristic of the European television industries has therefore been the use of de/re-regulatory reforms at both national and EU levels to provide greater market opportunities for commercial television organisations. However, the priorities of liberalisation may suit the interests of EU firms but sit uncomfortably alongside the social and political priorities associated with pluralism and diversity.

Moreover, as this volume has shown, the consequences of market-driven policies have proved to be double-edged. Greater pressures have been placed on public service broadcasters across Europe with regard to their financing, organisational structures and programming policies. As the case for public funding has been weakened, so commercial competition has grown. Partial funding of a number of PSBs by advertising, and the expansionary policies of PSBs like the BBC, have attracted complaints from commercial rivals who feel that PSBs have an unfair competitive advantage in the marketplace. Some PSBs are taking up contradictory positions by seeking to maintain a balance between the normative principles of public service against consumer-driven demands in an increasingly competitive market.

However, the sustainability of the European television industries is questionable. In spite of optimistic predictions concerning the expansion of digital services, digital take-up has been variable within national television markets. There are still considerable technical, financial and creative hurdles that need to be overcome and the public has yet to be convinced of the merits of digital television. Some digital services collapsed under the weight of the heavy costs associated with overbidding for programming rights and poor consumer demand. The commercial failures of ITV Digital in Britain and Premiere in Germany showed that in spite of the financial background of the participating companies and the predicted profits of industry forecasters, digital services and their providers still face many uncertainties.

The collapse of a number of high-profile digital services has not only indicated the commercial difficulties of establishing new services but also reflected a more general malaise in the European television marketplace. Europe's television industries have had to face a general global economic downturn and have been affected by declining advertising revenues. The European television economy has been subject to the boom and bust principles which have characterised the development of modern multinational conglomerates. These forms of financial instability have seen Kirch Media (the owners of Premiere) fall into bankruptcy and the dissolution of Vivendi-Universal (now NBC-Universal), which overreached itself through high-risk commercial strategies. Even Europe's largest media conglomerate, the giant Bertelsmann, has been forced to pursue a policy of retrenchment.

This volume has shown that, despite the many reforms which accompanied the expansion of European television markets, uncertainties will continue to demarcate the national and pan-European markets' development. It remains to be seen how the European television industries will continue to adapt to a more unstable and volatile set of market conditions. What is clear is that the ideological values of plurality or enhancement of citizens' rights and national identity which have traditionally underpinned the European television industries have now been placed under greater pressure as industry and policy-makers have adopted commercial and public-choice philosophies. Across all of the European states surveyed, there has been a shift from public service traditions to the interests of consumer demand through the policies of privatisation and de/re-regulation. As part of this process, the European Commission has played a vital role in developing a Europe-wide liberalising framework through the Television Without Frontiers Directive.

These changes raise many questions about the purpose of television and audiovisual services in democratic societies, and whether they should continue to be conceived as having a public as well as a commercial worth. Television services do after all have an exchange value, which is not only defined by their economic or commercial worth, but also by their social and cultural functions. Technological change also raises questions about what form any future regulatory framework should take, and the principles which should underpin it. Regulators need to assess the effectiveness of traditional regulatory tools and determine the role of alternative forms of regulation in the era of market and industry convergence. Inevitably, the scale of this study leaves the complexities of certain matters in need of further discussion. Future studies are needed to provide regulators with insights as to how to combine economic regulation with certain elements of sectoral regulation in the communications sector, in order to meet the growing force of technological, economic, structural and social changes in the new era. It has not been possible here to explore the importance of independent production in detail. However, this undercapitalised sector accounted for over 40 per cent of programming (excluding news, sports, games and advertising) within the EU during 2000. The volume of production from independents is testimony to changes in programme supply away from inhouse production by broadcasters (European Commission, 2002b), and the growing importance of the independent production sector suggests future studies are needed to concentrate solely on its contribution to the European television landscape.

It has been our intention to provide an insight into the debates which have defined thinking within the industry, among policy-makers and in the academy itself. It is our hope that this book will add to these debates and, as a consequence, ensure that not only the concerns of commercial practitioners but also the interests of citizens come to the fore in any future discussions concerning the European television industries.

Bibliography

Achille, Yves and Bernard Miège. (1994) 'The Limits to the Adaptation Strategies of European Public Service Television'. *Media, Culture & Society* 16, no. 1: 31–46.

Allen, Rod. (1998) 'This Is Not Television . . .'. *Changing Channels: The Prospects for Television in a Digital World*. Ed. Jeanette Steemers. Luton: John Libbey Media/University of Luton Press. 59–71.

Alvarado, Manuel. (2000) 'The "Value" of TV Drama. Why Bother to Produce It?'. *Television and New Media* 1, no. 3: 307–19.

Anan, Nadja. (2002) Head of Series and Animation, ProSieben – Telephone Interview, 7 February.

Andersen. (2002) *Media Ownership Consultation Response*, Response to Consultation on Media Ownership Rules, 25 January. <www.culture.gov.uk/creative/index.html> (downloaded January 2003).

Andrews, Geoff. (2003) 'From Salesman to Statesman: The Postmodern Populism of Silvio Berlusconi'. Paper presented at the Can Vote, Won't Vote Conference, Goldsmith's College, 6 November, London.

Arata, Giovanna. (2002) Head of International Productions, Mediatrade, Gruppo Mediaset – Interview, Milan, 12 June.

Avis, Tim. (2000) 'Big Brother: Tracked across Markets', *C21*, November. <www.c21media.net/features/detail.asp?area=2&article=457> (downloaded 30 December 2003).

Battocchio, Fabrizio. (2002) Head of Format Department, RTI, Reti Televisive Italiane, Mediaset Group – Interview, Milan, 11 June.

Bausch, Hans. (1980) *Rundfunkpolitik nach 1945. Erster Teil*. München: Deutscher Taschenbuch Verlag.

BBC Worldwide. (2002) *Annual Review 2001/2002*. London: BBC Worldwide.

BBC Worldwide. (2003a) *Annual Review 2002/2003*. London: BBC Worldwide. <www.bbcworldwide.com/aboutus/corpinfo/annualreps/annualreport2003/default. html> (downloaded December 2003).

BBC Worldwide. (2003b) *Report and Financial Statements for the Year Ended 31 March 2003*. London: BBC Worldwide.

BBC Worldwide. (2003c) ' "Walking with . . ." Brand Is Monster Hit for BBC Worldwide'. BBC Worldwide Press Release, 15 July. <www.bbc.co.uk/pressoffice/

commercial/worldwidestories/pressreleases/2003/07_july/walking_with_brand.shtml>
(downloaded 29 September 2003).

BBC Worldwide. (2004) *Annual Review 2003/2004*. London: BBC Worldwide.
<www.bbcworldwide.com/aboutus/corpinfo/annualreps/review2004/default.htm>
(downloaded August 2004).

Bechelloni, Giovanni. (1998) 'Introduction'. *Imaginary Dreamscapes: Television Fiction in Europe*. Ed. Milly Buonanno. Luton: University of Luton Press. xiii–xviii.

Bellens, Didier. (2000) 'News Release: Merger of CLT-UFA, Pearson TV and Audiofina'. Brussels, 4 July: 1.

Berg, Klaus. (1986) 'Analyse und Bewertung des Niedersachen-Urteils des Bundesverfassungsgerichts vom 4. November'. *Media Perspektiven* 12: 799–802.

Biddiscombe, Ross. (2002) 'Ratings Round-up: Millionaire Marches across Europe'. *Television Europe*, 1 January. <www.tvinsite.com/international/index.asp?layout=print_page&doc_id=articleID=CA192473> (downloaded 6 June 2002).

Biltereyst, Daniël and Philippe Meers. (2000) 'The International Telenovela Debate and the Contra-Flow Argument: A Reappraisal'. *Media, Culture & Society* 22, no. 3: 393–413.

Blain, Neil and Rinella Cere. (1995) 'Dangerous Television: The *TV a Lucci Rosse* Phenomenon'. *Media, Culture & Society* 17, no. 3: 483–98.

Blanchard, Simon. (2001) 'The "Wrong Type" of Television: New Labour, British Broadcasting and the Rise and Fall of an Exports "Problem"'. Paper presented at AHRB Seminar, Birkbeck College, London, September.

Blumler, Jay. (1992) 'Public Service Broadcasting before the Commercial Deluge'. *Television and the Public Interest: Vulnerable Values in Western Europe*. Ed. Jay Blumler. London: Sage. 7–21.

Blumler, Jay. (1993) 'Meshing Money with Mission: Purity versus Pragmatism in Public Broadcasting'. *European Journal of Communications* 8, no. 4: 403–24.

Bonner, Frances. (2003) *Ordinary Television*. London: Sage.

Brants, Kees. (2004) 'Netherlands'. *The Media in Europe: The Euromedia Handbook*. Eds Mary Kelly, Gianpietro Mazzoleni and Denis McQuail. London: Sage. 145–56.

Brants, Kees and Els De Bens. (2000) 'The Status of TV Broadcasting in Europe'. *Television across Europe: A Comparative Introduction*. Eds Jan Wieten, Graham Murdock and Peter Dahlgren. London: Sage. 7–22.

Brants, Kees and Karen Siune. (1992) 'Public Broadcasting in a State of Flux'. *Dynamics of Media Politics*. Eds Karen Siune and Wolfgang Truetzchler. London: Sage. 101–15.

British Television Distributors' Association. (2003) 'Better Year for Overseas TV Sales in 2002'. Press Release, 19 March. <www.btda.org.uk> (downloaded March 2003).

British Television Distributors' Association. (2004) 'UK TV Exports Approach $1 Billion for the First Time'. Press Release, 13 May 2003. <www.btda.org> (downloaded June 2004).

Broadcast. (2004) 'Channel Overview'. 9 January: 35.

Broadcasters' Audience Research Board. (2003). 'Annual % Shares of Viewing (Individuals) (1981–2002)'. <www.barb.co.uk/TVFACTS.cfm?fullstory=true&newsid=11&flag=tvfacts> (downloaded January 2004).

BRU. (1985) *The Public Service Idea in British Broadcasting: Main Principles*. London: Broadcasting Research Unit.

Bulkley, Kay. (2002) 'Digital Dilemmas'. *Broadcast International*, 12 April: 16–17.

Bundesverfassungsgericht. (1971) 'Urteil des Bundesverfassungsgerichts vom 28 Februar 1961 (Fernsehurteil)'. *Rundfunk und Presse in Deutschland*. Eds Wolfgang Lehr and Klaus Berg. Mainz: Hase & Koehler. 221–56.

Bundesverfassungsgericht. (1986) 'Urteil des Bundesverfassungsgerichts vom 4. November 1986'. *Funk-Korrespondenz Dokumentation* 34, no. 45: D1–D46.

Buonanno, Milly. (1998) 'A Comparative Overview'. *Imaginary Dreamscapes: Television Fiction in Europe*. Ed. Milly Buonanno. Luton: University of Luton Press. 7–20.

Buonanno, Milly. (2000) 'A Comparative Overview'. *Continuity and Change: Television Fiction in Europe*. Ed. Milly Buonanno. Luton: University of Luton Press. 7–27.

Burt, Tim. (2002) 'Bertelsmann Holds Back on UK TV Expansion'. *Financial Times*, 1 August: 20.

Campaign for Press and Broadcasting Freedom. (2002) 'The Response of the Campaign for Press and Broadcasting Freedom to the Department of Trade and Industry Consultation Document Liberalising Trade in Services'. 22 December. <keywords.dsvr.co.uk> (downloaded March 2003).

Campbell, William. (2003) 'Background Information on Playboy TV UK'. Speech by Managing Director of Playboy TV UK – Minutes of the British Screen Advisory Council. London: BSAC, 3 July: 11–13.

Casey, John B. and Ken Aupperle. (1998) *Digital Television and the PC*, Hauppauge Computer Works, Inc., November. <www.digital-law.net/switch-off/technology.htm> (downloaded April 2002).

Cassy, John. (2003) 'Bertelsmann Battle over Family's Remote Control Fight between Owners and Managers Is Jeopardising Media Empire'. *Guardian*, 18 February: 23.

Chalaby, Jean K. (2002) 'Transnational Television in Europe. The Role of Pan-European Channels'. *European Journal of Communication* 17, no. 2: 183–203.

Chalaby, Jean K. (2003) 'Television for a New Global Order: Transnational Television Networks and the Formation of Global Systems'. *International Journal for Communications Studies* 65, no. 6: 457–72.

Charon, Jean-Marie. (2004) 'France'. *The Media in Europe.* Eds Mary Kelly, Gianpietro Mazzoleni and Denis McQuail. London: Sage. 65–77.

Chris, Cynthia. (2002) 'All Documentary, All the Time? Discovery Communications Inc and Trends in Cable Television'. *Television and New Media* 3, no. 1, February: 7–28.

Christmann, Sabine. (2003) 'Digital Television in Germany: Experiences of the Commercial Pay-TV Broadcaster Premiere'. Paper presented at the Conference on Digital Television in Europe: What Prospects for the Public?, organised by the Council of Europe, 3 November, Rome.

Clark, Thomas. (2002) 'Last Throw of Dice for Kirch'. *Broadcast: Broadcast International Section*, 12 April: 16.

Collins, Richard. (1989) 'The Language of Advantage: Satellite Television in Western Europe'. *Media, Culture & Society* 11, no. 2: 351–71.

Collins, Richard. (1994) *Broadcasting and Audio-visual Policy in the European Single Market.* London: John Libbey.

Collins, Richard and Christina Murroni. (1996) *New Media, New Policies.* Cambridge: Polity Press.

Cozens, Chris. (2002) 'Italian TV Drops Berlusconi Opponents'. *Guardian*, 27 June. <www.guardian.co.uk/Archive/Article/0,4273,4449166,00.html> (downloaded July 2002).

Crumley, Bruce. (2002) 'Battle Lines Drawn: The Firing of a Top TV Executive Causes a Public Outcry against Vivendi's Messier'. *Time: Europe Magazine* 159, no. 17, 29 April. <www.time.com/time/europe/magazine/article.0,13005,901020 429– 232500,00html> (downloaded 25 November 2003).

Cunningham, Stuart and Elizabeth Jacka. (1996*) Australian Television and International Mediascapes.* Cambridge: Cambridge University Press.

Dahlgren, Peter. (2000) 'Key Trends in European Television'. *Television across Europe.* Eds Jan Wieten, Graham Murdock and Peter Dahlgren. London: Sage. 23–34.

Darschin, Wolfgang and Heinz Gerhard. (2003) 'Tendenzen im Zuschauerverhalten'. *Media Perspektiven* 4: 158–66.

Darschin, Wolfgang and Camille Zubayr. (2003) 'Was leisten die Fernsehsender? Publikumsurteile über die Fernsehprogramme in den Jahren 1993 bis 2002'. *Media Perspektiven* 5: 206–15.

Davis, William. (1998) *The European Television Industry in the 21st Century.* London: FT Business Ltd.

Deans, Jason. (2003) 'The Rise and Fall of Michael Green'. *Guardian*, 21 October: 22.

De Bens, Els. (1998) 'Television Programming: More Diversity, More Convergence?'. *The Media in Question.* Eds Kees Brants, Joke Hermes and Liesbet van Zoonen. London: Sage. 27–37.

De Bens, Els and Hedwig de Smaele. (2001) 'The Inflow of American Television Fiction on European Broadcasting Channels Revisited'. *European Journal of Communication* 16, no. 1: 51–76.

De Bens, Els, Mary Kelly and Marit Bakke. (1992) 'Television Content: *Dallas*ification of Culture?'. *Dynamics of Media Politics: Broadcast and Electronic Media in Western Europe*. Eds Karen Siune and Wolfgang Truetzchler. London: Sage. 75–100.

Del Valle, David. (2001) 'The Morning After: Territory Guide to Spain'. *Television Business International*, December: 4–8.

De Mateo, Rosario. (2004) 'Spain'. *The Media in Europe*. Eds Mary Kelly, Gianpietro Mazzoleni and Denis McQuail. London: Sage. 225–36.

Department for Culture, Media and Sport. (1999a) *The Report of the Creative Industries Task Force Inquiry into UK Television Exports*. London: DCMS.

Department for Culture, Media and Sport. (1999b) *Building a Global Audience: British Television in Overseas Markets – A Report by David Graham and Associates*. London: DCMS.

Department for Culture, Media and Sport. (2000) 'Government Announces BBC Licence Fee Rises by #3 in Return'. <www.bipa.co.uk/getArticle.php?ID=90> (downloaded 17 June 2004).

Department for Culture, Media and Sport. (2001) *Creative Industries Mapping Document*. London: DCMS. <www.culture.gov.uk> (downloaded January 2003).

Department of National Heritage. (1994) *The Future of the BBC: Serving the Nation: Competing Worldwide*. London: HMSO.

Department of Trade and Industry/Department for Culture, Media and Sport. (2001) *Consultation on Media Ownership Rules*. November. <www.culture.gov.uk/creative/ index.html> (downloaded January 2003).

Department of Trade and Industry/Department for Culture, Media and Sport. (2002) *The Draft Communications Bill – The Policy*. London: TSO, May, Cm 5508–III.

Digital Television Group. (2003) <www.dtg.org.uk> 15 May (downloaded December 2003).

Doyle, Gillian. (2002) *Media Ownership*. London: Sage.

Dransfeld, Henning and Gabriel Jacobs. (2000) 'Digital Pay-TV: Regulating Ring-Fenced Monopolies'. *Is Regulation Still an Option in a Digital Universe?* Eds Tim Lees, Sue Ralph and Jo Langham Brown. Luton: University of Luton Press. 145–51.

Dupaigne, Michael and David Waterman. (1998) 'Determinants of US Television Fiction Imports in Western Europe'. *Journal of Broadcasting and Electronic Media* 42, no. 2: 208–20.

Dyson, Kenneth and Peter Humphreys with Ralgh Negrine and Jean-Paul Simon. (1988) *Broadcasting and New Media Policies in Western Europe*. London: Routledge.

EAO. (2001a) *Statistical Yearbook 2001*. Strasbourg: European Audiovisual Observatory.

EAO. (2001b) 'TV Fiction Programming: Prime Time Is Domestic, Off Prime Time Is American'. Based on the Fifth Eurofiction Survey, *Television Fiction in Europe. Report 2001*, 9 October. <www.obs.coe.int/about/oea/pr/pr_eurofiction_bis.html.en> (downloaded December 2002).

EAO. (2001d) *Television and Media Concentration – Regulatory Models on the National and the European Level*. Ed. Suzanne Nikoltchev. Strasbourg: European Audiovisual Observatory.

EAO. (2002) 'The Imbalance of Trade in Films and Television Programmes between North America and Europe Continues to Deteriorate', 9 April. <www.obs.coe.int/about/oea/pr/desequilibre.html.en> (downloaded 9 April 2002).

EAO. (2003a) 'Household Audiovisual Equipment-Transmission-Television Audience', *2003 Yearbook*, vol. 2. Strasbourg: European Audiovisual Observatory.

EAO. (2003b) 'Television Channels – Programme Production and Distribution', *2003 Yearbook*, vol. 5. Strasbourg: European Audiovisual Observatory.

EAO. (2004) 'Economy of the Radio and Television Industry in Europe, *2004 Yearbook*, vol. 1. Strasbourg: European Audiovisual Observatory.

Easter, Geraldine. (2002) Head of London Office, Holland Media Group – Interview, London, 4 January.

The Economist. (2002) Editorial 'The Two-humped Beast: A Merger Looks Inevitable, But Also Anti-competitive'. 17 October: 5.

Endemol. (2003) 'Corporate: Profile'. <www.endemol.com/profile.xtml> (downloaded 26 November 2003).

Euronews. (2003) 'Many Voices, One Vision'. <www.euronews.net/create_html.php?page=euronews&lng=1> (downloaded 25 November 2003).

European Commission. (1997a) *Protocol on the System of Public Broadcasting in the Member States*. <www.europa.eu.int/comm/dg10/avpolicy/key_doc/amsprot_en.html> (downloaded July 2002).

European Commission. (1997b) *Directive 97/36/EC Amending the 1989 'Television without Frontiers' Directive*, OJ L 202. Brussels: European Commission, 30 July.

European Commission. (1999a) *Principles and Guidelines for the Community's Audiovisual Policy in the Digital Age*. Brussels, COM 657 Final, 14 December.

European Commission. (1999b) *The 1999 Consultation on Audiovisual Services*. <www.europa.eu.int/comm/avpolicy/extern/gats2000/consultdoc_en.htm> (downloaded October 2002).

European Commission. (2000a) *Fourth Communication from the Commission to the Council and the European Parliament on the Application of Articles 4 and 5 of Directive 89/552/EEC 'Television without Frontiers' for the Period 1997–8*. COM (2000) 442 Final. Brussels: European Commission, 17 July.

European Commission. (2000b) *Background Document on the GATS*. 1 December.

<www.europa.eu.int/comm/avpolicy/extern/gats2000/conbg_en.htm>
(downloaded 22 August 2002).

European Commission. (2001a) *A Communication to the Spring European Council in Stockholm*. Brussels: European Commission, COM 140 Final, 23–4 March.

European Commission. (2001b) *Communication on the Application of State Aid Rules to Public Service Broadcasting*. Brussels: European Commission, 15 November.

European Commission. (2002a) 'Audiovisual Policy'.
<www.europa.eu.int/comm/ avpolicy/regul/regul_en.htm> (downloaded 5 February 2003).

European Commission. (2002b) *Fifth Communication from the Commission to the Council and the European Parliament on the Application of Articles 4 and 5 of Directive 89/552/EEC 'Television without Frontiers' for the Period 1999–2000*. COM (2002) 612 Final. Brussels: European Commission, 8 November.

European Commission. (2002c) *Commission Staff Working Document on 'Barriers to Widespread Access to New Services and Applications of the Information Society through Open Platforms in Digital Television and Third-Generation Mobile Communications'*. Brussels: European Commission, 4 February.
<www.europa.eu.int/information_society/topics/telecoms/regulatory/publiconsult/documents/211_29_en.pdf> (downloaded January 2003).

European Commission. (2003) *Fourth Report to the Council of Europe and the European Parliament on the Application of the TWF Directive*. Brussels: European Commission, 6 January.

European Commission. (2004) *Communication on the Future of the European Regulatory Audiovisual Policy*. COM (2003) 784 Final. Brussels: European Commission, 23 April.

European Council. (1989) *Council Directive 89/552/EEC of 3 October 1989 on the Coordination of Certain Provisions Laid down by Law, Regulation or Administrative Action in Member States Concerning the Pursuit of Television Broadcasting Activities*. Brussels: European Council.

Eurosport. (2003) 'About Eurosport TV'.
<www.eurosport.com/home/pages/V4/L0/S10000/sport_Lng0_Spo10000.shtml> (downloaded 24 November 2003).

Ewington, Tim. (2002) 'Consumers and Choices'. *Television and Beyond: The Next Ten Years*. London: Independent Television Commission. 32–9.

Extreme Sports. (2003) 'About Us'. <www.extreme.com/aboutus.asp> (downloaded 25 November 2003).

Fenati, Barbara and Nora Rizza. (1992) 'Schedules and Programmes on Television in Italy'. *The New Television in Europe*. Ed. Alessandro Silj. London: John Libbey. 151–90.

Flottau, Heiko. (1978) *Hörfunk und Fernsehen heute*. 2nd edition. München/Wien: Olzog.

Forgan, Liz and Damian Tambini. (2001) 'Content Regulation: A New Settlement'. *Communications Revolution and Reform.* Eds Damian Tambini with Liz Forgan, Stefaan Verhulst and Clare Hall. London: Institute for Public Policy Research. 45–64.

Fox Kids. (2003) 'Company Profile'. <www.foxkidseurope.com/company> (downloaded 19 November 2003).

Freedman, Des. (2002) 'Trading Culture: An Evaluation of the Impact of Current GATS Negotiations on European Broadcasting Policy'. Paper presented at the RIPE 2002 Conference, Broadcasting and Convergence: New Articulations of the Public Remit, 17–19 January, Tampere.

Fremantle. (2003) 'Profile'. <www.fremantlemedia.com/page.asp?partid=7> (downloaded 27 November 2003).

Fry, Andy. (2001) 'Entering Millionaire's Row'. *Broadcast International*, 5 October: 10–12.

Fry, Andy. (2002) 'European Broadcasters Fight Back', *C21*, 28 June. <www.c21media.net/news/detail.asp?area=4&article=3612> (downloaded 30 December 2003).

Galperin, Hernan. (1999) 'Culture Industries in the Age of Free-Trade Agreements'. *Canadian Journal of Communication* 24, no. 1: 49–77.

Galperin, Hernan. (2002) 'Can the US Transition to Digital TV Be Fixed? Some Lessons from Two European Union Cases'. *Telecommunications Policy* 26, no. 1: 3–15.

Gilder, George. (1992) *Life after Television: The Coming Transformation of Media and American Life*. New York: W. W. Norton.

Gitlin, Todd. (2000) *Inside Prime Time*, rev. edn. Berkeley: University of California Press.

Giudicelli, L. and E. Derieux. (2001) 'France'. *Television and Media Concentration – Regulatory Models on the National and the European Level*. Ed. Suzanne Nikoltchev. Strasbourg: European Audiovisual Observatory. 55–62.

Gomez, Alberto-Perez. (2001) 'Spain'. *Television and Media Concentration – Regulatory Models on the National and the European Level*. Ed. Suzanne Nikoltchev. Strasbourg: European Audiovisual Observatory. 29–46.

Gomez, Alberto Perez. (2002) Comision del Mercado de las Telecomunicaciones – Interview via email, 30 April.

Graham, Andrew. (1999) *Public Purposes in Broadcasting: Funding the BBC*. Luton: University of Luton Press.

Graham, Andrew. (2000) 'Public Policy Issues for UK Broadcasting'. *E-Britannia: The Communications Revolution*. Eds Steven Barnett, Virginia Bottomley, Martin Cave, Andrew Graham, Janice Hughes, Richard Inglewood, Charles Leadbeater, Graham

Mather, Tom McNally, Mark Oliver, Jean Seaton, Harry M. Shooshan and Wilf Stevenson. Luton: University of Luton Press. 93–108.

Graham, Andrew and Gavyn Davies. (1997) *Broadcasting, Society and Policy in the Multimedia Age*. Luton: University of Luton Press.

Grignaffini, Giorgio and Zelda Stewart. (2002) Director of Programming, Mediaset, and Acquisitions Executive, Mediatrade, Gruppo Mediaset – Interview, Milan, 12 June.

Hallenberger, Gerd. (2003) 'Eurofiction 2002: Trotz Krise überraschend stabiles Angebot'. *Media Perspektiven* 11: 490–9.

Hamelink, Cees. (1983) *Cultural Autonomy in Global Communications*. New York: Longman.

Harcourt, Alison and Claudio M. Radaelli. (1997) 'Limits to Technocratic Regulation in the European Union – The Case of Media Ownership Regulation'. Paper presented at the 47th Political Studies Association Conference, 8–10 April, University of Ulster.

Hardy, Jonathan. (2001) 'Border Crossings: Convergence, Cross-Media Promotion and Commercial Speech in UK Communications Policy'. Paper presented at the 51st Political Studies Association Conference, 10–12 April, University of Manchester.

Hargreaves, Ian. (2001) 'How to Turn off the Voters'. *Financial Times* (Creative Business section), 20 February: 5.

Häussermann, B. and A. Scheuer. (2001) 'Germany'. *Television and Media Concentration – Regulatory Models on the National and the European Level*. Ed. Suzanne Nikoltchev. Strasbourg: European Audiovisual Observatory. 7–18.

Hazelton, John. (2002) 'From Millionaire to Weakest Link?'. *Broadcast International*, 12 April: 28.

Henten, Anders, Rohan Samarajiva and William H. Melody. (2003) *Designing Next Generation Telecom Regulation: ICT Convergence or Multisector Utility?* Report on the WDR Dialogue Theme 2002, January. <www.regulateonline.org> (downloaded January 2003).

Herfurth, Hans Wolfgang. (2002) Head of International Relations/Programme Purchase, WDR – Interview, Cologne, 22 February.

Herman, Edward and Robert McChesney. (1997) *The Global Media: The New Missionaries of Global Capitalism*. London and Washington: Cassell.

Hesmondhalgh, David. (2002) *The Cultural Industries*. London: Sage.

Hibberd, Matthew. (2001) 'The Reform of Public Service Broadcasting in Italy'. *Media, Culture & Society* 23, no. 2: 233–57.

Hickethier, Knut. (1996) 'The Media in Germany'. *Markets & Myths – Forces for Change in the European Media*. Eds Anthony Weymouth and Bernard Lamizet. London and New York: Longman. 100–33.

Higham, Nick. (2003) 'European Debates Continental Television'. *BBC online: BBCi*

News, 15 July. <news.bbc.co.uk/1/hi/entertainment/tv_and_radio/3065569.stm> (downloaded 24 November 2003).

Hill, Annette. (2002) '*Big Brother*. The Real Audience'. *Television and New Media 3*, no. 3: 323–40.

HIT. (2001) *Annual Report and Accounts 2001*. London: HIT Entertainment PLC.

HIT. (2002) *Annual Report and Accounts 2002*. London: HIT Entertainment PLC.

HIT. (2003) *Annual Report and Accounts 2003*. London: HIT Entertainment PLC.

Hobsbawm, Eric. (1994) *Age of Extremes*. London: Michael Joseph.

Hodgson, Jessica. (2003) '*Pop Idol* Scores a $1bn Hit in US Market'. *The Observer* (Business section), 7 September: 1.

Hoffmann-Riem, Wolfgang. (1992) 'Trends in the Development of Broadcasting Law in Western Europe'. *European Journal of Communication 7*, no. 2: 147–71.

Holtz-Bacha, Christina. (2003) 'Of Markets and Supply. Public Broadcasting in Germany'. *Broadcasting and Convergence: New Articulations of the Public Service Remit*. Eds Gregory Ferrell Lowe and Taisto Hujanen. Göteborg: Nordicom. 109–19.

Hooper, John. (2002a) 'Kirch on the Brink as Banks Step in: Last Attempt to Save 10,000 Jobs and £4bn Investors' Cash'. *Guardian*, 9 April: 22.

Hooper, John. (2002b), 'Sporting Spirit That Led to Collapse'. *Guardian*, 9 April: 22.

Hooper, John. (2002c) 'Bank Regulators Review Loans Made to Kirch'. *Guardian*, 11 April: 23.

Hooper, John. (2003) 'Berlusconi Stirs Media Bill Row'. *Guardian*, 17 December. <www.guardian.co.uk/international/story/0,3604,1108414,00.html> (downloaded January 2004).

Hooper, John and John Cassy. (2002) 'BSkyB Rules out Cash to Save KirchPayTV'. *Guardian*, 10 April: 24.

Horsman, Matthew. (1998) *Sky High: The Amazing Story of BSkyB – and the Egos, Deals and Ambitions That Revolutionised TV Broadcasting*. London: Orion Business Books.

Hoskins, Colin and Roger Mirus. (1988) 'Reasons for the US Dominance of International Trade in Television Programmes'. *Media, Culture & Society 10*, no. 4: 499–515.

Hoskins, Colin, Stuart McFadyen and Adam Finn. (1997) *Global Television and Film: An Introduction to the Economics of the Business*. Oxford: Oxford University Press.

Hoskins, Colin, Stuart McFadyen, Adam Finn and Anne Jäckel. (1995) 'Film and Television Co-production. Evidence from Canadian-European Experience'. *European Journal of Communication 10*, no. 2: 221–43.

Hughes, Janice and Charlie Marshall. (2002) 'Developing Technologies'. *Television and Beyond: The Next Ten Years*. London: Independent Television Commission. 22–31.

Huhn, Manuela. (2002) Programme Acquisition Executive, RTL Television –
Interview, Cologne, 21 February.

Humphreys, Peter. (1996) *Mass Media and Media Policy in Western Europe*.
Manchester: Manchester University Press.

Humphreys, Peter and Matthias Lang. (1998) 'Digital Television between the
Economy and Pluralism'. *Changing Channels: The Prospects for Television in a Digital
World.* Ed. Jeanette Steemers. Luton: University of Luton Press. 9–35.

IDATE. (2000) *Development of Digital Television in the European Union*. Montpellier:
European Institute of Audiovisual Media and Telecommunications.

Iosifidis, Petros. (1997a) 'Pluralism and Media Concentration Policy in the European
Union'. *Javnost/The Public* 4, no. 1: 85–104.

Iosifidis, Petros. (1997b) 'Methods of Measuring Media Concentration'. *Media,
Culture & Society* 19, no. 3: 643–63.

Iosifidis, Petros. (2001) *Reform of Cross-Media Ownership Rules.* London: DCMS.
<www.communicationswhitepaper.gov.uk> (downloaded 20 December 2002).

Iosifidis, Petros. (2002a) 'Digital Convergence: Challenges for European Regulation'.
Javnost/The Public 9, no. 3: 27–48.

Iosifidis, Petros. (2002b) 'The Limits of Competition Policy: Does the EC Competition
Framework Ensure Media Diversity and Plurality?'. *Intermedia* 30, no. 2: 22–5.

Iosifidis, Petros. (2003) 'Media Concentration and the Communications White Paper'.
Diversity or Anarchy?. Eds Sue Ralph, Helen Manchester and Colin Lees. Luton:
University of Luton Press. 208–16.

ITC. (2002) *A Review of the UK Programme Supply Market.* London: Independent
Television Commission.

Jarvis, Colin. (2001) Director of Programming and Operations, BBC Worldwide –
Telephone Interview, 12 December.

Jeancolas, Jean-Pierre. (1998) 'From the Blum-Byrnes Agreement to the GATT
Affair'. *Hollywood and Europe.* Eds Geoffrey Nowell-Smith and Steven Ricci.
London: British Film Institute. 47–60.

Jeremy, Denise. (2001) 'Animating Ideas That Float'. *Broadcast International*,
5 October: 29–30.

Jeremy, Denise. (2002) 'France Shows Its True Colours'. *Broadcast International*,
4 October: 16.

Jezequel, Jean-Pierre and Andre Lange. (2000) *Economy of European TV Fiction,
Executive Summary.* Strasbourg: European Audiovisual Observatory.

Jezequel, Jean-Pierre and Guy Pineau. (1992) 'French Television'. *The New Television
in Europe.* Ed. Alessandro Silj. London: John Libbey. 429–521.

Johnson, Debra. (2000) 'Formats: What Did Millionaire Ever Do for Us?'. *C21*,
March. <www.c21media.net/features/detail.asp?area=2&article=478&t=7>
(downloaded 23 October 2003).

Johnson, Jo and James Harding. (2002) 'Messier Sits Tight and Tables Motions'. *Financial Times*, 29 May: 28.

Joint Committee on the Draft Communications Bill. (2002) *Draft Communications Bill*. Volume 1 Report. 25 July. HL Paper 169–I, HC 876–I. London: The Stationery Office.

Jowell, Tessa. (2002) 'Sorry Guys, We're Still Talking'. *Financial Times*, 5 November: 5.

Jupiter MMXI. (2002) 'Digital TV Forecast Report'. 13 March.

Kapner, Fred. (2002) 'Italian TV Gamble Spells All Change for Murdoch'. *Financial Times*, 11 June: 31.

Kapner, Suzanne. (2003) 'US TV Shows Losing Potency around World'. *New York Times*, 2 January.

Katsoudas, Dimitrios. (1985) 'Greece: A Politically Controlled State Monopoly Broadcasting System'. *Broadcasting and Politics in Western Europe*. Ed. Raymond Kuhn. London: Frank Cass. 137–51.

Kehoe, Dermot. (2002) 'What Is the Purpose of the BBC in the Digital Age?'. Speech. 4 December. London: City University.

Keighron, Peter. (2003a) 'Attack of the Clones'. *Broadcast International*, 21 March: 13–18.

Keighron, Peter. (2003b) 'Bridging the Divide'. *Broadcast International*, 10 October: 10.

Kelly, Mary and Wolfgang Truetzchler. (1997) 'Ireland'. *The Media in Western Europe*. Ed. Bernt Stubbe Østergaard. London: Sage. 110–25.

Kelly, Mary, Gianpietro Mazzoleni and Denis McQuail. (2004) *The Media in Western Europe*. 3rd edn. London: Sage.

Kjellberg, Gudrun. (2002) Acquisitions Executive Fiction, SVT – Interview, Stockholm, 25 April.

Krüger, Udo Michael. (1996) 'Tendenzen in den Programmen der großen Fernsehsender 1985–1995'. *Media Perspektiven* 8: 418–40.

Krüger, Udo Michael. (2002) 'Inhaltsprofile öffentlich-rechtlicher und privater Hauptprogramme im Vergleich'. *Media Perspektiven* 10: 512–30.

Krüger, Udo Michael and Thomas Zapf-Schramm. (1997) 'ARD 3 – mit stabilem Programmprofil im Wettbewerb behauptet'. *Media Perspektiven* 12: 638–51.

Krüger, Udo Michael and Thomas Zapf-Schramm. (2001) 'Die Boulevardisierungskluft im deutschen Fernsehen'. *Media Perspektiven* 7: 326–44.

Krüger, Udo Michael and Thomas Zapf-Schramm. (2002) 'Öffentlich-rechtliches und privates Fernsehen: Typische Unterschiede bleiben bestehen'. *Media Perspektiven* 4: 178–89.

Krüger, Udo Michael and Thomas Zapf-Schramm. (2003) 'Wandel der Unterhaltungsformate im Fernsehen bei robuster Spartenstruktur'. *Media Perspektiven* 3: 102–14.

Kuhn, Raymond. (1985) 'France and the "New Media"'. *Broadcasting and Politics in Western Europe*. Ed. Raymond Kuhn. London: Frank Cass. 50–66.

Kuhn, Raymond. (1995) *The Media in France*. London: Routledge.

Kuhn, Raymond and James Stanyer. (1999) 'Television and the State'. *Television Broadcasting in Contemporary France and Britain*. Eds Michael Scriven and Monia Lecomte. Oxford: Berghahn Books. 2–15.

Kuiper, Els. (2002) Programme Buyer Youth, VPRO – Interview, Hilversum, 1 February.

Lagardère, Jean-Luc. (2000) *Report on the Annual General Meeting and the Extraordinary Meeting of Lagardère SCA*. 23 May. <www.lagardere.com/us/info_financieres/actionnaires_ag_compte_rendu00.shtml> (downloaded 15 January 2004).

Lamizet, Bernard. (1996) 'The Media in France'. *Markets & Myths – Forces for Change in the European Media*. Eds Anthony Weymouth and Bernard Lamizet. London and New York: Longman. 76–99.

Leveaux, Sophie. (2002) Creative Director, Service Acquisitions, TF1 – Interview, Paris, 21 March.

Levitt, Ted. (1983) *The Marketing Imagination.* London: Collier-Macmillan.

Levy, A. L. David. (1997) 'The Regulation of Digital Conditional Access Systems: A Case Study in European Policymaking'. *Telecommunications Policy* 21, no. 7: 661–76.

Levy, A. L. David. (1999) *Europe's Digital Revolution: Broadcasting Regulation, the EU and the Nation State.* London: Routledge.

Lidén, Maria. (2002) Acquisitions Executive Documentaries, TV4 – Interview, Stockholm, 24 April.

Liikanen, Erkki. (2000) 'E-Europe: Evolution or Revolution?'. Helsinki. <www.europa.eu.int/ISPO/docs/services/docs/2000/April/speech_00_151_en.doc> (downloaded 20 April 2002).

Liikanen, Erkki. (2001) 'IT in the Future eEurope eLearning'. Speech. Helsinki. 15 June.

Lovegrove, Nick and Luis Enriquez. (2002) 'Promoting Investment and Quality'. *Television and Beyond: The Next Ten Years.* London: Independent Television Commission.

Machill, Marcel. (1998) 'Euronews: The First European News Channel as a Case Study for Media Industry Development in Europe and the Spectra of Transnational Journalism Research'. *Media, Culture & Society* 20, no. 3: 427–50.

Marsden, Chris and Stefaan Verhulst. Eds (1999) *Convergence in European Digital TV Regulation*. Oxford: Blackstone Press.

Mastrojanni, R. and M. Cappello (2001) 'Italy'. *Television and Media Concentration – Regulatory Models on the National and the European Level*. Ed. Suzanne Nikoltchev. Strasbourg: European Audiovisual Observatory. 47–53.

Mazzoleni, Gianpietro. (2003) 'Medienpluralismus in Italien zwischen Politik und Marktwettbewerb'. *Media Perspektiven* 11: 517–29.

McAnany, Emile G. and Kenton T. Wilkinson. (1996) 'Introduction'. *Mass Media and Free Trade*. Eds Emile G. McAnany and Kenton T. Wilkinson. Austin: University of Texas Press. 3–29.

McGougan, Julian. (1999) 'The Challenge of Convergence to Audiovisual Regulation: Is the Current Regulatory Framework Approaching Its Sell-by Date?'. *Convergence in European Digital TV Regulation*. Eds Chris Marsden and Stefaan Verhulst. Oxford: Blackstone Press. 175–90.

McKinsey. (1999) *Public Service Broadcasting around the World. A McKinsey Report for the BBC.* <www.bbc.co.uk/info/bbc/pdf/McKinsey.pdf> (downloaded 3 December 2000).

McKinsey. (2002) *Comparative Review of Content Regulation*. 1 May. <www.itc.org.uk> (downloaded 6 February 2003).

McQuail, Denis. (1986) 'Kommerz und Kommunikationstheorie'. *Media Perspektiven* 10: 633–43.

McQuail, Denis. (1995) 'Western European Media: The Mixed Model under Threat'. *Questioning the Media*. Eds John Downing, Ali Mohammadi and Annabelle Sreberny-Mohammadi. London: Sage. 147–64.

McQuail, Denis. (1998) 'Commercialization and Beyond'. *Media Policy*. Eds Denis McQuail and Karen Siune. London: Sage. 107–27.

McQuail, Denis and Karen Siune: (1998) Eds *Media Policy*. London: Sage.

Miller, Toby. (1996) 'The Crime of Monsieur Lang: GATT, the Screen and the New International Division of Cultural Labour'. *Film Policy: International, National and Regional Perspectives*. Ed. Albert Moran. London: Routledge. 72–84.

Milmo, Dan. (2002) 'Kirch Crash Takes Toll on Banking Sector'. *Guardian*, 9 April: 23.

Milmo, Dan. (2003a) 'Saban Seals Deal for ProSieben'. *Guardian*, 12 August: 24.

Milmo, Dan. (2003b) 'Vivendi Says Farewell to Its Universal Vision'. *Guardian*, 9 October: 23.

Milner, Mark. (2002) 'Vivendi Debt: Down to the Wire'. *Guardian*, 16 May: 24.

Misert, Tamara. (2002) Acquisitions Manager, Telecinco – Interview, Madrid, 26 June.

Moran, Albert. (1998) *Copycat TV: Globalisation, Program Formats and Cultural Identity*. Luton: University of Luton Press.

Mozzetti, Francesco. (2002) Acquisitions Manager, Children's Programmes, Mediatrade, Gruppo Mediaset – Interview, Milan, 12 June.

MTVE. (2003) 'About Us'. <www.mtveurope.com/about_us.html> (downloaded 14 November 2003).

Müller, Suzanne. (2002) Head of Children's Programmes, ZDF – Interview, Mainz, 20 February.

Murdock, Graham. (1990) 'Redrawing the Map of the Communications Industries:

Concentration and Ownership in the Era of Privatisation'. *Public Communication: The New Imperatives.* Ed. Marjorie Ferguson. London: Sage. 1–15.

Murdock, Graham. (2000) 'Digital Futures in the Age of Convergence'. *Television across Europe: A Comparative Introduction.* Eds Jan Wieten, Graham Murdock and Peter Dahlgren. London: Sage. 35–57.

Murdock, Graham and Peter Golding. (2001) 'Digital Possibilities, Market Realities: The Contradictions of Communications Convergence'. *The Socialist Register.* Eds Leo Panitch and Colin Leys. London: Merlin Press. 111–29.

Muscara, Piero and Eleanora Zamparutti. (2000) 'Italy: *Big Brother* Sparks Ratings Battle'. *C21*, September. <www.c21media.net/features/detail.asp?area2&article=468> (downloaded 23 October 2003).

Mutimer, Tim. (2002) 'Formats Must Tune into National Psyche'. *C21*, 4 February. <www.c21media.net/news/detail.asp?area=4&article=2474> (downloaded 20 December 2003).

Negrine, Ralph and Stylianos Papathanassopoulos. (1990) *The Internationalisation of Television.* London: Pinter.

Negroponte, Nicholas. (1995) *Being Digital.* New York: Hodder & Stoughton.

Neil, Garry. (2002) 'General Agreement on Trade in Services: A Growing Threat to Cultural Policy'. *International Network for Cultural Diversity*, 3 May. <www.incd.net/paper03.html> (downloaded 20 July 2002).

New Media Markets. (2003) 'Italian Merger Through'. 21, no. 13, 4 April.

Noam, Eli. (1998) 'Digital Convergence and the Next Cyber Trade Wars'. Paper presented at the Convergence and the Internet IDATE Conference, Montpellier. <www.idate.fr/maj/conf/actes98/noam/index.html> (downloaded 11 October 2001).

Nobre-Correia, J-M. (1997) 'Portugal'. *The Media in Western Europe.* Ed. Bernt Stubbe Østergaard. London: Sage. 185–93.

Nordenstreng, Kaarle and Tapio Varis. (1974) *Television Traffic – A One Way Street.* Paris: Unesco.

NOS. (2000) *Hilversum Summary.* Hilversum: NOS.

O'Carroll, Lisa. (2003) 'Puttnam Withdraws Opposition to Media Bill after Jowell Compromise'. *Guardian*, 2 July.

OECD. (2000a) *A New Economy? The Changing Role of Innovation and Information Technology in Growth.* Paris: Organisation for Economic Cooperation and Development.

OECD. (2000b) *Telecommunications Regulations: Institutional Structures and Responsibilities.* DSTI/ICCP/TISP(99)15/FINAL. Paris: Organisation for Economic Cooperation and Development.

OFTEL. (2001) *The Benefits of Self- and Co-Regulation to Consumers and Industry.*

London: Office of Telecommunications. July.
<www.oftel.gov.uk/publications/about_oftel/2001/self0701.htm#chapter1>
(downloaded 16 July 2002).

Oliver, Mark. (2002) 'Towards a New Equilibrium'. *Television and Beyond: The Next
Ten Years*. London: Independent Television Commission. 40–55.

Oreja, Marcellino. (1999) 'Self-Regulation in the Media'. 19–21 April.
<www.europa.eu.int/comm/avpolicy/legis/key_doc/saarbruck_en.htm>
(downloaded 5 July 2002).

Østergaard, Bernt Stubbe. (1998) 'Convergence: Legislative Dilemmas'. *Media Policy:
Convergence, Concentration & Commerce*. Eds Denis McQuail and Karen Siune.
London: Sage. 95–106.

Österlund-Karinkanta, Marina. (2004) 'Finland'. *The Media in Europe*. Eds Mary
Kelly, Gianpietro Mazzoleni and Denis McQuail. London: Sage. 54–64.

Padovani, Cinzia. (2003) 'Redefining Public Service Broadcasting in Italy:
Radiotelevisione Italiana 1990–2001'. *Television and New Media* 2, no. 3: 141–53.

Padovani, Cinzia and Michael Tracey. (2003) 'Report on the Condition of Public
Service Broadcasting'. *Television and New Media* 4, no. 2: 311–53.

Palmer, Michael and Claude Sorbets. (1997) 'France'. *The Media in Western Europe*.
Ed. Bernt Stubbe Østergaard. London: Sage. 56–74.

Palmer, Michael and Jeremy Tunstall. (1990) *Liberating Communications: Policy Making
in France and Britain*. Oxford: Blackwell.

Papathanassopoulos, Stylianos. (2002) *European Television in the Digital Age: Issues,
Dynamics and Realities*. Oxford: Polity Press.

Papathanassopoulos, Stylianos. (2004) 'Greece'. *The Media in Europe*. Eds Mary Kelly,
Gianpietro Mazzoleni and Denis McQuail. London: Sage. 91–102.

Peasey, Jeanette. (1990) *Public Service Broadcasting in Transition: The Example of West
Germany*. Unpublished PhD thesis. Bath.

Pennington, Adrian. (2001) 'The Market That Bob Helped Build'. *Broadcast
International*, 5 October: 40–1.

Petersen, Vibeke (1992) 'Commercial Television in Scandinavia'. *The New Television
in Europe*. Ed. Alessandro Silj. London: John Libbey. 617–24.

Petley, Julian. (2002a) 'A War of Words'. *Red Pepper*, August.
<www.redpepper.org.uk/natarch/x-communications-bill.html>

Petley, Julian. (2002b) 'Legalised Piracy'. *Campaign for Press and Broadcasting Freedom*,
December. <www.keywords.dsvr.co.uk> (downloaded 10 March 2003).

Pinto, Manuel and Helena Sousa. (2004) 'Portugal'. *The Media in Europe*. Eds Mary
Kelly, Gianpietro Mazzoleni and Denis McQuail. London: Sage. 180–90.

Price, Monroe E. (2002) *Media and Sovereignty: The Global Information Revolution and
Its Challenge to State Power*. Cambridge, MA: The MIT Press.

Pugnetti, Guido. (2002) Head of Acquisitions, Rai Cinema – Interview, Rome, 14 June.

Purvis, Stuart. (1999) 'Euronews Improves Output and Distribution under ITN'. *EBU Yearbook*. Geneva: European Broadcasting Union.

Raboy, Mark. (1995) 'Public Service Broadcasting in the Context of Globalisation'. *Public Broadcasting for the 21st Century.* Ed. Mark Raboy. Luton: University of Luton Press. 1–19.

Radaelli, Claudio M. (1999) *Technocracy and the European Union*. London: Longman.

Ramos, Carlos Martinez. (2002) Fiction Series Acquisitions, TVE Television Espanola – Interview, Madrid, 24 June.

Real, Michael M. (1996) *Exploring Media Culture: A Guide*. Thousand Oaks, CA: Sage.

Reding, Vivienne. (2001) 'Position by Mrs Reding on Cultural Policy and WTO in the Framework of the 58th Mostra Internazionale d'arte cinematographica'. Venice, 7 September. <www.europa.eu.int/comm/avpolicy/legis/venise_en.pdf> (downloaded 17 June 2004).

Reding, Vivienne. (2002) 'The Review of the TVWF Directive'. Speech presented at the European Voice Conference on 'Television Without Frontiers'. Brussels, 21 March. <www.europa.eu.int/comm/avpolicy/legis/pressrel/euvoice_en.pdf> (downloaded 17 June 2004).

Robertson, Roland. (1994) 'Globalisation or Glocalisation?'. *Journal of International Communications* 1, no. 1: 33–52.

Robertson, Roland. (1995) 'Glocalisation: Time–Space and Homogeneity–Heterogeneity'. *Global Modernities*. Eds Mike Featherstone, Scott Lash and Roland Robertson. London: Sage. 25–44.

Rodier, Melanie. (2002) 'The Battle for the Airwaves'. *Broadcast International*, 4 October: 32–5.

Roe, Keith and Gust De Meyer. (2000) 'Music Television: MTV-Europe'. *Television across Europe.* Eds Jan Wieten, Graham Murdock and Peter Dahlgren. London: Sage. 141–57.

Root, Antony. (2001) President, Granada Entertainment – Interview, Los Angeles, 20 September.

Rouse, Lucy. (2001) 'Are Imports on the Slide?'. *Broadcast International*, 5 October: 38–9.

Rouse, Lucy. (2003) 'The Future of Formats'. *Broadcast*, 6 June: 26–7.

Rowe, David. (1996) 'The Global Love-Match: Sport and Television'. *Media, Culture & Society* 18, no. 2: 565–82.

RTL. (2003) *RTL Company Profile*. <www.rtlgroup.com/corporate> (downloaded 16 January 2004).

Saló, Gloria. (2002) New Projects Manager, Telecinco – Interview, Madrid, 26 June.

Sartori, Carlo. (1996) 'The Media in Italy'. *Markets and Myths.* Eds Anthony
    Weymouth and Bernard Lamizet. London: Longman. 134–72.

Sassoon, Donald. (1985) 'Italy: The Advent of Private Broadcasting'. *The Politics of
    Broadcasting.* Ed. Raymond Kuhn. London: Croom Helm. 119–57.

Scannell, Paddy. (1989) 'Public Service Broadcasting and Modern Public Life'. *Media,
    Culture & Society* 11, no. 2: 135–66.

Schiller, Herbert. (1976) *Communication and Cultural Domination*. New York: M. E.
    Sharpe.

Schiller, Herbert. (1991) 'Not Yet the Post-Imperialist Era'. *Critical Studies in Mass
    Communication* 8, no. 1: 13–28.

Schiller, Herbert. (1992) *Mass Communications and American Empire*. 2nd edn.
    Boulder, CO: Westview Press.

Schulz, Wolfgang and Thorsten Held. (2001) *Regulated Self-Regulation as a Form of
    Modern Government: Study Commissioned by the German Federal Commissioner for
    Culture and Media Affairs*. Hamburg: Hans-Bredow-Institut.

Scott, Kevin. (2003) 'Northern Exposure'. *Television Business International*,
    March–April: 73–6.

Screen Digest. (2003) *European Programming Rights Markets*. July.
    <www.screendigest.com/rep_mip.html> (downloaded 22 November 2003).

Screen Digest (2004) Personal communication.

Scriven, Michael and Monia Lecomte. Eds (1999) *Television Broadcasting in
    Contemporary France and Britain*. Oxford: Berghahn Books.

Servon, Lisa J. (2002) *Bridging the Digital Divide: Technology, Community and Public
    Policy*. Oxford: Blackwell.

Sinclair, John. (1996) 'Culture and Trade: Some Theoretical and Practical
    Considerations'. *Mass Media and Free Trade.* Eds Emile G. McAnany and Kenton T.
    Wilkinson. Austin: University of Texas Press. 30–60.

Sinclair, John, Elizabeth Jacka and Stuart Cunningham. (1996) 'Peripheral Vision'.
    New Patterns in Global Television. Eds John Sinclair, Elizabeth Jacka and Stuart
    Cunningham. Oxford: Oxford University Press. 1–32.

Siune, Karen and Olof Hultén. (1998) 'Does Public Broadcasting Have a Future?'.
    Media Policy: Convergence, Concentration and Commerce. Eds Denis McQuail and
    Karen Siune. London: Sage. 23–37.

Siune, Karen and Wolfgang Truetzchler. Eds (1992) *Dynamics of Media Politics:
    Broadcast and Electronic Media in Western Europe*. London: Sage.

Smadja, Catherine. (2003) 'Digital Broadcasting in the UK'. Paper presented at the
    Conference on Digital Television in Europe: What Prospects for the Public?
    Organised by the Council of Europe, 3 November, Rome.

Smith, Anthony. (1998) 'Television as a Public Service Medium'. *Television: An International
    History*. 2nd edn. Ed. Anthony Smith. Oxford: Oxford University Press. 38–54.

Sparks, Colin. (1995) 'The Future of Public Service Broadcasting in Britain'. *Critical Studies in Mass Communication* 12, no. 3: 325–41.

Steemers, Jeanette. (2001) 'In Search of a Third Way: Balancing Public Purpose and Commerce in German and British Public Service Broadcasting'. *Canadian Journal of Communication* 26, no. 1: 69–87.

Steemers, Jeanette. (2002) 'Selling British Television in Western Europe'. Paper presented at the Trading Culture Conference, AHRB Centre for British Film and Television Studies, 19 July, Sheffield Hallam University.

Stewart, Zelda. (2002) Acquisitions Executive, Mediatrade, Gruppo Mediaset – Interview, Milan, 12 June.

Strategy Analytics. (2002a) *UK Dominates European Digital TV*. January.

Strategy Analytics. (2002b) *Digital TV in 73% of European Homes by 2008*. May. <www.strategyanalytics.com/press/PRSK012.htm> (downloaded 11 September 2003).

Strategy Analytics. (2003) *Digital TV Prices Will Fall to 36 Euros by 2007.* August. <http://quickstart.clari.net/qs_se/webnews/wed/bo/Bstrategy-analytics.RwyT_DaQ. html> (downloaded 21 October 2003).

Straubhaar, Joseph. (1991) 'Beyond Media Imperialism: Asymmetrical Interdependence and Cultural Proximity'. *Critical Studies in Mass Communication* 8, no. 1: 39–59.

Swann, Dennis. (1988) *The Retreat of the State*. London: Harvester Wheatsheaf.

Syvertsen, Trine and Eli Skogerbø. (1998) 'Scandinavia, Netherlands and Belgium'. *Television: An International History*. 2nd edn. Ed. Anthony Smith. Oxford: Oxford University Press. 223–33.

Tambini, Damian. (2001) 'Through with Ownership Rules? Media Pluralism in the Transition to Digital'. *Communications Revolution and Reform.* Eds Damian Tambini with Liz Forgan, Stefaan Verhulst and Clare Hall. London: Institute for Public Policy Research. 21–44.

Tambini, Damian and Stefaan Verhulst. (2001) 'The Transition to Digital and Content Regulation: The Paradigm Shift'. *Communications Revolution and Reform.* Eds Damian Tambini with Liz Forgan, Stefaan Verhulst and Clare Hall. London: Institute for Public Policy Research. 5–20.

Teather, David. (2002) 'Messier Heads for the Exit: Corporate Chaos as Fourtou Is Lined up to Take over at Vivendi as Empire Dream Fades'. *Guardian*, 2 July: 19.

TBI. (2002) *TBI Yearbook 2003.* London: Television Business International.

Tettenborn, Sabine. (2002) Director of Coproductions, Kirch Media – Interview, Munich, 18 February.

Thomas, Adam, Chris Groner and Simon Dyson. (2003) *European Television.* 7th edn. London: Informa Media Group.

Thussu, Daya K. (2000) *International Communication: Continuity and Change*. London: Arnold.

Torrance, Caroline. (2001) Head of International Drama, Granada International –
    Interview, London, 30 October.

Tracey, Michael. (1983) *Das Unerreichbare Wunschbild – Ein Versuch über Hugh Greene
    und die Neugrundung des Rundfunks in Nordwestdeutschland nach 1945*. Hamburg:
    Kohlhammer-Grote.

Tracey, Michael. (1988) 'Popular Culture and the Economics of Global Television'.
    Intermedia 16, no. 2: 9–25.

Tracey, Michael. (1998) *The Decline and Fall of Public Service Broadcasting*. Oxford:
    Oxford University Press.

Trappel, Josef. (2004) 'Austria'. *The Media in Europe*. Eds Mary Kelly, Gianpietro
    Mazzoleni and Denis McQuail. London: Sage. 4–15.

Tryhorn, Chris. (2003a) 'News Corp Returns to Profit'. *Guardian*, 13 August: 24.

Tryhorn, Chris. (2003b) 'ITV Merger Gets Go-ahead: Granada and Carlton Can Keep
    Their Advertising Sales Division'. *Guardian*, 7 October: 24.

Tunstall, Jeremy. (2004) 'The United Kingdom'. *The Media in Europe.* Eds Mary Kelly,
    Gianpietro Mazzoleni and Denis McQuail. London: Sage. 262–73.

Tunstall, Jeremy and David Machin. (1999) *The Anglo-American Media Connection*.
    Oxford: Oxford University Press.

Van Miert, Karel. (1997) 'A European View on Opening up Networked Industries to
    Competition: The Telecommunications Example'. Paper presented at the VIIIth
    International Antitrust Conference, 27 October, Berlin.
    <www.europa.eu.int/comm/competition/speeches/text/sp1997_056_en.html>
    (downloaded 17 June 2004).

Varis, Tapio. (1984) 'The International Flow of Television Programs'. *Journal of
    Communication* 34, no. 1: 143–52.

Varis, Tapio. (1985) *The International Flow of Television Programmes*. Paris: Unesco.

Vilches, Lorenzo. (1996) 'The Media in Spain'. *Markets & Myths – Forces for Change in
    the European Media*. Eds Anthony Weymouth and Bernard Lamizet. London and
    New York: Longman. 173–201.

Viljoen, Dorothy. (2002) *Art of the Deal.* 3rd edn. London: PACT.

Villagrasa, Jose-Marie. (1992) 'Spain: The Emergence of Commercial Television'.
    The New Television in Europe. Ed. Alessandro Silj. London: John Libbey.
    337–425.

Von Hennet, Thomas. (2002) Head of Documentaries, ProSieben – Interview,
    Munich, 19 February.

Walker, Aalia and Kevin Scott. (2002) 'Holding Steady'. *Television Business
    International*, August–September: 25–9.

Waller, Ed. (2002a) 'Fox Lines up Two UK Dramas'. *C21*, 30 October.
    <www.c21media.net/news/detail.asp?area=4&article=4604> (downloaded 1
    December 2003).

Waller, Ed. (2002b) 'Endemol Format Delivers for TLC'. *C21*, 10 May. <www.c21media.net/news/detail.asp?area=4&article=3254> (downloaded 1 December 2003).

Westcott, Tim. (2002) 'European Broadcasting: How the Mighty Have Fallen'. *Television Europe*, 1 January: 5.

Weymouth, Anthony. (1996) 'Introduction: The Role of the Media in Western Europe'. *Markets & Myths – Forces for Change in the European Media.* Eds Anthony Weymouth and Bernard Lamizet. London and New York: Longman. 1–36.

Wheeler, Mark. (1997) *Politics and the Mass Media.* Oxford: Blackwell.

Wheeler, Mark. (2000) 'Research Note: The "Undeclared War" Part II'. *European Journal of Communication* 15, no. 2: 253–62.

Wheeler, Mark. (2001) 'Regulating Communications in the UK'. *Convergence* 7, no. 3: 28–35.

Wheeler, Mark. (2003) 'UK Perspectives: A "Third Way" in British Communications Policy?'. Paper presented at the Workshop on Cultural Industries, University of Versailles, November 14–15.

Wildman, Steven and Stephen Siwek. (1988) *International Trade in Films and Television Programs.* Cambridge, MA: Ballinger.

Windhorst, Natalie. (2002) Programme Buyer, VPRO – Interview, Hilversum, 31 January.

Winstone, Keely. (2002) 'The (Mis)management of *Millionaire*'. *C21*, February. <www.c21media.net/features/detail.asp?area=2&article=2586> (downloaded 23 October 2003).

ZDF. (1988) *ZDF Jahrbuch 1988.* Mainz: ZDF.

LIST OF ILLUSTRATIONS

Whilst considerable effort has been made to correctly identify the copyright holders, this has not been possible in all cases. We apologise for any apparent negligence and any omissions or corrections brought to our attention will be remedied in any future editions.

Operación Triunfo, Gestmusic/Televisión Española; *Tatort*, ARD; *News at Ten*, ITN; *V Graham Norton*, So Television; *The Bill*, Fremantle Media/Thames Television; *Men Behaving Badly*, Hartswood Films/Thames Television; *Pop Idol*, 19 Television/Thames Television; *Dr Zhivago*, E-Vision/Epsilon TV Productions/Granada Productions/Granada Television/WGBH Boston; *Un Posto al sole*, Grundy Productions Italy/RAIFormat; *Who Wants to Be a Millionaire?*, Celador Productions.

Index

Page numbers in **bold** type indicate detailed analyses/case studies; those in *italics* denote illustrations; *n* = endnote; *t* = table/diagram